Leckie
the education publisher
for Scotland

Higher
ENGLISH

Revision + Practice
2 Books in 1

Contents

Contents

Contents

Contents

ebook 📖

To access the ebook version of this Revision Guide visit
www.collins.co.uk/ebooks
and follow the step-by-step instructions.

ANSWERS Check your answers to the practice test papers online:
https://collins.co.uk/pages/scottish-curriculum-free-resources

Acknowledgements

What Sport Tells Us About Life by Ed Smith on p21–22/19–20 published by Penguin Books Ltd; *Youth subcultures: what are they now?* by Alexis Petridis on p24 is reproduced by permission of Guardian News & Media Ltd; *Crow Country* by Mark Cocker on p25 published by Vintage and reprinted by permission of The Random House Group Limited; *Your child is going to experiment: what teenagers really think* by Suzanne Moore on p29 is reproduced by permission of Guardian News & Media Ltd; *Dangerous Liaisons* by Lucy Mangan on p32–33 are reproduced by permission of Guardian News & Media Ltd; *Stop criticising private schools, start learning from them* on p35–36 © Telegraph Media Group Limited 2014; *Secret Teacher: jargon is ruining our children's* education on p36–38 is reproduced by permission of Guardian News & Media Ltd; *Want to silence a two-year-old? Try teaching it to ride a motorbike* by Charlie Brooker on p38–40 is reproduced by permission of Guardian News & Media Ltd; *Post-traumatic stress disorder is the invisible scar of war* by Stuart Tootal on p40/41–42 © Telegraph Media Group Limited 2014; *The Greatest Show on Earth* by Richard Dawkins on p45–46, published by Jonathan Cape and reprinted by permission of The Random House Group Limited; *Science lessons should tackle creationism and intelligent design* by Professor Michael Reiss on p47–48 is reproduced by permission of Guardian News & Media Ltd; *All My Sons* by Arthur Miller on p49 are reproduced by permission of The Wylie Agency (UK) Ltd; *Othello* William Shakespeare p50, 94–95 is in the public domain; *Romanno Bridge* by Andrew Greig on p56 is reproduced by permission of Quercus Publishing; *Darkness and Light* by Kathleen Jamie/Findings, Kathleen Jamie p167–168 Sort of Books, 2005; 'Pilate's Wife' by Carol Ann Duffy on p61 are reproduced by permission of Pan Macmillan, Reproduced with permission of the Licensor through PLSclear; 'Mrs Icarus' by Carol Ann Duffy on p62 are reproduced by permission of Pan Macmillan, reproduced with permission of the Licensor through PLSclear; *Ambulances* by Philip Larkin on p64 published by Faber & Faber; 'Heliographer' by Don Paterson on p65 published by Faber & Faber; *In a snug room* by Norman MacCaig from *The Poems of Norman MacCaig* on p65–66 is reproduced by permission of Birlinn Ltd.; 'Head of English' by Carol Ann Duffy on p67 © Carol Ann Duffy from *Collected Poems* and reproduced by permission of the author c/o Rogers, Coleridge & White Ltd, reproduced with permission of the Licensor through PLSclear; 'Thrushes' by Ted Hughes on p68 published by Faber & Faber; 'Waterfall' by Seamus Heaney on p68 published by Faber & Faber; *The Slab Boys* by John Byrne on p76–79, 164–165, p207–208 reproduced by permission of Casarotto Ramsay & Associates Ltd; *Sunset Song* by Lewis Grassic Gibbon on p80–81, 179–180, 222–223 is in the public domain; 'Nil Nil' by Don Paterson on p82 reproduced by permission of Rogers, Coleridge and White and Faber & Faber; *Aging* by Paulina Porizkova on p158–159 published in The Huffington Post; *Sorry, Rosie Huntington-Whiteley, but I don't buy into this idea of a female shelf life* by Barbara Ellen on p160–161 published in the Observer and reproduced by permission of Guardian News & Media Ltd; *The Cheviot, the Stag and the Black, Black Oil* by John McGrath on p167–168, p210–212 reproduced by permission of Bloomsbury Methuen Drama, an imprint of Bloomsbury Publishing Plc; *Men Should Weep* by Ena Lamont Stewart on p170–171, p213–215 reproduced by permission of Alan Brodie Representation; 'Mother and Son' by Iain Crichton Smith from *The Red Door: The Complete English Stories 1949–76* on p173 reproduced by permission of Birlinn Ltd, reproduced with permission of the Licensor through PLSclear; *The Eye of the Hurricane* by George Mackay Brown on p175–176 reproduced by permission of Jenny Brown Associates; *The Strange Case of Dr Jekyll and Mr Hyde* by Robert Louis Stevenson on p177–178, 220 is in the public domain; *The Cone-Gatherers* by Robin Jenkins on p181–18, 224–225 reproduced by permission of Canongate Books Ltd; 'Mrs Tilscher's Class' by Carol Ann Duffy from *Collected Poems* on p186–187 © Carol Ann Duffy and reproduced by permission of the author c/o Rogers, Coleridge & White Ltd, reproduced with permission of the Licensor through PLSclear; 'Last Supper' by Liz Lochhead from *A Choosing: Selected Poems by Liz Lochhead* on p188–189 reproduced by permission of Birlinn Ltd. Reproduced with permission of the Licensor through PLSclear; 'Basking Shark' by Norman MacCaig from *The Poems of Norman MacCaig* on p191 reproduced by permission of Birlinn Ltd, Reproduced with permission of the Licensor through PLSclear; 'An Autumn Day' from *White Leaping Flame/Caoir Gheal Leumraich, A: Sorley Maclean: Collected Poems,* Reproduced with permission of the Licensor through PLSclear; 'Nil Nil' by Don Paterson on p195–196 reproduced by permission of Rogers, Coleridge and White and Faber & Faber; *Why We Sleep* by Matthew Walker Ó Matthew Walker 2018, published by Penguin Books Ltd p202–203; 'Who can afford forty winks?' by Arianne Huffington p203–204 are reproduced by permission of Guardian News & Media Ltd 'Home' by Iain Crichton Smith from *The Red Door: The Complete English Stories 1949–76* on p216–217 reproduced by permission of Birlinn Ltd, reproduced with permission of the Licensor through PLSclear; *The Wireless Set* by George Mackay Brown on p218–219 reproduced by permission of Jenny Brown Associates; 'Valentine' by Carol Ann Duffy from *Collected Poems* on p229 reproduced by permission of Pan MacMillan and author c/o Rogers Coleridge & White Ltd, reproduced with permission of the Licensor through PLSclear; 'My Rival's House' by Liz Lochhead from *A Choosing: Selected Poems by Liz Lochhead* on p231–232 reproduced by permission of Birlinn Ltd, reproduced with permission of the Licensor through PLSclear; 'Visiting Hour' by Norman MacCaig from *The Poems of Norman MacCaig* on p234–235 reproduced by permission of Birlinn Ltd, reproduced with permission of the Licensor through PLSclear; 'The Circle' by Don Paterson from *Rain* on p239–240 published by Rogers, Coleridge and White and Faber & Faber; 'XIX I Gave You Immortality' by Sorley MacLean on p236- 237 Day' from *White Leaping Flame/Caoir Gheal Leumraich, A: Sorley Maclean: Collected Poems,* Reproduced with permission of the Licensor through PLSclear; *The Return of John MacNab* by Andrew Greig on p54–55 is reproduced by permission of Quercus Publishing; *Laidlaw* by William McIlvanney on p55 are reproduced by permission of Canongate Books; 'A Poet's Welcome to His Love-Begotten Daughter' by Robert Burns on p183–184 is in the public domain; 'To A Mouse' by Robert Burns on p226–227 is in the public domain;

Who needs this book?

If you are studying Higher English this year you will already be aware of the challenges that face you: you might know someone who has sat previous versions of this exam; you might have looked at an SQA past paper; your teacher might have talked about the 'big jump' required from National 5 English. Whatever your thoughts and feelings about Higher English, there is no doubt that it can appear a rather daunting prospect and one that a good number of candidates find difficult each year.

Higher English can sometimes appear daunting simply because of the importance placed on this qualification. Even with all the changes to SQA exams in recent years, the status of Higher English remains unchanged. You might require a pass in this subject in order to gain entry to the university or college course that you have always wanted to do. Potential employers will often require job applicants to have a pass in Higher English because it shows you are an effective thinker and communicator – someone who can read and write and talk and listen at a detailed and complex level. To put it simply, our society *values* Higher English. Higher English requires hard work from you but obtaining this qualification will give *you* more choices in life.

But you should also *enjoy* the experience of studying for this qualification. Whatever literature you study and whatever language activities you undertake as part of your course you should come out at the end with a real sense that you have experienced something worthwhile – something that has made you look at yourself, other people and the world in a different way.

This book is designed to help you cope with the challenges you will face as you work your way towards the final examination. It is designed to maximise your chances of success. Think of it as your own secret weapon in your battle against the mighty Scottish Qualifications Authority (SQA). Who needs this book? You do.

Course structure and assessment

First of all the good news. If you have already studied English at National 5 level you will recognise most of the elements of your new Higher course.

The assessments

In order to pass Higher English (the SQA calls it 'gaining a course award'), you will have to pass the Performance – Spoken Language assessment and the **external assessment** (the exam and the Portfolio of Writing). The Performance – Spoken Language assessment is marked by your teachers and the external assessment is marked by the SQA.

The external assessment

The following external assessment will be marked by the SQA:

- A Portfolio of Writing worth **30 marks**. You have to send **two** pieces of writing to the SQA. One must be **creative**. The SQA guidelines specify the following possibilities for your creative piece:
  - ➤ a personal reflective essay
  - ➤ a piece of prose fiction (e.g. short story, episode from a novel)
  - ➤ a poem or set of thematically linked poems
  - ➤ a dramatic script (e.g. scene, monologue, sketch).

- One piece of writing must be **discursive**. The SQA guidelines specify the following possibilities for this piece:
  - ➤ a persuasive essay
  - ➤ an argumentative essay
  - ➤ a report
  - ➤ a piece of transactional writing.

You will be given opportunities to plan, draft and redraft these pieces but they must be all your own work. You can even write one or both pieces in Scots if you want. Each folio piece is marked out of **15**. It is vital that you work hard on your portfolio because it is the one piece of external assessment that is totally under your control.

Further external assessment by the SQA is as follows:

- Exam Question Paper 1 – Reading for Understanding, Analysis and Evaluation (**1 hour and 30 minutes**), worth **30 marks**. In this paper you have to answer questions on two non-fiction passages.
- Exam Question Paper 2 – Critical Reading (**1 hour and 30 minutes**). This consists of:
  - ➤ Section 1 – questions on Scottish texts (one context question), worth **20 marks**. In this part of the paper you will answer questions on a Scottish text or an extract from a Scottish text you have already studied.

➤ Section 2 – one critical essay, worth **20 marks**. In this part of the paper you will be given a choice of essay topics. You will write about a text (or texts) you have studied during your course. You can choose from Drama, Prose (fiction or non-fiction), Poetry, Film and Television Drama. You can even write about a Language topic if you wish.

In your course you will probably study three different genres of texts, including one or perhaps two of the specified Scottish texts.

The SQA has specified the following Scottish texts for study from 2019 onwards but you should note that this list might change every few years or so.

Drama   *The Slab Boys* by John Byrne   *The Cheviot, The Stag and The Black, Black Oil* by John McGrath   *Men Should Weep* by Ena Lamont Stewart
Prose   **Short stories** by Iain Crichton Smith. *The Red Door, The Telegram, Mother and Son, Home*   **Short stories** by George Mackay Brown. *A Time to Keep, The Wireless Set, The Eye of the Hurricane, Andrina*   *The Strange Case of Dr Jekyll and Mr Hyde* by Robert Louis Stevenson   *Sunset Song* by Lewis Grassic Gibbon   *The Cone-Gatherers* by Robin Jenkins
Poetry   **Robert Burns**   *Holy Willie's Prayer, Tam O'Shanter, To a Mouse, A Poet's Welcome to his Love-Begotten Daughter, To a Louse, A Red, Red Rose*   **Carol Ann Duffy**   *War Photographer, Valentine, Originally, Mrs Midas, In Mrs Tilscher's Class, The Way My Mother Speaks*   **Liz Lochhead**   *The Bargain, My Rival's House, View of Scotland/Love Poem, Last Supper, Revelation, Box Room*   **Norman MacCaig**   *Assisi, Visiting Hour, Aunt Julia, Basking Shark, Hotel Room, 12th Floor, Brooklyn Cop*   **Sorley MacLean**   *Hallaig, Shores, An Autumn Day, I Gave You Immortality, Kinloch Ainort, Girl of the Red-Gold Hair*   **Don Paterson**   *Waking with Russell, 11:00: Baldovan, The Ferryman's Arms, Nil Nil, Rain, The Circle*

You will use your knowledge of these texts to answer the question on Scottish texts **and** (if you study more than one set text) to write a critical essay.

The marks for your external assessment will be added up and converted into a grade from A–D.

In order to give yourself the best possible chance to succeed in this subject, you *must* be prepared to spend a significant amount of your own time studying and revising.

It is a good idea to keep a record of your assessments as you work your way through the course. Your teacher or tutor will probably provide you with one or you can use something like the record shown on the following pages.

Higher English student record

	Outcome	Date: Pass/fail:	Reassessment date: Pass/fail:
Spoken Language	• Employs relevant detailed and complex ideas and/or information using a structure appropriate to purpose and audience. • Communicates meaning effectively through the selection and use of detailed and complex spoken language. • Uses aspects of non-verbal communication. • Demonstrates listening skills by responding to detailed and complex spoken language.		

Writing portfolio			
Creative	**Title**	**Estimated mark/15**	**Selected for folio?**
a personal essay/ reflective essay			
a piece of prose fiction (e.g. short story, episode from a novel)			
a poem or set of thematically linked poems			
a dramatic script (e.g. scene, monologue, sketch)			

Writing portfolio			
Discursive	**Title**	**Estimated mark/15**	**Selected for folio?**
a persuasive essay			
an argumentative essay			
a report for a specified purpose			
a piece of transactional writing			
		Total folio estimate	**/30**

You must send **one discursive** and **one creative** piece of writing (max. 1300 words each) to the SQA. Your Writing Portfolio is worth 30% of your final grade.

Prelim examination		
	Marks	**Comments**
Reading	**/30**	
Scottish text question	**/20**	
Critical essay	**/20**	
	Total /70	

Final estimate > SQA	**Overall percentage**	**Grade/band**
Prelim + Writing Portfolio (70% + 30%)		

Genres of literature

You should study at least three **different** genres of literature as part of your course and as preparation for the final exam.

The only compulsory requirement is the need to study at least **one** of the specified Scottish texts so there is a wide variety of possible combinations of texts to study.

For example, the literature element of your course might involve you studying:

- Poetry – the six specified poems by Don Paterson
- Prose – *The Cone-Gatherers*
- Drama – *Othello*

OR

- Poetry – the six specified poems by Carol Ann Duffy
- Prose – *One Flew over the Cuckoo's Nest*
- Drama – *A View from the Bridge*

OR

- Poetry – a selection of poems by contemporary writers
- Prose – *Sunset Song*
- Film and TV drama – *Goodfellas*

OR

- Poetry – the six specified poems by Robert Burns
- Prose – the four specified stories by George Mackay Brown
- Drama – *Men Should Weep*

OR

- Poetry – a selection of Philip Larkin's poems
- Prose – *The Strange Case of Dr Jekyll and Mr Hyde*
- Drama – *The Slab Boys*

OR

- Poetry – the six specified poems by Norman MacCaig
- Prose – a selection of non-fiction texts
- Drama – *Macbeth*

Some texts are common to National 5 and Higher (the MacCaig poetry and *The Cone-Gatherers* are two examples of this). If you studied any of these texts for National 5, don't overlook them as possible choices in the question on Scottish texts.

TOP TIP

Make sure that you study a wide range of literature/media during your course – you will get far more out of the course if you do so. It will also mean that you are more likely to encounter texts which interest you and candidates nearly always answer more effectively on texts they have enjoyed.

One other thing to bear in mind is that you are allowed to write a critical essay on **any text** as long as it is on a **different genre** from the text you chose in the questions on Scottish texts section of the paper. This means that you could, for example, write a critical essay on the Norman MacCaig poem printed in the question on Scottish texts, providing that you didn't answer on poetry in that section.

Let's say 'Aunt Julia' was the MacCaig poem printed in the Scottish texts section and the following question appeared in the critical essay section:

> *Choose a poem which features a relationship.*
>
> *Discuss how the poet's presentation of this relationship adds to your understanding of the central concerns of the poem.*
>
> SQA, Specimen Paper, Higher English 2018

You could then use 'Aunt Julia' as the subject of your essay. This would have the obvious advantage of not requiring you to agonise over whether you have remembered lines of the poem to use to support your line of argument in the essay – it's all there in front of you!

LECKIE
the education publisher
for Scotland

Higher
ENGLISH

Revision Guide

Iain Valentine

Reading for understanding, analysis and evaluation

The external assessment (the SQA examination) requires you to show the following skills:

- *understanding of the writer's ideas and/or views by recasting content from the passage in their own words*
- *understanding of vocabulary in context*
- *analysis of language (word choice, figurative language, sentence structure, tone, punctuation, etc.)*
- *understanding of text structure (opening, conclusion, development of argument, linkage, etc.)*
- *evaluation of the writer's techniques or the overall impact of the text*
- *inferring meaning*
- *summarising: understanding of the writer's ideas through identifying and isolating key points or main ideas in one passage, and, through comparison, in both passages (SQA, 2018)*

Understanding, analysis, evaluation

The sorts of questions you can expect in the examination paper fall into the following categories.

1. Questions that test your **understanding** of the writer's ideas (*what* the writer is trying to say). These tend to be the more straightforward questions in the examination.

2. Questions that test your skills of **analysis**. You will be asked to explain the techniques used by the writer (*how* the writer conveys his or her message). You will be asked to explain how the writer's use of language (which might include such things as word choice, imagery, sentence structure, sound and tone) helps to get across their point of view. You will also be asked how these techniques add to the impact of the passage.

3. Questions that ask you to **evaluate** how successful the writer is in using particular techniques or how effective they are in achieving the purpose of the writing.

TOP TIP

Each question will have a number of marks attached to it. Questions will be worth between **2** and **5** marks. The number of marks allocated to a question is generally a good guide to the length of answer required from you. A 2-mark question asking you to identify two basic points made in the passage will require a more concise answer than a 4-mark question which asks you to analyse a range of language features. Obviously you have to answer the question but don't waste time writing unnecessarily long answers – this is after all a test of your reading, not your writing. The 5-mark question asking you to identify key areas from both passages can be answered either in a series of bullet points or in a number of linked sentences – we'll look at this particular question in more detail later. Above all, you need to use the **1 hour and 30 minutes** you have to complete this paper as efficiently as you can; make sure you answer **all** the questions.

Passages

Passages for the Reading for Understanding, Analysis and Evaluation paper are always non-fiction.

This means that they could, for example, be taken from things like:

- a newspaper article
- a magazine article
- a popular science book
- a biography
- a piece of travel writing
- a report.

Passages might come from traditional print or online texts.

In order to get yourself familiar with the sort of writing found in these passages you could look at the SQA specimen paper and also the practice test papers provided in this book.

You should also seek out this kind of writing for yourself. Feature articles in newspapers such as *The Times, the Herald, the Guardian, the Telegraph, the Scotsman, the Independent* and their Sunday equivalents will all include examples of the kind of writing chosen for exam passages. You can access most of these online. Pay particular attention to articles written by a newspaper's regular columnists – these are likely to contain good examples of persuasive and argumentative writing.

There are also any number of blogs online that will provide you with appropriate reading material which might be useful for practice. Look out for reputable print or TV journalists who also write blogs. Following newspapers and journalists on Twitter will usually supply you with links to longer written pieces.

TOP TIP

Your school librarian will be of invaluable assistance in suggesting the 'right' sort of reading. Make a point of talking to them – they will only be too delighted to assist you.

TOP TIP

Once you've started finding examples of the kinds of passages used in the exam, practise making up questions on them. Thinking *'What might I be asked about this part of the passage?'* is an excellent way of making yourself really focus on the language techniques used by a writer.

Types of questions: understanding

If you have already done National 5 English, you will be familiar with some of the things that you will be asked at Higher. Let's look at some examples of questions that you might find in a Higher paper.

Questions that test your understanding

> Referring to lines 8–11, identify **two** ways in which 'our prison system is not fit for purpose'.
>
> Read lines 22–33. According to the writer in lines 24–26, in what ways are online shoppers different to those who shop on the High Street?
>
> Explain in detail why the writer thinks that women 'can never achieve full equality' (line 31).
>
> Explain the cause of the 'pessimism' expressed by the economist (line 4).
>
> Explain why the writer does not believe that 'humanity's journey has a positive destination' (line 15).
>
> Re-read lines 50–55. Identify any four reasons given in these lines for abandoning the wave power project.
>
> According to lines 43–47, why does the writer believe 'our online identities are merely artificial constructs'?

Notice that you are always told where to look for the answer in the passage with a reference to the line number(s). Key words in this category of question are often words and phrases such as **explain**, **give reasons for**, **according to the writer what is …**, **why and identify**.

For all questions that test your understanding, you **must** attempt to answer in your own words as far as possible. You **must not** simply copy down the words of the passage. Remember that you are not always reminded of this requirement in individual questions at Higher. There is an assumption that you will answer questions using your own words (there are, of course, questions that do require you to quote from the passage as part of your answer but these are dealt with below). Identifying and explaining the ideas of a passage is not only a test of your ability to understand these ideas, it is also a test of your vocabulary. That is why it is so important you read as widely as possible during this course.

TOP TIP

If you are asked to 'identify' something in the passage, simply supply the answer in a concise form or name.

Locate, translate

As a first step in answering this kind of question you should first of all **locate** the part of the passage that will supply you with the answer and underline or highlight it – remember that the exam paper is for you to use as you like – and then **translate** it into your own words. If you can't remember **locate**, **translate**, then think about the following commands in your computer's word processing software:

FIND [   ]

REPLACE WITH [   ]

Let's see how that works in practice.

Look at the following extract from Ed Smith's book, *What Sport Tells Us About Life*. It is taken from a chapter that discusses the concept of 'amateurism'. Then look at the question which follows it.

One generation's favourite idea is despised by the next as old-fashioned rubbish. That is what happened to amateurism.

At its peak, the character-building philosophy of amateurism defined British attitudes to sport. A century ago 'amateur' was a compliment to someone who played sport simply for the love of it – it is derived, after all, from the Latin for 'to love'. The word professional, on the other hand, scarcely existed as a noun.

How the wheel has turned. In fact, the words have almost completely swapped meanings. 'Professional' now has a definition so broad that almost anyone who has held down a job for a few months can call himself a 'true professional'. And amateurism has become a byword for sloppiness, disorganisation and ineptitude.

Question: Explain what, according to the writer, the current meanings of the words 'professional' and 'amateur' are.

2

The first thing to do is to **locate** the parts of the passage that will supply us with the answer. Remember you will find it helpful to <u>underline</u> or highlight the appropriate words.

One generation's favourite idea is despised by the next as old-fashioned rubbish. That is what happened to amateurism.

At its peak, the character-building philosophy of amateurism defined British attitudes to sport. A century ago 'amateur' was a compliment to someone who played sport simply for the love of it – it is derived, after all, from the Latin for 'to love'. The word professional, on the other hand, scarcely existed as a noun.

How the wheel has turned. In fact, the words have almost completely swapped meanings. 'Professional' now has a definition so broad that almost anyone who has held down a job for a few months can call himself a 'true professional'. And amateurism has become a byword for sloppiness, disorganisation and ineptitude.

The next step is simply to **translate** or paraphrase the highlighted or underlined text into your own words.

Answer: It's hard to say exactly what 'professional' means as so many people regard themselves as one and 'amateurism' has become another name or label for poor performance.

TOP TIP

Remember you can mark up or highlight the exam paper in any way that you find helpful.

This answer shows that the appropriate parts of the passage have been identified and that the writer's words have been successfully **glossed** by the candidate.

Remember you are dealing with 'detailed and complex' language at Higher level so you are always likely to come across words with which you might be unfamiliar. When this happens, don't just give up. Use the following tactics:

Look at the rest of the sentence and the other sentences immediately before and after the word again – **the context**. This might give you some idea of a possible meaning.

Words are made up of **roots** and **stems**. Are there any clues there? For example, if you didn't know what the word 'laudable' meant you might still be reminded of the word 'applaud' and so be able to work out that 'laudable' means 'praiseworthy'.

Is there another word, or phrase, close to the word, that appears to have a similar meaning?

Is there another word or phrase, close to the word, that suggests the opposite meaning? Is the writer trying to indicate a contrast of some kind?

Does the writer make use of an example that might help to explain the meaning of the word?

Above all, don't get thrown by the unfamiliar – try to work it out as best you can.

Now practise using what you have learned to answer a selection of questions on the rest of the extract from Ed Smith's book. Check your answers on page 132. The questions all test your **understanding**. In the exam there will probably be a maximum of three 2-mark questions.

The age of the amateur has passed
Worse luck

One generation's favourite idea is despised by the next as old-fashioned rubbish. That is what happened to amateurism.

At its peak, the character-building philosophy of amateurism defined British attitudes to sport. A century ago 'amateur' was a compliment to someone who
5 played sport simply for the love of it – it is derived, after all, from the Latin for 'to love'. The word professional, on the other hand, scarcely existed as a noun.

How the wheel has turned. In fact, the words have almost completely swapped meanings. 'Professional' now has a definition so broad that almost anyone who has held down a job for a few months can call himself a 'true professional'. And
10 amateurism has become a byword for sloppiness, disorganisation and ineptitude.

'The amateur, formerly the symbol of fair play and a stout heart,' as the literary critic D.J. Taylor put it, 'became the watchword for terminal second-rateness and lower-rung incompetence.' Have we thrown the baby out with the bathwater?

There is no doubt that the survival of amateur rhetoric so far into the twentieth
15 century was a bizarre anachronism, even by British standards. When Fred Titmus made his debut for Middlesex at cricket in 1949, his progress to the wicket was accompanied by a loudspeaker announcement correcting an error on the score-card: 'F.J. Titmus should, of course, read Titmus, F.J.' A gentleman was allowed his initial before the surname; a professional's came after. People felt these things
20 mattered.

There are countless stories about grand but hopeless amateurs insisting that far more talented pros call them 'Mr' – even on the field of play.

Clearly the amateur ideal – in its snobbery, exclusivity and sometimes plain silliness – assisted in its own demise. But now professionalism has had a good
25 crack of the whip, perhaps it is time we drew stock about where that ideal has taken us. And as we wave amateurism goodbye, could there be anything in its wreckage that might be worth salvaging?

First of all, we might consider whether amateurism allowed for a broad church of personalities, and encouraged an instinctiveness and individuality that is well
30 suited to producing success in sport. Secondly, perhaps amateurism left people alone more – and it might be that great players respond well to being left alone.

It is a truism that there is a creative element to the best sport. We crave creative midfield footballers, creative managers and creative leadership. Alongside their creativity, sportsmen are often lauded when they seem inspired – we talk of an
35 inspired spell of bowling, an inspired tactical move or an inspirational act of defiance. The language of sporting excellence draws heavily from the arts – for the very good reason that playing sport has much in common with artistic expression.

What do we mean when we talk of creativity and inspiration? Perhaps we can never fully understand the answer. Many of the most inspired sporting
40 achievements, like great works of art or innovation, spring from parts of our personalities which resist rational analysis, let alone professional planning. Where does a writer find inspiration for a novel? Where do scientific ideas come from,

how does an entrepreneur come up with a new business idea? There will be an element of self-awareness in all these processes – a management of talent,
45 a regulation of originality – but also a good amount of instinct. Forces beyond rationality lead creative people to follow certain paths and not others. Like strikers with an instinct for where to be in the penalty area, something takes them into different (and better) creative territory.

Crucially, the wisest of these original minds
50 know better than to over-analyse the sources of their inspiration. They do not undermine the muse by trying to master her. Whatever works should be left well alone. 'If the word "inspiration" is to have any meaning,' wrote T.S. Eliot, 'it must
55 mean that the speaker or writer is uttering something which he does not wholly understand – or which he may even misinterpret when the inspiration has departed from him.' After all, 'inspiration' derives linguistically from the
60 concept of breath – once breathed out it is gone.

Bob Dylan has argued that inspiration needs to be protected from too much 'grown-up' self-analysis: 'As you get older, you get smarter and that can hinder you because you try to gain
65 control over the creative impulse.' Many sportsmen, in the same way, succeed not despite inexperience, but because of it. Experience brings wisdom to some, but over-analysis to most. Sometimes, we simply learn new impediments to creative self-expression. You've got to unlearn them.

Ed Smith, *What Sport Tells Us About Life*

Questions

		Marks
1.	Re-read lines 1–2. Explain in your own words what has happened to amateurism.	2
2.	Re-read lines 14–22. Identify **two** examples of what the writer terms 'bizarre anachronism'.	2
3.	Re-read lines 28–31. Explain in your own words **two** possible advantages of amateurism.	2
4.	Re-read lines 38–48. Explain in your own words what 'many of the most inspired sporting achievements' have in common with 'great works of art or innovation'.	2
5.	Re-read lines 61–68. Explain in your own words what makes many sportsmen successful.	2

Check your answers on page 132.

Types of questions: analysis

Analysis questions

Questions that test your skills of **analysis** are generally more challenging. Here is a selection.

Analyse how the writer's use of language in lines 10–15 emphasises her dislike of celebrity culture. You should refer in your answer to such features as sentence structure, word choice, imagery, contrast, tone ...

Re-read lines 22–28. By referring to at least two examples, analyse how the writer's use of imagery highlights the contrast between rural and urban communities.

By referring to at least two features of language in lines 17–27, analyse how the writer conveys his attitude towards social media. You should refer in your answer to such features as sentence structure, word choice, contrast, tone ...

Re-read lines 7–17. By referring to at least two features of language in lines 21–37, analyse how the writer conveys the seriousness of the situation faced by the journalists.

Notice that the key word in all these questions is **analyse**.

Other key words in this type of question are the technical terms **word choice**, **language**, **tone**, **sentence structure and imagery**. Sometimes the question will remind you that these are the techniques to analyse, sometimes the question will just use the term **features of language**. As soon as you see this term, a checklist should start running automatically in your head: word choice, imagery, sentence structure, sound, tone, punctuation ...

FEATURES OF LANGUAGE

☐ word choice
☐ imagery
☐ sentence structure
☐ sound
☐ tone
☐ punctuation

In order to answer questions that require you to analyse the writer's use of language features, the first thing you must do is refer to the technique(s) being used by the author (usually accompanied by quotation). Unfortunately, there are no marks for this part of your answer. The second thing you must do is comment on how the particular technique is used. The marks are awarded for your comments. An appropriate reference to a language feature and a detailed or insightful comment will usually get you 2 marks; a reference plus a more basic comment will be worth 1.

Let's see how that works in practice.

Read the following extract from an article by music journalist Alexis Petridis on youth subcultures and the question that follows.

I'm trying to investigate the state of youth subcultures in 2014. It seems a worthwhile thing to do. You hardly need a degree in sociology to realise that something fairly dramatic has happened to them over the past couple of decades; you just need a functioning pair of eyes. When I arrived at secondary school in the mid-80s, the fifth and sixth forms, where uniform requirements were relaxed, looked like a mass of different tribes, all of them defined by the music they liked, all of them more or less wearing their tastes on their sleeves. There were goths. There were metallers. There were punks. There were soulboys, at least one of whom had made the fateful decision to try and complete his look by growing a moustache, the bum fluff result pathetic in the extreme. There were Morrissey acolytes, and even a couple of ersatz hippies, one of whom had decorated his Adidas holdall with a drawing of the complex front cover of Gong's 1971 album *Camembert Electrique*: a pretty ballsy move, given the derision that hippies had suffered during punk, and at the hands of the scriptwriters of *The Young Ones*.

From an article by Alex Petridis in the *Guardian*, Thursday 20 March 2014

Question: Analyse how the writer's use of language emphasises the wide variety of youth subcultures the writer encountered when he was at school. You should refer in your answer to such features as sentence structure, word choice, imagery, contrast, tone ...   **2**

To answer this question, look for appropriate language features, quote/refer to them and then comment on their connotations. Your answer should include at least two of the following:

Word choice

'mass' suggests a large number.

'different tribes' suggests assorted, almost primitive, groups.

Sentence structure

Repetition. 'There were ... There were ...' emphasises the number of different groups.

Listing. 'goths ... metallers ... punks ... soulboys' indicates the range of subcultures.

Short sentences. 'There were goths. There were metallers.' highlights that each group was separate from the others.

Let's look at how to deal with each language feature in more detail.

To comment on **word choice** simply quote the appropriate word (or words) and comment on the **connotations** of that word. In other words make sure you say what that word **suggests** rather than just what it **means**. Remember that the writer will have chosen that particular word carefully for the specific effect it will create.

Answers on word choice can be written very economically and effectively like this:

Word   suggests   reference to connotations/effect of word

For example:

'sunset' suggests something coming to an end/death.

'thorny' suggests something difficult or painful to deal with.

'rationale' suggests a more sophisticated reason/things have been thought through logically.

'maternal' suggests a caring attitude.

'pedestrian' suggests something very ordinary.

Now let us consider questions about imagery.

An image is just a picture in words. In the kind of non-fiction writing used in the Reading for Understanding, Analysis and Evaluation exam paper, a writer will use imagery to help illustrate a point being made or to achieve a particular effect.

Look at how the nature writer Mark Cocker describes a flock of crows.

> It is no longer a flock of birds. Each occasion I see these protean swirls rise they act like ink-blot tests drawing images out of my unconscious. Sometimes they seem like something you saw before you left the womb, before your eyes first opened, an entopic vision buried deep beneath the avalanche of waking experience: black dust motes sinking steadily through the gentle oil of sleep. Tonight the flock blossoms as an immense night flower and, while beautiful and mysterious, it always stirs something edgy into my sense of wonder. It is the feeling that in viewing the unnumbered and unnumberable birds, I am tipped towards the state of confusion which that inchoate twisting swerve so perfectly represents.
>
> Mark Cocker, *Crow Country*

Here is one way to answer questions on imagery (your teacher/tutor might suggest other equally valid approaches). First of all explain the 'root' of the image and say what is being compared with what. Think about what the two things have in common and what the writer is suggesting by making this comparison. Then go on to say why this makes the image effective or otherwise.

You might be asked the following question about imagery:

Question: By referring to at least one example, analyse how the writer's use of imagery conveys his experience of watching crows.

To answer this question, find the images used by the writer, explain the 'root' of these images and go on to comment on what they suggest about the experience.

A possible answer might look like this:

The writer compares watching a flock of crows to undergoing an 'ink-blot' test. Depending on what we see in them, ink-blot tests are designed to reveal things in our subconscious and the writer's use of this simile effectively suggests the many different patterns formed by the crows and the deep and powerful effect watching them has on him.

Now see if you can comment in the same way on the following images:

- like something you saw before you left the womb
- an entopic vision buried deep beneath the avalanche of waking experience
- black dust motes sinking steadily through the gentle oil of sleep
- the flock blossoms as an immense night flower.

> **TOP TIP**
>
> Make sure you are able to identify techniques such as simile, metaphor and personification so that you can respond effectively to questions on imagery.

Types of questions: analysing sentences – structure and punctuation

Sometimes a question will ask you directly about sentence structure and/or punctuation but don't forget to consider these if the question asks about the writer's use of **language**.

In answering questions on sentence structure and punctuation you must identify the technique that is being used and then comment on what effect it has. As always, there are no marks awarded for the reference you make – for example, you get nothing for pointing out that

The writer uses a list in line 55.

Marks are allocated depending on the quality of your **comment** on the effect of the list. Structure your answer by referring first of all to the technique and then adding your comment.

The list in line 55 ('the carefree, the careworn, the innocent, the guilty, the indolent, the industrious ...') suggests the wide variety of personalities in the room.

Any time you are asked about sentence structure, a checklist of possible features should start running in your head.

Ask yourself, is it a long sentence? A short sentence? A list …?

Once you've spotted the technique, think about the effect it creates. The following table gives you a reminder of different sentence features and their effects.

Feature — types of sentence	Possible effects
Statement	• conveying facts • making assertions
Question	• involves the reader • indicates writer reflecting on or considering things • a series of questions might suggest bewilderment/puzzlement
Rhetorical question	• invites the reader to think • invites the reader to share the writer's opinion
Exclamation	• expresses emotion (surprise, anger, etc.)
Command (imperative)	• instructions • can suggest friendly informality (*Bring a friend …; Imagine you are …*)
Minor sentence	• impact • informality • suspense
Sentence in a paragraph of its own	• impact • drama

Feature — structure	Possible effects
Long sentence	To describe (amongst other things): • physical length • a complex process • a series of activities • something tedious or boring
Short sentence	• (dramatic) impact
List	• number of examples • reinforcement of an idea • range or variety
Repetition	• emphasis (always say **what** it emphasises)

Inversion	• changes focus/emphasis of the sentence to the displaced word(s)
Climax	• builds up to something (say **what** that is)
Anti-climax	• builds up and then descends to something contrasting with what has gone before (often used for humorous effect)
Antithesis	• contrasting ideas (look at **what** is being contrasted and why)

Feature — punctuation	Possible effects
Capitalisation	indicates • names • titles • significance
Inverted commas '...'	indicate • names • titles • direct speech • quotation • writer using word ironically
Comma ,	separates • clauses • items in a list
Colon :	introduces • a list • an expansion of an idea • a quotation
Semi-colon ;	• 'hinge' in a balanced sentence • separates phrasal items in a list
Dash –	• introduces an explanation or expansion of an idea • introduces an aside or afterthought from the writer
Parenthesis – – or ( ) or , ,	indicates extra information included in the sentence (remember that you must comment on **what** the extra information **adds** to the sentence)
Ellipsis ...	• indicates words missing • suggests a list could continue • interruption • hesitation

Here is an extract from an article on teenagers and their parents by the journalist Suzanne Moore. Look at it and try to explain what effects are achieved by the writer's use of sentence structure.

'Your child is going to experiment': what teenagers really think

It's so unfair. No one understands you. People who actually have no idea tell you what to do all the time. About anything. Everyone patronises you or exchanges knowing looks when you say something really important. No one sees you as an individual any more but just as some kind of generic blob. No one is there when you feel really lonely. No one is there when you discover something completely weird  about the world. No one is there when you are too tired to pick up the remote control. No one gets quite how boring all of this is.

This is how it feels to be the parent of a teenager. Not all the time. Some of the time. I can't tell you how to do it, but I can reassure you that you are probably doing it *all* wrong. There are experts in adolescence, apparently. There are manuals that are fine if you accept that you just need to change the settings on teenagers until their lights flash on and off. Teenagers are bracketed with toddlers in terms of targeted user guides. This seems naff, but there is no one these days apparently not in need of some dumbed-down cognitive behavioural therapy. Strangely, I happen to believe teenagers – er, much like us grown-ups – are all different.

I am currently on my third teenager (she is 13; my older ones are in their 20s), but the real truth is that I am on my fourth. Me! I was a teenager. It is this experience more than anything that informs my parenting. For I know I was pretty much formed as a person by 14, and I haven't changed that much since. That may be a good thing or a bad thing. Your relationship to your adolescent is often hooked into the relationship you have with your own adolescence. So many irrational fears, hopes and denials come from this nowhere land.

That's why, when your child starts the journey of separating from you, you may react in all sorts of strange ways. You as a parent may feel suddenly out of control. Of yourself as well as of your child.

Many people seem anxious that what is seen as adolescent behaviour kicks in long before the teen years, at about 10. By this I mean the stereotypical way that we define this phase: wanting stuff, being sarcastic, needing to be alone sometimes, caring too much about being included or excluded from particular groups, demanding the impossible, being oversensitive, easily hurt and inexplicably angry. All the while doing daft things. None of these behaviours belongs to any one age group, but we tend to see teenagers' emotional lives as somehow always excessive and exaggerated.

From an article by Suzanne Moore in *the Guardian*, Thursday 14 June 2014

You should have spotted:

- the short emphatic statement at the start of the passage, 'It's so unfair', to introduce the writer's complaints
- the use of the minor sentence 'About anything' to bluntly reinforce the sense of unfairness
- the repetition of 'No one ... No one ...' to effectively suggest the sense of the writer's feelings of isolation/lack of empathy from others
- the use of parenthesis ' – er, much like us grown-ups –' to add a conversational aside that acknowledges what the two groups have in common
- the use of the colon to introduce a list of stereotypical teenage behaviours
- the use of 'but' in 'None of these behaviours ..., but we tend to see ...' to indicate the contrast between reality and our perception of teenage behaviour.

Did you spot any other features?

The link question

You'll need to quote in your answer ('Referring to specific words and/or phrases ...').

Any link in a chain is joined to what comes before it and what follows after.

There are always four parts to your answer:

1. Quote the words in the link sentence which refer back to what the writer has already said.
2. Say clearly what ideas they introduce or how they are connected to the next part of the passage.
3. Quote the words in the link sentence which introduce what the writer goes on to say next.
4. Say clearly what ideas they introduce or how they are connected to the next part of the passage.

Here is an example from an old SQA Higher paper:

Read lines 17–29 of passage 2.

Q. Referring to specific words and/or phrases, show how the sentence 'The trouble ... sports drugs.' (lines 22–23) performs a linking function in the writer's argument.

The trouble is that such questioning has long been abandoned in the culture of sports drugs.

Answer:

'such questioning' refers back to the questions asked in the previous paragraph about why a canoeist would cheat in this way.

'abandoned in the culture of sports drugs' introduces the idea that these questions are no longer even an issue and that people have to take drugs just to compete.

Tone

Tone is sometimes a difficult thing to identify in a piece of writing. It's much easier to spot when someone is talking to you. You immediately know for example if the person is angry, bitter or enthusiastic. We can all usually tell when someone is being sarcastic ('Yeah, Higher English is so easy'). The tone someone uses when speaking reveals their attitude to what they are saying.

> **TOP TIP**
> Don't say the writer is being sarcastic unless you are absolutely certain of this. Too many candidates use this as a kind of automatic response to questions about tone!

It's the same in writing. The tone a writer adopts will reflect his or her attitude to their subject matter.

You need to be able to identify when a writer is being ironic or nostalgic or angry or serious or enthusiastic or humorous or …

When you are faced with a question in the RUAE paper which asks you to 'Comment on the writer's tone …' you must first identify which tone you think the writer has adopted and go on to explain how the language features used help to establish the tone. Look at how the writer uses techniques such as word choice, imagery and sentence structure to suggest this tone.

Try this

Read the extracts on the next two pages by *Guardian* journalist Lucy Mangan. They are from an article in which she discusses the novel *Twilight* and the film of the same name.

Look at the highlighted pieces of text and try to explain how they contribute to the **critical** tone she adopts (it's clear she's not a fan). The first section has been done for you.

See if you agree with the comments on pages 132–133.

> **TOP TIP**
> Always look carefully at the information given to you about each passage in the exam. It can sometimes give you a clue to the overall tone of the passage.

Dangerous liaisons

As most teenage girls in Britain will already know, Twilight – a tale of love between a young woman and a vampire – has now been made into a movie. It will no doubt be a huge hit. But what a shame it's not more like Buffy, writes Lucy Mangan.

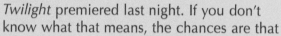

Twilight premiered last night. If you don't know what that means, the chances are that you are neither a teenage girl nor mother or teacher of same. If you were, you would know instantly that today is the day the first book in Stephenie Meyer's internationally bestselling vampire romance saga comes to the big screen.

The idea for the book came in a dream, says Meyer, a Mormon who performed the impressive feat of typing the subsequent 500-page narrative one-handed with a baby on her lap and two other children under five playing round her feet.

Looking at the synopsis of *Twilight*, sceptics and cynics might ask if this was a dream that came to the author after she fell asleep in front of an episode of Joss Whedon's television series *Buffy the Vampire Slayer*, which also centred round the relationship between a high school girl and a 'good' vampire who couldn't have sex for fear that he would turn evil again. Sceptics and cynics who have actually read *Twilight* or seen the film, however, will simply roll their eyes at their misguided brethren and say, 'If only.'

If only Meyer had taken Buffy as her template. If only she had used that groundbreaking series as her foundation and built on it. If only there was a Whedonesque intelligence and modern, feminist sensibility informing *Twilight* and its successors. If only.

You should have spotted:

- the repetition of 'If only …' to highlight the writer's low opinion of Meyer's work compared to Buffy
- that the minor sentence to end the paragraph adds impact and drives the writer's message home.

Now go on to look at the rest of the article.

What you have instead in Meyer's work is a depressingly retrograde, deeply anti-feminist, borderline misogynistic novel that drains its heroine of life and vitality as surely as if a vampire had sunk his teeth into her and leaves her a bloodless cipher while the story happens around her. Edward tells her she is 'so interesting … fascinating', but the reader looks in vain for his evidence.

Far more important, however, is the nature of the relationship between Bella and Edward. In interviews, Meyer claims that the theme of the *Twilight* saga is choice, because Edward chooses not to behave as his nature impels him to. Alas, the only choice Bella gets to make is to sacrifice herself in ever-larger increments.

It sounds melodramatic and shrill to say that Bella and Edward's relationship is abusive, but as the story wears on it becomes increasingly hard to avoid the comparison, as she gradually isolates herself from her friends to protect his secret, and learns to subordinate her every impulse and movement to the necessity of not upsetting Edward and his instincts.

Edward, of course, has warned her not to be alone with him. To those less enamoured of Meyerworld, the implication is that Bella chooses to put herself in danger and the further implication is that she must therefore bear full responsibility for the consequences (which, in the way of vampire romances, are not entirely confined to hugs and puppies).

In the book (though, naturally, less so in the film, as she is still physically present on screen), despite being the narrator, Bella all but disappears as a character. The few signs of wit and independence she exhibits at the beginning of the book, when she is starting her new school, have long been abandoned in favour of mute devotion to Edward, which by the end is so slavish that she asks him to turn her into a vampire too, so that he needn't be frightened of killing her any more.

Now, teenage readers – or viewers, although the film loses much of the written detail of Bella and Edward's relationship, which in this case could be classed as a good thing – aren't idiots. But they are young, inexperienced and underinformed, and that makes them vulnerable to influences they are exposed to uncritically.

Edward is no hero. Bella is no Buffy. And *Twilight*'s underlying message – that self-sacrifice makes you a worthy girlfriend, that men mustn't be excited beyond a certain point, that men with problems must be forgiven everything, that female passivity is a state to be encouraged – are no good to anyone. It should be staked through its black, black heart.

Did you spot any other features which contribute to the critical tone?

Types of questions: evaluation

Evaluation questions ask you to evaluate **how successful** the writer is in using particular techniques or **how effective** he or she has been in achieving the purpose of the writing.

Effectiveness of a paragraph

A common question you might encounter in the RUAE paper is one which asks you to evaluate the effectiveness of a particular paragraph. Often it is the final paragraph that you get asked about but the question might also be about the opening one (or indeed any particular paragraph that is important to the writer's line of thought). Let's look at how to deal with such a question. Here is an example:

Evaluate the effectiveness of the final paragraph as a conclusion to the passage as a whole. You should refer in your answer to ideas and to language.

To answer this kind of question, always begin with a comment on the effectiveness. Make some kind of *evaluative* judgement.

So you should begin your answer as follows:

The final paragraph is very effective because ...

You are, of course, perfectly at liberty to say the paragraph is *not* very effective (perhaps the ideas are rather obvious and/or some of the language is a bit clichéd) or that some parts of it are effective but others are not. This is all very acceptable providing you support your evaluative comment with good use of evidence. Having said all that, it is usually much easier to say that the particular bit of writing you have been asked to look at *is* effective.

Once you've made your initial evaluative statement go on to provide evidence to support your judgement. You should consider ideas and language.

Ideas

Some things to consider:

- Does the paragraph sum up some of the points made earlier in the passage?
- Does it refer to anything from the opening of the passage (a common technique which gives a nice sense of 'circularity' in the structure of the article)?
- Does it include a clear statement of the writer's opinion?

Language

Identify techniques as you would for questions elsewhere in the passage, for example:

- sentence structure
- word choice
- imagery
- sound
- tone
- punctuation.

Comment on how these features help to reinforce the effectiveness of the paragraph.

Here is a sample answer to the question, 'How effective do you find the final paragraph as a conclusion to the writer's argument?'

The final paragraph acts as a very effective conclusion to the passage. It returns to the topic introduced in the very first paragraph – that the internet needs to be reclaimed from the giant tech companies. The short sentence 'But we can do it' clearly suggests the writer's belief that change is possible. The emphatic tone of the two closing minor sentences, 'For us now. And for our Children.' signals the profound importance of this issue.

Notice how this answer refers to ideas (mentioning the return to the topic from the opening paragraph) and to particular features of language (the short sentence and the two concluding minor sentences).

All of the above applies to a question on a final paragraph but you can essentially take the same approach if you are asked about an opening paragraph. In *that* case look for:

Ideas

- Does it introduce the topic in an interesting and engaging way?
- Are things mentioned which then reappear later in the passage?
- Does it give us a hint of the writer's personality and their approach to the subject?

Language

- sentence structure
- word choice
- imagery
- sound
- tone
- punctuation

Now try putting your knowledge of language features to the test by reading the following passages on private schools, education jargon and allowing toddlers to play video games. *Identify* and *comment* on:

- word choice
- imagery
- sentence structure
- tone.

Passage 1: Stop criticising private schools, start learning from them

Former Chancellor, Lord Lamont, is absolutely right to say we should take more pride in our private schools, and see them as "great national assets".

Private schools are renowned the world over: a British success story increasingly being exported, with top schools like Cranleigh, Dulwich, Harrow, Marlborough and Wellington, all setting up overseas subsidiaries in the Far and Middle East.

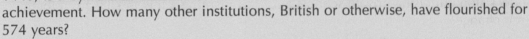

Meanwhile Eton itself, founded in 1440, is a byword in educational achievement. How many other institutions, British or otherwise, have flourished for 574 years?

So why are so many, as Lord Lamont observes, so critical of private schools? Is this pure envy?

Whatever the reason, it's not enough simply to sit back and take pride in these excellent institutions. We need to learn what makes them successful and translate some of the attitudes, some of the culture, to the maintained sector too.

What an irony: Britain has probably the best independent schools in the world; but on the other side of the "Berlin Wall", has a maintained sector increasingly languishing behind our competitors, as the PISA tests revealed.

So what makes private schools special? First and foremost, the "can do" attitude they foster amongst pupils. Success, achievement, ambition, pride: these are not dirty words, to be avoided at all costs, but are embedded in the ethos of all independent schools – often seen in their mottos.

Cheltenham College's is typical: "Labor Omnia Vincit" ("Work Conquers All"). Or how about "Industria", the motto of Tony Blair's alma mater, Fettes College (often regarded as "Scotland's Eton"), exhorting its pupils to work harder.

The fact such mottos are still unashamedly in Latin, itself makes a statement about excellence: "You don't know the meaning? Why not look it up and learn something?"

Apart from "Floreat Etona", "May Eton Flourish" (no shortage of pride there), one of the most famous mottos is Winchester College's "Manners makyth man".

This may sound unfashionable, until you remember that Winchester, founded in 1382, has been around for over 600 years – even predating Eton. Surely that's something to take pride in?

In contrast, every time I pass a comprehensive, I am struck by the bland, meaningless "mission statements" posted proudly outside school gates. Usually these run something along the lines of "excellence for everyone", or "achievement for all", or some such other woolly, waffly, slogan. How exactly is this to be achieved, I find myself wondering?

Next, private schools encourage competition – and not just in the classroom itself, with well-publicised grading systems and form orders, so everyone knows exactly how they stand, but also on the sports field.

Competitive sport is, sadly, on its way out in too many maintained schools. But in the private sector, sport flourishes: with regular rugby, soccer, cricket fixtures. This is why 40 per cent of medals at the London Olympics were won by former private pupils. When will we realise that "competition" too is not taboo?

Crucially, private schools also give every pupil a sense of community and belonging. They achieve this through their "house" systems. No matter how large the school, from two hundred to the huge size of Eton, boys and girls will be split into smaller, friendlier, school houses of fifty or sixty pupils.

Fierce rivalries between houses are engendered; fierce loyalties develop. A strong sense of identity and confidence is the end result.

So let's stop criticising private schools and start learning a few lessons from them for a change.

The author teaches English at a top independent boarding school.

From an article in *the Telegraph*, 29 July 2014

Passage 2: Secret Teacher: jargon is ruining our children's education

Ugly words – such as learning objectives, non-negotiables and targets – are meaningless to young pupils and put too much pressure on them too soon.

"What do you do when you get to school in the morning?" a colleague asked a younger member of my family recently. "Well, when we get to class, we get out our books and start on our non-negotiables," replied the child, who is in year 2. "What are they?" the colleague inquired. "Don't know" was the answer.

This is a perfect example of what is bothering me as a primary school teacher – educational jargon that is passed on to our children. At no point during my own education was I ever aware of non-negotiables, targets, levels, learning objectives or success criteria. But my teachers still taught me a great deal and it was pretty obvious that I was learning. Where I stood in the academic pecking order was the teacher's business, not mine.

But the constant jargon that teachers are forced to use is rubbing off on our students. Not only is this meaningless for them but it's increasingly making their academic performance their responsibility too. Do primary school children really need that kind of pressure when they're so young?

Despite my objections, this year I prepared a group of year 6 children to have a go at the Sats level 6 papers. Level 6 is designed for children aged 14, but these students were very secure at level 5. One girl in particular found this process really difficult and, when I found her in tears after a practice test, it was clear from our conversation that however much I tried to explain that level 6 was miles ahead of where she was supposed to be, it hadn't really sunk in.

"Why are you so upset?" I asked.

"Because I just don't think I'm going to get a level 6 in reading, and that's my target."

"Really? Did I ever tell you that was your target?"

"No, but I'm doing the paper."

"Well, what will happen if you don't get the level 6? What level will you get instead?"

"I'll just get a level 5."

"And do you know what level most children leave primary school with? Level 4b, so it's not just a level 5 – you're already higher than average."

"Oh."

"Just do the best that you can."

"Ok, thanks Miss. And you won't be disappointed if I don't get level 6?"

"No, not at all. If you try your hardest I'll be happy with whatever you get."

By dragging children into a stupid numbers game with us, we do them a great disservice. They don't respond well to the pressure, and levels and targets don't tell the tale of their primary education. But many schools make children believe it really matters. Of course it matters to teachers and management, because that is what we as professionals are judged on, but it is of little consequence to the children themselves.

In the same vein, schools conduct their own type of Pavlov's dog experiment by conditioning students to think that they are only learning when they use the correct buzzwords. Learning that takes place outside of the objective is rarely valued or recognised, and teachers who train under this rigid system never realise there was ever another way.

Learning is apparently pointless unless it has a clear "objective" shared with the children, and children cannot possibly achieve anything unless they follow the success criteria. While these concepts are amazing tools for professionals when used with care and thought, too often the jargon leads to boring teaching. And teachers only feel obliged to cling on to these terms to get approval from other adults.

Children are expected to jump perfectly through adult-designed hoops in other ways too. The question most often asked of children in a lesson observation is: "What you are learning?" Should the child dare to reply by enthusiastically telling the adult about what they are doing, then the teacher is penalised because the learning objective isn't clear enough. For many children, this is an extremely demanding question and one many will not be developmentally ready for. When a child plays with Lego they don't say, "I'm developing my sense of spatial awareness and 3D shapes, as well [as] elementary engineering and architecture." Rather, they say: "Look at the house I built!" Should we really expect them to respond any differently?

Teachers need to claim back their intellectual confidence and decide what is best for their children, exercising professional judgment without fear of criticism. Too much of children's time is wasted telling them in great detail what skills they are developing as if they were able to stand outside of themselves and see the wider application of these skills.

Thankfully I now work in an environment where the management appreciate that learning does not have to take a set format. I don't feel obliged to tick their boxes and this is good for the children and for me. I know exactly what I'm going to teach, giving clear guidance on what is expected and direction on how to get things done. But I rarely mention the ugly words learning objectives, success criteria and targets. The principles are there but the jargon isn't. And guess what? They still learn.

From an article in *the Guardian*, 9 August 2014

Passage 3: Want to silence a two-year-old? Try teaching it to ride a motorbike

I decided to introduce my son to video games. We soon found one he liked … and I mean really, really liked.

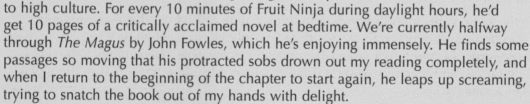

After a while my son was shunning his regular toys in favour of "the Motorbike Game", as he calls it (it's actually called Trials Fusion).

So I decided to introduce my two-year-old son to the world of video games. Before you accuse me of hobbling my offspring's mind, I'd like to point out that a) television is 2,000 times worse, so shove that up your Night Garden and b) I also decided to counterbalance the gaming with exposure to high culture. For every 10 minutes of Fruit Ninja during daylight hours, he'd get 10 pages of a critically acclaimed novel at bedtime. We're currently halfway through *The Magus* by John Fowles, which he's enjoying immensely. He finds some passages so moving that his protracted sobs drown out my reading completely, and when I return to the beginning of the chapter to start again, he leaps up screaming, trying to snatch the book out of my hands with delight.

Like any self-respecting 2014 toddler, he can swipe, pat and jab at games on a smartphone or tablet, but smartphone games aren't real games. They're interactive dumbshows designed to sedate suicidal commuters. And they're not just basic but insulting, often introducing themselves as free-to-play simply so they can extort money from you later in exchange for more levels or less terrible gameplay. Either that or they fund themselves with pop-up adverts that defile the screen like streaks on a toilet bowl.

I don't want him playing that horrible rubbish. I want him mainlining proper games as quickly as possible. And proper games are played with a keyboard and a mouse, or a weighty controller embellished with an intimidating array of buttons and sticks and triggers – one that melts ergonomically into any experienced gamer's hands, but makes newcomers feel like they've just picked up a Rubik's Cube designed by Salvador Dalí.

So I handed him a controller. I tried him on Super Mario World, but he didn't understand that you could move *and* jump at the same time, which limited the fun. My fun, not his. He was perfectly happy to press one button repeatedly to make Mario leap up and down on the spot. But he wouldn't time the jumps properly. He kept getting killed by the same Goomba, endlessly waddling towards him. It was excruciating to watch. So I switched the Nintendo off and tried a different console. He screamed with enthusiasm, or possibly despair. Maybe even hunger. It was getting quite late.

Eventually, after a few more missteps, I stumbled across the perfect game: Trials Fusion. It looks like an action game, but it's actually more of a physics-based puzzle. You're meant to continually adjust the stance of a motorcyclist so he doesn't fall off as he rides at speed over spectacular courses full of ramps and chasms. Despite its high difficulty level, he could make entertaining progress just by pressing the accelerator. The rider fell off all the time, but when he did he plummeted into ravines and bashed against photorealistic scenery, screaming in terror. My son found this hilarious, which is fine, OK, because it *is* hilarious. After each tumble he hurriedly tapped "retry", which is the second button he learned to locate.

Things soon escalated. One afternoon he threw a tantrum in a supermarket and I, in desperation, downloaded the iPhone version of "the Motorbike Game" (which is what he calls it), and handed it to him as he writhed screaming in the trolley seat. Bingo. Instant calm. He couldn't have been happier. Or quieter. I had to prise it from his hands later with a shoehorn, but that seemed a reasonable exchange for 30 minutes of peace.

But as with free-to-play games, the price was higher; the sting came later. Shortly afterwards, we went on holiday. He had a meltdown on the plane, so out came the Motorbike Game. Wouldn't sit still in a restaurant. Out came the Motorbike Game. Strayed perilously near the pool. Motorbike Game. It was too tempting: like having a toddler with a pause button. Inevitably, he got hooked. Hopelessly hooked.

I want the Motorbike Game. I want the Motorbike Game. That's all I heard all week, apart from him singing the theme music. Just like smoking, each individual cigarette satiated the immediate craving, while increasing his overall dependence.

Worst of all, in the iPhone version – which surprise, surprise masquerades as "free" – the bike runs out of fuel now and then, and the only way to refill the tank it is to wait for a countdown to expire (slightly harder for a two-year-old than completing a tapestry), watch an advert (evil) or to purchase in-game petrol from the App Store.

I first became aware of this when he screamed and hurled the phone across a restaurant table in a fury. I caved in immediately and, illustrating everything that's wrong with human progress, found myself spending real money on non-existent petrol for a non-existent motorbike in a desperate bid to appease an infant. Spending money to shut him up felt transgressive and undignified – but worse still, I was literally fuelling his addiction.

On our return we realised he was shunning his regular toys in favour of the Motorbike Game. There was nothing else for it. He had to go cold turkey. The Motorbike Game had to die. I deleted it from the phone and hid the Xbox controller. Neither action went down well. Having been introduced in order to avert meltdowns, the Motorbike Game was now causing them on an epic scale.

Eventually, after several days of endless and often furious requests for the Motorbike Game, he passed through the five stages of grief and came out the other side.

I walked into the kitchen where he sat calmly on the floor, playing with his wooden blocks for the first time in a week.

"That's nice," I cooed encouragingly. "What are you doing?"

"I'm playing the Motorbike Game", he replied, a little sadly.

I looked again. He was re-enacting the game. One block was the motorbike. The rest were the scenery.

It wasn't as good as the original. But it was, at least, his own.

From an article by Charlie Brooker in *the Guardian*, 11 August 2014

Now read the following article by Stuart Tootal, a former soldier who served in Afghanistan. Answer the questions which follow using the techniques you have learned so far. Check your answers on pages 133–135.

Post-traumatic stress disorder is the invisible scar of war

Not all Afghan veterans will suffer from mental trauma – but we owe a debt to those who do

1. As a soldier, I used to be sceptical about the significance of post-traumatic stress disorder (PTSD) – about the idea that strong men could be reduced to a shadow of their former selves by the experience of war. I might have stayed that way, had I not found myself commanding troops in Afghanistan.

2. In 2006, 3 Para was the first UK combat unit to be sent into Helmand province. Fifteen of my battle group were killed in action, and another 46 seriously wounded. By the time we returned to Britain, any cynicism had disappeared.

3. The fighting 3 Para engaged in has been described as the most intensive combat experienced by the British Army since the Korean War. Isolated bases came under constant attack from enemy assaults, mortars and rocket fire. Patrols were close-combat affairs in high-standing crops, where the Taliban could often be heard moving in the next stand of maize prior to the start of a firefight. The increasing sophistication of roadside bombs became an enduring dread.

4. While we, and the other Army and Marine units that followed us, served valiantly and admirably, the experience of Helmand left a mark on all of us: the loss of close friends and comrades, combat fatigue, the constant stress of facing death or serious injury. But while most of us readjusted to the peacetime world and reintegrated with our families, for some the mental trauma had become too deeply embedded.

5. Since 2006, hundreds of thousands of British troops have fought in Afghanistan. Numerous studies have indicated that between 10 and 20 per cent of soldiers returning from these combat zones are suffering, or will suffer, from PTSD. Yesterday, the charity Combat Stress announced that it has seen a 57 per cent increase in the number of Afghanistan-related referrals over the past year, from 228 to 358. Given the estimated incubation period of between seven to 14 years, there are bound to be many more.

6. But like shellshock during the First World War, and combat fatigue in the Second, PTSD remains a contentious issue. Official MoD (Ministry of Defence) figures claim that only 4 per cent of soldiers will suffer from it, although they accept that the level will be slightly higher for infantry units and among reservists (at 5 and 6 per cent respectively). But this calculation is based on a study completed in 2009. Since then, the UK has been at war for another five years, and thousands more have served. Additionally, the study did not track veterans, so cannot take account of the delayed onset of PTSD – which can often manifest itself when veterans leave the familiar environment of the military and enter civilian life.

7. This is not to suggest that the MoD has not acted. Post-tour decompression; education and training to identify and manage PTSD; 24-hour mental health lines; joint initiatives with the NHS – all have been put in place over the past few years. The Service charities have also worked hard to address the issue. However, there is still more that we can do, especially in regard to supporting those who leave the military. In 2012, 50 soldiers and veterans took their own lives – more than the number of combat casualties in the same year. And I continue to hear stories from former soldiers whose treatment for PTSD has fallen short of where it should be.

8. Given the number of British troops that have been exposed to the dehumanising effects of war in Afghanistan and the likely incubation periods associated with the condition, there is a compelling case to review the statistics and address the gaps in provision. But we also need to avoid exaggerating the extent of the mental trauma, and maligning those who suffer from it.

9. By no means will everyone who has served on combat operations succumb to PTSD – and even then, the condition does not prevent them from leading normal lives or holding down a meaningful job, with proper treatment and managerial support. My current employer, Barclays, has helped 2,350 veterans since 2010 via its Armed Forces Transition, Employment and Resettlement programme, and a small number have suffered from PTSD.

10. Our Servicemen and women are a remarkable fraternity, 'born from smoke, danger and death'. They know what real fear is and have to live with the consequences of the application and receipt of lethal force. Yet they are continuously prepared to risk life and limb in places such as Afghanistan to do the nation's bidding.

11. While not all will suffer from mental trauma, even the bravest of soldiers can succumb to the condition. We need to work together in the state, military and private sectors to understand and address PTSD as an invisible scar of war, and the natural – but treatable – consequence of combat.

Written by Stuart Tootal and published in
the Daily Telegraph on 13 May 2014.

Re-read paragraphs 1–3.

1. a) Explain in your own words the change in Stuart Tootal's attitude to PTSD. **3 marks**

   b) Analyse how two examples of the writer's language in these paragraphs convey the reality of combat. **4 marks**

Re-read paragraph 4.

2. Analyse how the writer uses sentence structure and word choice to highlight the soldiers' experiences in Afghanistan and their experiences in the 'peacetime world'. **4 marks**

Re-read paragraphs 6–8.

3. Explain what might be a reason for the level of PTSD being 'slightly higher for infantry units and reservists'. **2 marks**

4. Identify and explain the writer's use of irony in paragraph 7. **2 marks**

5. Explain in your own words the **four** main points the writer makes in paragraph 8. **4 marks**

Re-read paragraph 11.

6. The writer describes PTSD as 'an invisible scar of war'. Explain the meaning of this image and analyse its effect. **3 marks**

Consider the text as a whole.

7. Identify evidence in the passage of the support offered to serving soldiers and veterans. Answer in your own words. **4 marks**

Questions on both passages

The question on both passages is the only question that follows the second passage in the Reading for Understanding, Analysis and Evaluation paper. Here is an example from the SQA Higher Specimen Paper:

Look at both passages.

Both writers express their views about the importance of trees.

Identify three key areas on which they agree. You should support the points by referring to important ideas in both passages.

You may answer this question in continuous prose or in a series of developed bullet points.

Notice that you are asked to identify the **key areas of agreement** in this question but you could also be asked to identify the key areas on which they **disagree**, or even the key areas of agreement **and** disagreement – so don't be thrown by this if it appears in your exam. The question is essentially a test of your ability to recognise what is at the heart of each passage. **It is always worth 5 marks.** When answering a question about the key areas in each passage, make sure you can identify and summarise what seem to be the main points the writer has made. Look again at the topic sentences of each paragraph – they should provide you with helpful reminders.

You can answer this question in continuous prose or in a series of developed bullet points but you might find the following 'template' helpful.

Answer

Key Area of Agreement #1: *write the first area of agreement here.*

- Evidence from passage 1: *this should be in the form of a quotation from the passage and a more generalised comment/summary by you to show your understanding of the idea presented by the writer of passage 1.*

- Evidence from passage 2: *this should be in the form of a quotation from the passage and a more generalised comment/summary by you to show your understanding of the idea presented by the writer of passage 2.*

Then **repeat** for Key Area of Agreement #2, #3 and so on.

Always try to identify at least **three** key areas in your response to this question.

Reading for Understanding, Analysis and Evaluation exam paper

Now you have had some practice with the kinds of questions asked in the Higher exam, have a go at this full length Reading for Understanding, Analysis and Evaluation paper. There are two passages and questions. Read each passage carefully and then answer the questions. Use the techniques explained earlier in the chapter and, once you have finished, check your answers against the suggested answers on pages 136–140.

Passage 1

In this passage, which is taken from an introduction to a book about evolution, the scientist Richard Dawkins describes some of the difficulties faced by those teaching the topic in schools.

TOP TIP

For extra realism, try completing past papers or practice papers 'against the clock'. Allow yourself **1 hour and 30 minutes** to complete all the questions.

ONLY A THEORY

Imagine that you are a teacher of Roman history and the Latin language, anxious to impart your enthusiasm for the ancient world – for the elegiacs of Ovid and the odes of Horace, the sinewy economy of Latin grammar as exhibited in the oratory of Cicero, the strategic niceties of the Punic Wars, the generalship of Julius Caesar and the voluptuous
5   excesses of the later emperors. That's a big undertaking and it takes time, concentration, dedication. Yet you find your precious time continually preyed upon, and your class's attention distracted, by a baying pack of ignoramuses (as a Latin scholar you would know better than to say 'ignorami') who, with strong political and especially financial support, scurry about tirelessly attempting to persuade your unfortunate pupils that
10 the Romans never existed. There never was a Roman Empire. The entire world came into existence only just beyond living memory. Spanish, Italian, French, Portuguese, Catalan, Occitan, Romansh: all these languages and their constituent dialects sprang spontaneously and separately into being, and owe nothing to any predecessor such as Latin. Instead of devoting your full attention to the noble vocation of classical scholar
15 and teacher, you are forced to divert your time and energy to a rearguard defence of the proposition that the Romans existed at all: a defence against an exhibition of ignorant prejudice that would make you weep if you weren't too busy fighting it.

If my fantasy of the Latin teacher seems too wayward, here's a more realistic example. Imagine you are a teacher of more recent history, and your lessons on
20 twentieth-century Europe are boycotted, heckled or otherwise disrupted by well-organized, well-financed and politically muscular groups of Holocaust-deniers. Unlike my hypothetical Rome-deniers, Holocaust-deniers really exist. They are vocal, superficially plausible, and adept at seeming learned. They are supported by the president of at least one currently powerful state, and they include at least one bishop
25 of the Roman Catholic Church. Imagine that, as a teacher of European history, you are continually faced with belligerent demands to 'teach the controversy' and to give 'equal time' to the 'alternative theory' that the Holocaust never happened but was invented by a bunch of Zionist fabricators. Fashionably relativist intellectuals chime in to insist that there is no absolute truth: whether the Holocaust happened is a matter of personal
30 belief; all points of view are equally valid and should be equally 'respected.'

The plight of many science teachers today is not less dire. When they attempt to expound the central and guiding principle of biology; when they honestly place the living world in its historical context – which means evolution; when they explore and explain the very nature of life itself, they are harried and stymied, hassled and bullied,
35 even threatened with loss of their jobs. At the very least their time is wasted at every turn. They are likely to receive menacing letters from parents, and have to endure the sarcastic smirks and close-folded arms of brainwashed children. They are supplied with state-approved textbooks that have had the word 'evolution' systematically expunged, or bowdlerized into 'change over time'. Once, we were tempted to laugh this kind of thing
40 off as a peculiarly American phenomenon. Teachers in Britain and Europe now face the same problems.

The Archbishop of Canterbury has no problem with evolution, nor does the Pope (give or take the odd wobble over the precise palaeontological juncture when the human soul was injected), nor do educated priests and professors of theology. This is a
45 book about the positive evidence that evolution is a fact. It is not intended as an anti-religious book. I've done that, it's another T-shirt, this is not the place to wear it again. Bishops and theologians who have attended to the evidence for evolution have given up the struggle against it. Some may do so reluctantly, some enthusiastically, but all except

the woefully uninformed are forced to accept the
50 fact of evolution. They may think God had a hand in
starting the process off, and perhaps didn't stay his
hand in guiding its future progress. They probably
think God cranked the universe up in the first place,
and solemnized its birth with a harmonious set of
55 laws and physical constants calculated to fulfil some
inscrutable purpose in which we were eventually to
play a role. But, grudgingly in some cases, happily
in others, thoughtful and rational churchmen and
women accept the evidence for evolution.

60   Evolution is a fact. Beyond reasonable doubt, beyond serious doubt, beyond sane,
informed, intelligent doubt, beyond doubt evolution is a fact. The evidence for evolution
is at least as strong as the evidence for the Holocaust, even allowing for eye witnesses to
the Holocaust. It is the plain truth that we are cousins of chimpanzees, somewhat more
distant cousins of monkeys, more distant cousins still of aardvarks and manatees, yet
65 more distant cousins of bananas and turnips... continue the list as long as desired. That
didn't have to be true. It is not self-evidently, tautologically, obviously true, and there
was a time when most people, even educated people, thought it wasn't. It didn't have
to be true, but it is.

Richard Dawkins, *The Greatest Show on Earth*

Questions on passage 1

		Marks
1.	Read lines 1–6. Using your own words as far as possible, identify some of the things that make teaching Roman history and the Latin language a 'big undertaking' (line 5).	4
2.	Analyse the writer's use of language in lines 6–10 to convey what he feels about the threat posed by the 'ignoramuses' (line 7).	2
3.	Referring to specific language features, how effective do you find lines 14–17 as an introduction to the writer's ideas?	4
4.	Explain in your own words the characteristics of the 'Holocaust-deniers' (line 21).	2
5.	By referring to at least **two** features of language in lines 25–30, analyse how the writer conveys his disapproval of the situation faced by the hypothetical history teacher.	4
6.	Read lines 31–41. Analyse the writer's use of language in this paragraph to highlight his feelings of sympathy for science teachers today. You should refer in your answer to such features as word choice, sentence structure, imagery …	4
7.	Re-read lines 50–59. By referring to at least one example, analyse how the writer's use of imagery reinforces his view of those who hold creationist beliefs.	2
8.	Analyse the writer's use of language in the final paragraph to emphasise his position on this subject.	3

Passage 2

*The following passage is adapted from an article written by Professor Michael Reiss,
Director of Education at The Royal Society, published in the Guardian.*

Science lessons should tackle creationism and intelligent design. What should science
teachers do when faced with students who are creationists? Definitions of creationism
vary, but about 10% of people in the UK believe that the Earth is only some 10,000 years
old, that it came into existence as described in the early parts of the Bible or the Qur'an
5　and that the most evolution has done is to split species into closely related species.

At the same time, the overwhelming majority of biologists consider evolution to be
the central concept in biological sciences, providing a conceptual framework that
unifies every aspect of the life sciences into a single coherent discipline. Equally, the
overwhelming majority of scientists believe that the universe is of the order of about 13 to
10　14 billion years old.

Evolution and cosmology are understood by many to be a religious issue because they
can be seen to contradict the accounts of origins of life and the universe described in
the Jewish, Christian and Muslim scriptures. The issue seems like an ongoing dispute
that has science and religion battling to support the credibility of their explanations.

15　I feel that creationism is best seen by science teachers not as a misconception but as a
world view. The implication of this is that the most a science teacher can normally hope to
achieve is to ensure that students with creationist beliefs understand the scientific position.
In the short term, this scientific world view is unlikely to supplant a creationist one.

So how might one teach evolution in science lessons, say to 14 to 16-year-olds? Many
20　scientists, and some science educators, fear that consideration of creationism or intelligent
design in a science classroom legitimises them.

For example, the excellent book *Science, Evolution, and Creationism* published by the US
National Academy of Sciences and Institute of Medicine, asserts: 'The ideas offered by
intelligent design creationists are not the products of scientific reasoning. Discussing these
25　ideas in science classes would not be appropriate given their lack of scientific support.'

I agree with the first sentence but disagree with the second. Just because something lacks
scientific support doesn't seem to me a sufficient reason to omit it from a science lesson.
When I was taught physics at school, and taught it extremely well in my view, what I
remember finding so exciting was that we could discuss almost anything providing we
30　were prepared to defend our thinking in a way that admitted objective evidence and
logical argument.

So when teaching evolution, there is much to be said for allowing students to raise any
doubts they have (hardly a revolutionary idea in science teaching) and doing one's best
to have a genuine discussion. The word 'genuine' doesn't mean that creationism or
35　intelligent design deserve equal time.

However, in certain classes, depending on the comfort of the teacher in dealing with
such issues and the make-up of the student body, it can be appropriate to deal with the
issue. If questions or issues about creationism and intelligent design arise during science
lessons they can be used to illustrate a number of aspects of how science works.

40　Having said that, I don't believe that such teaching is easy. Some students get very
heated; others remain silent even if they disagree profoundly with what is said.

I do believe in taking seriously and respectfully the concerns of students who do not
accept the theory of evolution, while still introducing them to it. While it is unlikely

that this will help students who have a conflict between science and their religious beliefs
45 to resolve the conflict, good science teaching can help students to manage it – and to learn more science.

Creationism can profitably be seen not as a simple misconception that careful science teaching can correct. Rather, a student who believes in creationism has a non-scientific way of seeing the world, and one very rarely changes one's world view as a result of a
50 50-minute lesson, however well taught.

Question on both passages

		Marks

9. Both writers express their views about the teaching of evolution and creationism. Identify key areas on which they disagree. In your answer, you should refer in detail to both passages.

You may answer this question in continuous prose or in a series of developed bullet points.

5

How to study drama

The first thing to remember when analysing a drama text is that it is something that has been created to be performed. Although a play has much in common with a novel in terms of characterisation, theme, etc. it is a very different kind of text and the best critical essays will recognise this.

Stage directions offer you vital information about how the play is to be presented to the audience and also provide you with an insight into the central concerns that the dramatist is exploring. If you are dealing with a play by Shakespeare, the stage directions will be minimal. In a modern play, they may be far more detailed, as the following examples from Arthur Miller's *All My Sons* show. The extracts are taken from the beginning of act one.

> *The back yard of the Keller home in the outskirts of an American town. August of our era.*
>
> *The stage is hedged on right and left by tall, closely planted poplars which lend the yard a secluded atmosphere. Upstage is filled with the back of the house and its open, unroofed porch, which extends into the yard some six feet. The house is two storeys high and has seven rooms. It would have cost perhaps fifteen thousand in the early twenties when it was built. Now it is nicely painted, looks tight and comfortable, and the yard is green with sod, here and there plants whose season is gone. At the right, beside the house, the entrance of the driveway can be seen, but the poplars cut off view of its continuation downstage. In the left corner, downstage, stands the four-foot-high stump of a slender apple tree whose upper trunk and branches lie toppled beside it, fruit still clinging to its branches.*

These stage directions at once inform us of the setting in time and place ('an American town' suggests the universality of what will unfold). The apple tree reduced to a stump is an important symbol in the play.

Miller's stage directions also give us a very clear idea of the central character, Joe Keller, from the outset.

> *Keller is nearing sixty. A heavy man of stolid mind and build, a businessman these many years, but with the imprint of the machine-shop worker and boss still upon him. When he reads, when he speaks, when he listens, it is with the terrible concentration of the uneducated man for whom there is still wonder in many commonly known things. A man whose judgements must be dredged out of experience and a peasant-like common sense. A man among men.*

Chapter 2: How to study drama

Of course it is not only through stage directions that we learn about the characters. What they do (their actions), what they say, and how they interact with other characters all suggest to the audience how the dramatist intends us to regard them and you should pay close attention to all of these when you are studying the text. Look out for techniques such as **soliloquy**, when a character's innermost thoughts and feelings are revealed to the audience. In the following example, Shakespeare ensures the audience is made aware of Iago's plans:

> *Cassio's a proper man: let me see now;*
> *To get his place and to plume up my will*
> *In double knavery. How? How? Let's see.*
> *After some time, to abuse Othello's ear*
> *That he is too familiar with his wife;*
> *He hath a person and a smooth dispose*
> *To be suspected, framed to make women false.*
> *The Moor is of a free and open nature,*
> *That thinks men honest that but seem to be so,*
> *And will as tenderly be led by th'nose*
> *As asses are.*
> *I have't. It is engendered. Hell and night*
> *Must bring this monstrous birth to the world's light.*
> Othello I.3.386–398

Pay close attention to how a character develops and changes during the course of the play. Does your response to a character change as the action unfolds? Does the character match the definition of any common dramatic types, e.g. the tragic hero, whose downfall is the result of some flaw in their character?

Relationships are usually at the heart of any play. Look at how the dramatist presents them to the audience and how they are used to explore the central concerns of the play. Consider the use of **dialogue**. Is it **naturalistic** or are some speeches clearly meant to have **symbolic** significance? Look at how lighting and other staging techniques help to give prominence to some speeches. Find the lines that seem to encapsulate the central concerns of the play.

Look carefully at how the play is structured. The Ancient Greeks thought that tragedy should follow the following pattern: *exposition* (or introduction); *rising action* (or complication); *crisis* (some sort of turning point); *falling action* (showing the forces operating against the hero); *catastrophe* (usually the death of the tragic hero). However, not all tragedies fit neatly into this pattern. Many modern plays have a much looser structure than the five acts of Shakespeare's tragedies, but you should still be able to spot **key scenes**, **turning points** and the **climax** of the action. Another technical term you should be able to use is **dénouement**. This refers to the part of the play when the outcome is revealed to the audience. How do you react to this?

Finally, consider what you think the dramatist's message is for the audience. What are the central concerns or themes of the play? How effective are the various dramatic techniques used in helping to convey these themes?

How to study prose fiction (novels and short stories)

Note taking advice

In addition to the tasks you do in the classroom related to the literature you are studying for the Critical Reading paper, it is a really good idea to make your own notes about the texts. This will encourage you to think about your own response to the writing as well as providing you with extra material to help in your revision. These notes need not be lengthy but they should be detailed enough to be helpful to you.

For novels and short stories you should make notes on:

- the structure of the story – straightforward beginning, middle, end? Flashbacks? Key scenes?
- the narrator – who is telling us the story? What are the consequences of this?
- the main characters – name, age, appearance, personality. Convincing? How does the writer use them to explore the central concerns of the text?
- the writer's style – write down examples. Look out for techniques such as imagery and symbolism.
- the mood or atmosphere of the story
- the theme(s) – what is the writer trying to make us think about?
- your personal reaction to the text
- similarities and differences between short stories by the same writer

For drama texts you should consider:

- setting
- stage directions
- stage craft – lighting, music, sound effects
- plot structure – exposition, development, climax, key scenes, turning points
- the main characters – costume, dialogue, actions, realistic or symbolic?
- the mood or atmosphere
- the theme(s) – what issues does the playwright want the audience to think about?
- your personal reaction to the play

For poetry:

- connotations of the title
- content – what is the poem about?
- theme(s)
- poetic voice – the poet? Or a persona adopted by the poet?
- form and structure – stanza pattern, line length, metre, rhythm, rhyme
- other techniques – word choice, imagery, sentence structure

- tone
- mood
- your personal reaction to the poem

For film and TV drama:
- setting
- plot
- structure
- genre conventions – is this text typical of its kind?
- characterisation
- representation
- stereotypes
- editing
- montage
- music and sound
- special effects
- dialogue
- mise-en-scène
- camera angles
- mood or atmosphere
- your personal reaction to the film or TV drama

When you read a novel or a short story as part of your Higher course you need to be able to do more than just offer an opinion on it ('I really liked that.'; 'That was the dullest book I've ever read.'). You have to be able to analyse the techniques used by the writer in constructing the text and be able to say how effective you find them.

Structure

In some ways you are already an expert in this area. You've been hearing and reading and watching stories all your life. You already know how stories 'work'. You expect stories to have a beginning, a middle and an end. A more sophisticated description of this structure is as follows:

Exposition. The situation that exists at the start of the story. The reader is introduced to the characters, the setting is described and we are given an idea of what is going on. This is sometimes described as the 'equilibrium'.

↓

Complication. Something happens to disturb the 'equilibrium' described at the start of the story and creates a problem for the central character(s).

↓

Development. The 'chain of events' that takes place as characters attempt to deal with the problem.

↓

Climax. The most exciting part of the story. Events come to a head.

↓

Resolution. The strands of the plot are all worked out and a 'new equilibrium' is established.

A good number of the stories you will study will follow this pattern or 'classic narrative structure'. However, you need to be aware that a writer will sometimes play about with this structure in order to achieve particular effects. The writer might begin *in medias res*, in the middle of things, at some point in the development. This adds impact to the start of the story and will sometimes make it more dramatic. The writer might then use flashback to give the reader details of the exposition. The writer might not use any exposition at all until the end, leaving the reader to try and work out what is happening and why as the story goes along. There might be no resolution and the reader is left to ponder what happens next. Some modern writers have abandoned traditional structure entirely and leave you as the reader to create one as best you can as you read the 'story'.

The narrator

Ask yourself who is telling the story. Is it told by a character in the story in the **first person (I, me, we, us)**? If so, how does this affect our experience of reading the story? This technique might make us sympathise with the character as they become our 'representative' in the story – especially if they tell us their thoughts and feelings. Beware the **unreliable narrator** – a narrator who might not be telling us the truth or who might not know the truth of what is going on.

Is the story told in the **third person**, i.e. by someone who is not 'in' the story? If so it might be an **omniscient narrator** who can tell us everything that is going on and what all the characters are thinking. It might be a **limited narrator** who only tells us about a few characters and their actions and tells us much less about other characters and actions. It might be a **demonstrative narrator** who only reports what characters *say* and *do* leaving the reader to work out the motives behind these actions.

Characterisation

It is very important to remember the simple truth that characters in novels and short stories are not real. It is not your job to treat them as if they are real people with all the hopes, fears, failings and neuroses that make up our personalities, even though the writer might present them to us in a very convincing way. What is important is for you to be able to analyse *how* the characters are created by the writer.

Characters can be created through what they say – the dialogue in the story – and what they do – their actions. Remember that nothing is in a story by accident. Everything means something. Look at this extract from the opening chapter of a novel by the Scottish writer Andrew Greig. Notice how economically Greig introduces the characters of Murray and Tricia to the reader through what they say and what they do. The extract is a good example of the **omniscient narrator** at work and you should notice how skilfully the writer suggests the characters' thoughts.

> Even in Kirkintilloch the sun was shining as Murray Hamilton eased the screws off the front licence plate on his old Kawasaki. His – eleven-year-old sat on the steps of the council house with her guitar, hesitating between one chord and the next. His boy Jamie was kicking a football against the lean-to.
>
> 'So,' Tricia said, 'is this the end of a glittering political career?'
>
> He took the new plate from her and squinted into the light. Five years on the Council till he'd resigned, a thousand committee meetings, ten thousand doorsteps – and what had changed?

'Time to try anither way, Trish.'

The thread caught in the bolt and he began to tighten.

'You'll not be much of a dad in jail.'

He put down the spanner.

'I'll stop right now if you want me tae.'

Behind them Eve at last found the new chord and strummed it cautiously.

'I just said be careful. And don't get hurt.'

'Right darlin.'

Tricia began loosening the rear plate. She glanced at her husband's bowed head and for the first time saw that his tight red-gold hair was starting to thin around the crown, and the edge of his beard was touched with grey like the first touch of frost. Still, she grinned, as she put the screws down carefully beside her. Might as well be a bit daft before we're all past it.

Andrew Greig, *The Return of John MacNab*

When describing a character to the reader, sometimes the narrator will just give the reader details of the character's appearance.

John Rhodes, when he came, was big and fair ... The face was slightly pockmarked. The eyes were pleasantly blue.

William McIlvanney, *Laidlaw*

But often the narrator's word choice or use of imagery will have *connotations* that the reader is expected to pick up on. What does the simile in the next extract suggest about John Rhodes?

'Hullo, you,' he said to Laidlaw and sat down across the table from them. 'Ye'll hiv a drink.'

'A whisky for me,' Laidlaw said. 'With water.'

'I won't bother, thank you,' Harkness said.

The blue eyes turned on him like a blowtorch lit but not yet shooting flame.

William McIlvanney, *Laidlaw*

Sentence structure

Don't forget to look for the effects created by the writer using sentences of different lengths and types. For example, the use of very long sentences with lots of punctuation might suggest things happening quickly or all at once. A series of short sentences might suggest rising tension or fear.

Mood

You should think of the *mood* of a piece of writing as the feeling or emotion or *atmosphere* the writer is trying to create. Is it happy, gloomy, bleak, sympathetic ... ? This can be achieved by reference to things such as the weather (just think about the different moods suggested by a storm on an isolated moor and a morning of bright sunshine on a holiday beach) or to different colours (black has connotations very different to that of white).

Look at this extract from the opening of another of Andrew Greig's novels. By closely examining word choice, imagery and sentence structure, see if you can spot *how* Greig creates a gloomy or downbeat mood.

A man on a motorbike finally came to the end of the road.

He sat astride contemplating gate, padlock, chain. Once he would have felt compelled to do something about those. Instead he switched off, unstrapped his helmet and let sound in.

Eight miles into the Rothiemurchus Forest, towards the end of a short winter's day, the world was quiet. No human voices, no birdsong, just a hiss of water from melting snow, damp wind seeping through the pines.

He got stiffly off the bike, clipped the helmet over the handlebars, climbed the gate and walked up the snowy path through the dark wood. He wore camouflage trousers and jacket but did not look like a soldier – at least, not from a war that anyone had won. After a hundred yards he paused, tossed the ignition key into the undergrowth and trudged on ...

... He took a smaller path and then a smaller one off that. At a ghostly intersection he stood in the rapidly fading light, pulled off his gloves and hurled one after the other into the darkness under the trees.

A while later, he unstrapped his watch, dropped it without breaking stride. He had no further need of time.

The last days had been a matter of discarding, in order, the remaining things that mattered to him. There was little left now. The pack was empty so he hung it dark and drooping on a branch, like a crow left by gamekeepers.

Andrew Greig, *Romanno Bridge*

How to study prose non-fiction

Prose non-fiction texts suitable for study at this level might come from the following kinds of writing: essays; travel writing; autobiography; journalism. George Orwell's non-fiction work continues to be very popular in schools and is often used as the basis for critical essay work in the Critical Reading paper.

Many of the features and techniques that you will see in your study of prose fiction can also be applied to the study of prose non-fiction. The following list would provide a focus for your note taking on a prose non-fiction text:

- ideas
- structure (of the piece as a whole)
- description of setting
- description of people
- portrayal of relationships
- point of view/bias
- vivid/effective description
- word choice
- imagery
- symbolism
- significant events
- evidence
- paragraph/sentence structure
- tone
- style
- writer's thoughts and feelings
- effect on the reader
- theme
- any other features you consider significant

Here are two examples of the sort of critical essay questions set by SQA in recent years:

*Choose a non-fiction text which presents a distinctive account of a place **or** an event **or** a person.*

*By referring to appropriate techniques, discuss how the account effectively creates a sense of the place **or** the event **or** the person.*

SQA, Past Paper, Higher English 2019

Choose a non-fiction text which has made you think differently about an important moral or social issue.

With reference to appropriate techniques, discuss how the writer has caused you to view the issue differently.

SQA, Specimen Paper, Higher English 2018

You can see that they are not too dissimilar from what you are asked to do for prose fiction. Any analysis must always make reference to 'appropriate techniques'.

- Here is an example of the sort of notes you might make when studying a prose non-fiction text. The text is taken from *Darkness and Light* by Kathleen Jamie, an account of a trip she takes to Shetland.

A reference to the dark as something to be endured.

An impression of her fellow passengers. The writer is an observer of the scene.

Humorous tone? Or maybe condescending?

Incidental details to give a sense of setting.

Typical of the writer's style. Short sentence. List. Almost 'poetic' expression.

Writer's desire for darkness. Darkness described as 'wholesome' as if it's healthy or good for you.

Some of the old hands, the Shetland folk for whom the crossing holds no novelty, were already laid flat out on benches. They had a long night ahead; it would take fourteen dark hours before they were in Lerwick for breakfast. Many were students heading home for Christmas. Some were planted in the bar. There was a man with a proper Fair Isle jersey, a girl with a hand-knit tourie. Throughout the whole of the boat – you'd to work hard to find a place to avoid it – Muzak was playing. Christmas hits of yore. Paul McCartney. The only place you could avoid Paul McCartney was a lounge with subdued lighting and big reclining chairs. There were prints on the walls, a set of three, showing a cartoon sea with a stripy lighthouse, a fishing-boat, and below the blue waves, three huge, stupid, cheerful fish. *The Shetland Times,* which a number of the passengers were reading, bore the headline 'Day of Reckoning Looms for Fishing'.

I'd wanted dark. Real, natural, starry dark, solstice dark, but you can't argue with the moon, and the moon was almost full. It shone through a smir of cloud, spreading its diffused light across the water. The moon had around it an aura of un-colours, the colours of oil spilled on tarmac.

Secretly, I'd been hoping for a moment at sea where there was no human light. 360 degrees of winter sea, the only lights those carried by the ship itself. I wanted to be out in the night wind, in wholesome, unbanished darkness. But the *Hrossa* was,

Vivid description of the seascape at night.

after all, only a ferry, and would hug the coast. Nevertheless, I went outside often, to stand shivering on its deck, but there was always a light somewhere. From the port side, small, northern Scottish towns, Brora, perhaps, or Helmsdale, were an orange smudge against the darker line of land. From the starboard side I could look out at the moonlit, fishless sea. Some hours out, I saw three brash lights, in a line to the east, the seaward side. I took them for other vessels but they were too piled up and intense. They were North Sea oil platforms, and even at this distance they looked frenzied. Maybe this was where the *Solar Prince* and the *Viking Warrior* were bound – on the urgent business of oil. As the ferry drove on, the rigs grew smaller, until they were at the edge of vision, at the edge of the night, as I imagine distant icebergs must look, only on fire.

Threatening image? Contrast fire/ice.

Then, alone on the metal deck, damp and moonlit, just when I fancied darkness might be complete, I heard a faint call. The boat throbbed on, leaving behind a wave as straight as a glacier. A human call. I must have been mistaken, but listened and – it came again. I scanned the water, there were only the waves, the wide, oil-dark sea. It gave me a fright, and had anyone else been out on deck I might have tugged their arm and said Listen! I'm glad I was alone, because, so help me, it was only Elton John. Elton John, piped though a speaker onto the deck. The music was so nearly drowned out by the ship's engines that I'd just caught the top notes. I bent down, stuck my ear next the speaker and, yes, it was Elton John singing, of all things: 'Don't let the sun go down on me'. I gave up on the dark then, and went below for a drink.

Build-up of tension then humorous anti-climax.

Irony given the text's central concerns of light and dark.

Around midnight, the pilot boat came out to accompany the ferry between the archipelago of low islands into Kirkwall. On all their reefs and hazards, warning lights winked.

Word choice is apt (nautical terms) and effective.

Reference to danger.

Source: *Findings*, Kathleen Jamie, Sort of Books, 2005.

How to study poetry

When you are first faced with a poem you should approach the text by asking the following questions:

Understanding	What is the poem about?	*Look at the content, mood, attitude of the poet, subject or aspect of life revealed in the poem.*
Analysis	Who is speaking?	*The poet? Or has a persona been adopted? How do you know?*
Analysis	How is the poem structured?	*Regular structure or not? Look at stanza form, line length, rhyme, rhythm.*
Analysis	What other techniques have been used?	*Look at word choice, imagery (simile, metaphor, personification), sentence structure, sound.*
Evaluation	How effective are the poet's methods in conveying the meaning of the text to the reader?	*Think about your reaction to the poem as a piece of literature.*

Annotate your copy whenever possible. Mark it in any way that helps you to think about the text. There will be lines you find difficult to understand but don't forget that the poem is not a 'puzzle' with only one 'solution' or 'right answer'. Ambiguity is an important concept in poetry – any poem might have more than one 'meaning'.

Here's a reminder of some of the technical terms you need to know:

Alliteration	Words beginning with the same consonant sound. Creates a pattern of sounds for a particular effect. Wee, sleekit, cowrin', tim'rous beastie, O, whit a panic's in thy breastie! Thou need na start awa sae hasty, 　　Wi' bickering brattle! 　　　　Robert Burns, 'To a Mouse'	
Association	Poems usually *suggest* more to the reader than they state. Poets want you to make associations based on the words on the page. Allusions, references, analogies, images, metaphors and similes all help you to employ associations.	
Caesura	A pause within a line of poetry. Such pauses can break up the rhythm or metre of a poem. A thing of beauty is a joy forever: Its loveliness increases; it will never Pass into nothingness; but still will keep A bower quiet for us, and a sleep Full of sweet dreams, and health, and quiet breathing. 　　　　John Keats, 'Endymion'	

Connotation	What the word *suggests* rather than what it simply *means* (denotation), e.g. 'sunset' means the time of day when the sun slips below the horizon (denotation), but 'sunset' might also suggest ending, something drawing to a close, or even something like death (connotation).
Dramatic monologue	A poem in which an imaginary speaker addresses an imaginary audience. In 'My Last Duchess' Robert Browning adopts the persona of the Duke of Ferrara negotiating terms prior to acquiring his latest wife. The poem reveals what happened to his previous wife! That's my last Duchess painted on the wall, Looking as if she were alive. I call That piece a wonder, now: Frà Pandolf's hands Worked busily a day and there she stands. Robert Browning, 'My Last Duchess'
Elegy	A serious and formal poem usually inspired by a person's death.
Ellipsis	Missing out words from a sentence.
End-stopped line	A line of poetry that ends in a pause of some kind – indicated by appropriate punctuation.
Enjambment	Where the meaning, punctuation and sound of a poem do not stop at the end of a line but run on into the next. These two verses of a poem by Carol Ann Duffy show examples of both end-stopped lines and enjambment. I longed for Rome, home, someone else. When the Nazarene Entered Jerusalem, my maid and I crept out, Bored stiff, disguised, and joined the frenzied crowd, I tripped, clutched the bridle of an ass, looked up And there he was. His face? Ugly. Talented. He looked at me. I mean he looked at *me*. My God. His eyes were eyes to die for. Then he was gone, His rough men shouldering a pathway to the gates. Carol Ann Duffy, 'Pilate's Wife'
Free verse	Poetry that has no regular rhyme or rhythm. Theme, images and layout are likely to provide a poem written in free verse with form.

Imagery	Pictures in words. Poets use images to make us recreate imaginatively what is being described. See how economically Norman MacCaig does this in his poem 'February – Not Everywhere'.
	Such days, when trees run downwind, their arms stretched before them. Such days, when the sun's in a drawer and the drawer locked. When the meadow is dead, is a carpet, thin and shabby, with no pattern and at bus stops people retract into collars their faces like fists. And when, in a firelit room, mother looks at her four seasons, at her little boy, in the centre of everything, with still pools of shadows and a fire throwing flowers. Norman MacCaig, 'February – Not Everywhere'
Inversion	Changing around (inverting) the usual or expected sequence of words in a sentence. Inversion enables a poet to draw attention to a particular word or idea.
Lyric	A shorter poem, which expresses the poet's thoughts and feelings.
Metaphor	The simplest way to think of this is comparison where one thing is described as being something else. Look again at 'February – Not Everywhere' (above) for some good examples.
Metre	The regular pattern of stressed and unstressed syllables in a poem.
Parody	A poem that imitates another for comic effect.
Persona	An identity assumed by the poet. Remember that the 'I' in the poem may not actually be the poet, it could be an entirely imaginary person. I'm not the first or the last to stand on a hillock, watching the man she married prove to the world he's a total, utter, absolute, Grade A pillock. Carol Ann Duffy, 'Mrs Icarus'
Rhyme	Words that have identical sounds, usually at the ends of lines. The rhyme inevitably links the words rhymed and hence their meanings and associations. 'Half-rhyme' is a rhyme that *almost* rhymes.

Rhyme scheme	The pattern of rhyme within a poem. Letters are used to indicate rhymes and non-rhymes, with the first line of a poem being *a*, and the second being *a* or *b* according to whether it rhymes with the first line or not.

Here are some familiar traditional rhyme schemes:

The ballad: *abcb*

The limerick: *aabba*

The 'Habbie' stanza often used by Burns: *aaabab*

The Shakespearean Sonnet: *abab cdcd efefgg*

My mistress' eyes are nothing like the **sun**;	a
Coral is far more red than her lips' **red**;	b
If snow be white, why then her breasts are **dun**;	a
If hairs be wires, black wires grow on her **head**.	b
I have seen roses damask'd, red and **white**,	c
But no such roses see I in her **cheeks**;	d
And in some perfumes is there more **delight**	c
Than in the breath that from my mistress **reeks**.	d
I love to hear her speak, yet well I **know**	e
That music hath a far more pleasing **sound**;	f
I grant I never saw a goddess **go**;	e
My mistress, when she walks, treads on the **ground**:	f
And yet, by heaven, I think my love as **rare**	g
As any she belied with false **compare**.	g

William Shakespeare, 'Sonnet 130'

Rhythm	The sense of 'movement' conveyed by the arrangement of stressed and unstressed syllables. The rhythm in the following poem is very obvious – say it aloud and you'll notice the four stressed syllables (or beats) in the first and third lines of each verse and the three stressed syllables in the second and fourth lines.

A slumber did my spirit steal;
I had no human fears:
She seemed a thing that could not feel
The touch of earthly years.
No motion has she now, no force;
She neither hears nor sees;
Rolled round in earth's diurnal course,
With rocks, and stones, and trees.

William Wordsworth, 'A Slumber Did My Spirit Steal'

Simile	A comparison introduced by words such as 'like' or 'as'. Closed like confessionals, they thread Loud noons of cities, giving back None of the glances they absorb. Philip Larkin, 'Ambulances'
Sonnet	A 14-line poem in one of the following forms: • the Italian sonnet, which consists of eight lines (the octave) rhyming *abbaabba*, and six lines (the sestet), rhyming *cdecde* or *cdccdc* or *cdedce* • the English (or Shakespearean) sonnet, which consists of three quatrains of four lines and a concluding rhyming couplet (*abab cdcd efef gg*) A sonnet is usually written in iambic pentameter – each line contains 10 syllables divided into five metric 'feet'. Each 'foot' consists of an unstressed syllable followed by a stressed syllable.
Stanza	Lines of poetry grouped together. Usually any pattern is repeated in following stanzas.
Stress	Emphasis put on a syllable or a word.
Symbol	Something that stands for or represents something. It is clear that 'The Sick Rose' by William Blake is not really a poem about a plant! Instead Blake uses the symbol of the rose to stand for something innocent or beautiful that is being corrupted. O Rose, thou art sick. The invisible worm That flies in the night In the howling storm Has found out thy bed Of crimson joy, And his dark secret love Does thy life destroy. William Blake, 'The Sick Rose'
Theme	The central concern or idea behind a poem.
Tone	The general mood of a poem and how the poet has signalled it to the reader.

Asking questions about poems

Now look at the following selection of poems. After you read each one ask yourself the following questions. Suggested answers for the first two poems are given on pages 141–143.

1. What is the poem about?
2. Who is speaking?
3. How is the poem structured?
4. What other techniques have been used?
5. How effective are the poet's methods in conveying the meaning of the text to the reader?
6. What is your personal reaction to the poem?

Heliographer

I thought we were sitting in the sky.
My father decoded the world beneath:
our tenement, the rival football grounds,
the long bridges, slung out across the river.
Then I gave myself a fright
with the lemonade bottle. Clunk –
the glass thread butting my teeth
as I bolted my mouth to the lip.

Naw ... copy me. It's how the grown-ups drink.
Propped in my shaky,
single-handed grip, I tilted the bottle towards the sun
until it detonated with light,
my lips pursed like a trumpeter's.

Don Paterson

In a snug room

He sips from his glass, thinking complacently
of the events of the day:
a flattering reference to him in the morning papers,
lunch with his cronies, a profitable deal
signed on the dotted line, a donation sent
to his favourite charity.

And he smiles,
thinking of the taxi coming
with his true love in it.

Everything's fine.

And Nemesis slips two bullets
into her gun
in case she misses with the first one.

                                    Norman MacCaig

Stopping by Woods on a Snowy Evening

Whose woods these are I think I know.
His house is in the village though;
He will not see me stopping here
To watch his woods fill up with snow.

My little horse must think it queer
To stop without a farmhouse near
Between the woods and frozen lake
The darkest evening of the year.

He gives his harness bells a shake
To ask if there is some mistake.
The only other sound's the sweep
Of easy wind and downy flake.

The woods are lovely, dark and deep.
But I have promises to keep,
And miles to go before I sleep,
And miles to go before I sleep.

                                    Robert Frost

Sonnet 18

Shall I compare thee to a summer's day?
Thou art more lovely and more temperate.
Rough winds do shake the darling buds of May,
And summer's lease hath all too short a date.
Sometime too hot the eye of heaven shines,
And often is his gold complexion dimmed;
And every fair from fair sometime declines,
By chance, or nature's changing course, untrimmed;
But thy eternal summer shall not fade,
Nor lose possession of that fair thou ow'st,
Nor shall death brag thou wand'rest in his shade,
When in eternal lines to Time thou grow'st.
So long as men can breathe, or eyes can see,
So long lives this, and this gives life to thee.

                                    William Shakespeare

Head of English

Today we have a poet in the class.
A real live poet with a published book.
Notice the inkstained fingers girls. Perhaps
we're going to witness verse hot from the press.
Who knows. Please show your appreciation
by clapping. Not too loud. Now

sit up straight and listen. Remember
the lesson on assonance, for not all poems,
sadly rhyme these days. Still. Never mind.
Whispering's as always, out of bounds –
but do feel free to raise some questions.
After all, we're paying forty pounds.

Those of you with English Second Language
see me after break. We're fortunate
to have this person in our midst.
Seasons of mist and so on and so forth.
I've written quite a bit of poetry myself,
am doing Kipling with the Lower Fourth.

Right. That's enough from me. On with the Muse.
Open a window at the back. We don't
want winds of change about this place.
Take notes, but don't write reams. Just an essay
on the poet's themes. Fine. Off we go.
Convince us that there's something we don't know.

Well. Really. Run along now girls. I'm sure
that gave you an insight to an outside view.
Applause will do. Thank you
very much for coming here today. Lunch
in the hall? Do hang about. Unfortunately
I have to dash. Tracey will show you out.

Carol Ann Duffy

Thrushes

Terrifying are the sleek thrushes on the lawn,
More coiled steel than living – a poised
Dark deadly eye, those delicate legs
Triggered to stirrings beyond sense – with a start a bounce, a stab
Overtake the instant and drag out some writhing thing.
No indolent procrastinations and no yawning states,
No sighs or head-scratchings. Nothing but bounce and stab
And a ravening second.

Is it their single-mind-sized skulls or a trained
Body, or genius, or a nestful of brats
Gives their days this bullet and automatic
Purpose? Mozart's brain had it, and the shark's mouth
That hungers down the blood-smell even to a leak of its own
Side and devouring of itself: efficiency which
Strikes too streamlined for any doubt to pluck at it
Or obstruction deflect.

With a man it is otherwise. Heroisms on horseback,
Outstripping his desk-diary at a broad desk,
Carving at a tiny ivory ornament
For years: his act worships itself – while for him,
Though he bends to be blent in the prayer, how
loud and above what
Furious spaces of fire do the distracting devils
Orgy and hossanah, under the wilderness
Of black silent waters weep.

Ted Hughes

Waterfall

The burn drowns steadily in its own downpour,
A helter-skelter of muslin and glass
That skids to a halt, crashing up suds.

Simultaneous acceleration
And sudden braking; water goes over
Like villains dropped screaming to justice.

It appears an athletic glacier
Has reared into reverse: is swallowed up
And regurgitated through this long throat.

My eye rides over and downwards, falls with
Hurtling tons that slabber and spill,
Falls, yet records the tumult thus standing still.

Seamus Heaney

How to study film and TV drama

You might already know how to study media texts from your work at National 5. If so, this section should serve as a useful reminder of the technical terms you need to be able to use in a critical essay. If you are coming to the study of 'Film and TV drama' for the first time, then this section will provide you with a brief introduction to the genre.

Studying a film or TV drama is similar to studying a prose fiction or drama text in many ways. The director of a film uses a range of techniques – just as a writer does – to create a narrative and so explore a central concern or theme. Concepts such as plot and characterisation are common to both film and literature and you should not find it too difficult to comment on these aspects of the text you are studying.

It is likely that the film or TV drama you are studying will follow the 'classical narrative' pattern of most 'mainstream' or commercial cinema releases. This means that the plot events of the film will follow a pattern of:

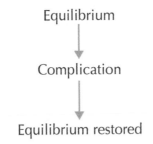

Equilibrium

Complication

Equilibrium restored

In fact, exactly the same sort of narrative structure that is explained in greater length in the section on *How to study prose fiction*.

If you think of any film you have seen in the cinema recently or a drama that you have watched on Netflix, you should be able to match the story told to the structure outlined above.

Camera

When writing about film and TV drama, you need to be able to analyse the effect of the different camera shots and angles chosen by the director. Remember that nothing appears on the screen by accident, *everything* is part of the director's 'art'.

Extreme long shot

Suitable for giving a view of a landscape and aerial views.

Long shot

Suitable for framing characters in their surroundings (and the background will be as important or more important than the characters).

Medium shot

Characters appear larger and dominate the screen. Useful for showing interaction between characters.

Close up

Used to highlight the significance of a character or object. A character's face might fill the screen to reveal a particular display of emotion. A director will sometimes use an extreme close up.

When a director uses a **low** camera angle it can suggest things like relative power or high status (it has the effect of making the subject seem larger).

A **high** angle (looking down on the subject) might suggest a character's relative lack of power or status. Remember to check from whose point of view we are seeing a shot.

Look out for other camera techniques such as a **tracking** shot, in which the camera moves alongside characters following their movements; **zooming** in or out and panning, in which the camera stays in the same place and swivels to the left or right. An example of a famous camera technique is the **dolly zoom** or **reverse tracking** shot in Steven Spielberg's *Jaws*, which is well worth looking at to see the disconcerting effect the director creates.

Mise-en-scène

This technical term covers everything you see on the screen, including **props**, **costume**, **lighting** and **special effects**. Again, nothing has been placed there by accident and you should be able to comment on the significance of all these elements. How are characters dressed? What does that red coat symbolise? Why is one character's face always harshly lit and another's always half in shadow? Why does the director repeatedly return to an image of a ticking clock? What does this or that object represent?

Editing

A director (usually in conjunction with a specialist film editor) chooses how the finished film appears to the audience by choosing how the various camera shots are joined together to construct a narrative. Usually a director will just **cut** from one shot to the next but look out for when a **fade** in or out is used. **Montage** is the process whereby different shots are placed together to create particular effects (such as to suggest increasing fear or tension).

Sound

You also need to say something about the use of sound. **Music** is an obvious tool used by directors to create a particular mood. It should be relatively easy for you to identify music that arouses emotions such sadness or excitement or apprehension in the audience. Don't forget to look at other sound techniques such as **sound effects**. **Dialogue** spoken by characters and any voice-over comes into this category. **Diegetic** sound refers to sound within the film itself (e.g. the sound of seagulls crying as a character walks along a harbour wall; the sound of breaking glass when a brick is thrown through a window). **Non-diegetic** sound refers to sound that is outwith the 'world' of the film (e.g. the sound of violins playing a sad melody after a character dies).

Here is an example of an extract from a critical essay on film. Note how techniques are referenced to support the analysis of a particular scene. This extract is from an answer written in response to the following question:

Choose a film or television drama in which there is a sequence which is particularly moving or humorous or shocking.

With reference to appropriate techniques, discuss how the film or programme makers succeed in engaging the viewer's emotions or reactions.

In the 'opera music' scene from 'The Shawshank Redemption', director Frank Darabont creates a sequence which is particularly moving. At the start of the sequence we see a close up of Andy Dufresne's hands as they carefully place the record on the turntable, which serves as a reminder of the typical care and attention to detail associated with this character's actions. The camera then slowly tracks up Andy's body, picking out his prison number en route — another reminder to the audience that prison has cost him his life and the identity he enjoyed 'on the outside'. The diagetic sound of the music begins to play and we see another close up of Andy's face as he listens to it. Andy's actions are humorously intercut with medium close ups of the prison guard in the adjacent toilet. This comic montage of Andy enjoying the high culture of opera while the prison guard can only read a comic entitled 'Jughead' reinforces the representation of Andy as a man of taste and sophistication and someone out of place in this environment. Low camera angles and close ups as Andy bars the entrance to the office help to reinforce his status and (in this instance) power. A wide shot shows the reaction of the inmates in the prison yard and Darabont gives us a montage of various other locations in the prison. We see Red and other prisoners react to the music in a workshop; we see patients in the prison sanatorium — in one case a man is literally raised up from his sick bed, again suggesting the power invested in Andy and his actions. We follow the prisoners' gaze through the window and the director cuts to a wide shot of the prisoners in the yard again. The camera rises and we are given a panoramic shot of the yard. The men all stand still and are struck dumb by the music. There is an obvious contrast between the drabness of the yard, and how they are dressed, and the exquisite beauty of Mozart's music, which continues to play over the shots. The viewer cannot help but be moved at this point by the men's reactions. Back in the office, a slow tracking shot follows the microphone cable back to the turntable. Red's voice returns in voice-over. He says he doesn't want to know what the two 'Italian ladies were singing about' because 'some things are best left unsaid'; an acknowledgement that beauty and art need not be explained to be enjoyed. Again, the viewer is moved by this reaction by a prison inmate to the events being shown. The director then continues with a close up of Andy, sitting back relaxed in the chair with a beatific smile on his face. His face is illuminated by the natural light falling on it through the slatted window blinds beside him. This is another example of how the director uses lighting to represent Andy as a morally good character.

SQA, Specimen Paper, Higher English 2018

Critical reading: Scottish texts – Questions

The Scottish text questions are found in Section 1 of the Critical Reading paper (the second paper in the examination).

You have to answer ONE question from

Part A, Drama

or

Part B, Prose (novels or short stories)

or

Part C, Poetry.

This part of the examination is worth **20 marks** in total and you should spend approximately **45 minutes** on it – you'll need the remaining 45 minutes to write a critical essay.

In the Scottish text questions there will be extracts printed from the drama and prose set texts. Poems will be printed in their entirety unless they are very long, in which case an extract will be printed.

Individual questions are worth **2**, **3** or **4 marks**. The final question is always worth **10 marks**.

Look at the following examples of the sort of questions you can expect to be asked about the printed extract.

Drama

- *Referring to two examples of dialogue explain what this reveals about ...*
- *Choose an example of humour in this extract and explain how it is used to engage the audience's sympathy for ...*
- *By referring closely to an example of stage directions or dialogue, analyse how the tension between the two characters is made clear to the audience in lines ...*

Prose

- *Analyse how the writer makes use of word choice and sentence structure in the final paragraph of the extract to suggest ...*
- *Analyse how the writer conveys a sense of isolation in lines 15–22.*
- *By referring closely to lines 1–13, explain how the writer makes the reader aware of the narrator's attitude towards ...*

Poetry

- *By referring closely to lines 1–9, show how MacCaig's use of poetic technique creates a vivid picture of the dwarf.*
- *Evaluate the effectiveness of the final stanza as a conclusion to the poem.*
- *The main themes of the poem are introduced in the title and first stanza. Identify **one** main theme and show how poetic technique is used to introduce this theme.*

Notice that these questions often require you to **refer closely**, to **analyse** and to **evaluate the effectiveness of** …

Comment on effect

When answering these questions it is important that you do not just name a technique or identify a feature in the passage – you must also comment on its effect.

Let's look at how this works in practice. Imagine that you've been asked a question about this part of 'Visiting Hour' (stanza 5) by Norman MacCaig.

> Ward 7. She lies
> in a white cave of forgetfulness.
> A withered hand
> trembles on its stalk. Eyes move
> behind eyelids too heavy
> to raise. Into an arm wasted
> of colour a glass fang is fixed,
> not guzzling but giving.
> And between her and me
> distance shrinks till there is none left
> but the distance of pain that neither she nor I
> can cross.

TOP TIP

In many ways these questions are quite similar to the sorts of questions you might be asked in the Reading for Understanding, Analysis and Evaluation paper. You can use the same approach to answer them.

Question: By referring closely to MacCaig's use of poetic techniques in stanza 5, show how he conveys a sense of the patient's isolation and weakness.

In your answer you might begin by choosing to focus on the lines

'A withered hand / trembles on its stalk';

the vivid metaphor used by MacCaig to describe the patient's hand and arm.

If you then wrote any of the following as part of your answer:

1. MacCaig says 'A withered hand / trembles on its stalk'.

2. MacCaig uses a metaphor 'A withered hand trembles on its stalk' to describe the patient.

3. MacCaig uses a metaphor 'A withered hand trembles on its stalk' to describe the patient's isolation and weakness.

you would not be awarded any marks because in the first one you are merely quoting the line; in the second you simply identify the technique as a metaphor, and in the third the words of the question are just tacked on at the end.

In order to gain the marks available for the question, of course you must identify the technique – but you must also make a suitable comment on the effect(s) of that technique or feature and what it suggests to the reader.

A successful answer would look something like:

MacCaig's use of the metaphor 'A withered hand / trembles on its stalk' suggests the patient's weakness by comparing the patient's arm to a decaying plant. This makes her seem less than human. 'Withered' suggests something dried up and dying. 'Stalk' exaggerates the thinness of the arm. 'Trembles' suggests a lack of control, again highlighting the patient's weakness.

You would then also comment on:

- 'white cave of forgetfulness'
- 'eyelids too heavy / to raise'
- 'arm wasted / of colour'
- 'glass fang is fixed'
- 'not guzzling but giving'
- 'the distance of pain that neither she nor I / can cross'

The final 10-mark question will require you to analyse and comment on a feature the printed text or extract has in common with the rest of the text (if it's a novel or a play) or with other texts by the same writer. You should organise your answer to the 10-mark question, using the suggested sub-headings, as follows:

Commonality

Bearing in mind what the question asks, make a broad, general statement about what the printed extract has in common with one or more of the other specified poems/short stories or with the rest of the play/novel. This is worth 2 marks.

Extract

Quote and comment on two elements of the printed extract which relate to the question being asked. This part of the answer is also worth 2 marks.

Other text(s)/other parts of the play/novel

Try to make up to six points (reference + comment) about the other text(s) or from elsewhere in the play/novel which relate to the question being asked. This part of the answer is worth 6 marks.

The acronym **CEO** (commonality, extract, other) might help you remember this structure.

The following pages contain three examples (drama, prose and poetry) of questions on Scottish texts.

Question on Scottish texts

Drama: *The Slab Boys*, by John Byrne

Read the extract below and then attempt the following questions. See pages 144–145 for the answers.

This extract is taken from the opening scenes of the play.

The Slab Room. Enter GEORGE 'SPANKY' FARRELL in dustcoat, drainpipe trousers, Tony Curtis hairdo, crepe-soled shoes. He crosses to his slab and starts working. Enter HECTOR MCKENZIE, similarly attired in dustcoat. He is shorter and weedier than SPANKY. He wears spectacles and carries a portable radio.

5 SPANKY: Hey ... where'd you get the wireless, Heck? Never seen you with that this morning.

HECTOR: Had it planked down the bog ... didn't want 'you-know-who' to see it.

SPANKY: Does it work? Give's a shot. (*Grabs radio.*) Where's Luxemburg?

HECTOR: Watch it, Spanky ... you'll break it! You can't get Luxemburg ... it's not
10 dark enough.

SPANKY: Aw – D'you need a dark wireless? I never knew that. Mebbe if we pull the aerial out a bit ... (*Does so. It comes away in his hand.*)

HECTOR: You swine, look what you've done!

SPANKY: Ach, that's easy fixed.

15 HECTOR: Give us it. (*Twiddles knobs. Gets Terry Dene singing 'A White Sport Coat'.*)

SPANKY: Good God, could you not've brung in a more modern wireless?
That's donkeys out of date.

HECTOR: I like it.

20 SPANKY: That's 'cos you're a tube, Hector.

(*Enter PHIL MCCANN in street clothes and carrying a portfolio under his arm. He sets folio down behind the door.*)

Morning, Phil. You're early the day. (*Consults wristwatch painted on wrist.*) 'S only half eleven.

25 PHIL: Anybody been looking for us?

SPANKY: Willie Curry was in ten minutes ago looking for that lemon yellow you promised but I told him you had diarrhoea and you'd take a big dish of it down to him later on.

PHIL: (*Changing into dustcoat*) Who belongs to the juke box?

30 HECTOR: 'S mines.

(*Enter WILLIE CURRY.*)

CURRY: Ha ... there you are, McCann. Where've you been this morning? Farrell there said you were unwell.

PHIL: Er ... um ... yes ...

35 CURRY: C'mon, what was up with you?

PHIL: Er ... touch of the ... er drawhaw.

CURRY: The what?

PHIL: Dee-oh-raw-ho ... the skitters ... it was very bad.

CURRY: Why didn't you come to me earlier? I could've got Nurse to have a look

40 at you ...

PHIL: No ... it's not what you'd cry a 'spectator sport', Mr Curly ...

CURRY: In future you report all illnesses to me ... first thing. How am I supposed to keep tabs on you lot if I don't know where the devil you are?

PHIL: I was down the lavvies ...

45 CURRY: You wouldn't get much done down there ...

PHIL: Oh, I wouldn't say that, Mr Corrie ...

CURRY: Godstruth, I don't know ... If I'd had you chaps out in Burma. Diarrhoea? There were men in my platoon fighting the Japanese with dysentery.

SPANKY: How did they fire it ... from chip baskets?

50 CURRY: Less of your damned cheek, Farrell. A couple of years in the Forces would smarten your ideas up a bit ... they'd soon have those silly duck's arse haircuts off you. And what've I told you about bringing that bloody contraption in ... eh? (*Picks up radio.*)

SPANKY: What contraption?

55 CURRY: How d'you expect to get any work done with that racket going on?

SPANKY: Pardon?

CURRY: Whoever owns this gadget can ask Mr Barton for it back.

(*Protests from boys.*)

I'll be calling back in five minutes and if you bunch are still lounging about

60 you're for the high jump, understand? Now, get on with it ... (*Exit.*)

PHIL: Chirpy this morning, eh?

CURRY: (*Popping head round the door*) Five minutes! (*Exit.*)

HECTOR: My bloody wireless! That was for my maw's Christmas present.

PHIL: Bless my boater, did you catch that, Cherry? A yuletide cadeau for the
65 squirt's mater and blow me if old Quelch ain't went and confiscated the blighter!

SPANKY: Christ, Nugent, that's torn it.

PHIL: Buck up, Pygmy Minimus ... Cherry and I'll think of something. Any ideas,
Cherry, old chap?

SPANKY: How about a set of cufflinks?

70 PHIL: I'll wager that beast, Bunter, had a fat finger in this ...

(*Enter JACK HOGG with ALAN DOWNIE.*)

Yaroo! ...

SPANKY: Yeugh ...

JACK: Morning, you chaps. Just showing the new lad round the Design Room.
75 This is our last stop.

PHIL: Natch. When're you off, Jacky boy?

JACK: Alan Downie ... George Farrell ... known to the riff-raff as 'Spanky' ...

SPANKY: Watch it, Jack. Howdy, Archie ...

JACK: And this is Phil McCann ...

80 PHIL: Hi, Andy ...

JACK: And last but by all means least Hector.

HECTOR: McKenzie ... hello.

JACK: This is the Slab Room, Alan ... where the colours are ground and dished for
the Designers ... you saw the patterns out there. What the lads do, basically, is dole
85 out a quantity of dry colour from those drums over there ... Persian red, rose pink ...

PHIL: ... bile green ...

SPANKY: ... acne yellow ...

JACK: ... dump it on to one of these marble diff slabs ... add some gum arabic to
prevent it flaking off the paper ... do we have some gum arabic? Then it's just a
90 matter of grinding ... (*demonstrates*). Bit of a diff from the studio, eh?

SPANKY: Why don't you vamoose, Jacky boy?

PHIL: Yeh, Plooky Chops ... them boils of yours is highly smittal.

JACK: I'm warning you, McCann.

PHIL: Keep away from me! Hector, fling us over the Dettol!

95 JACK: Jealousy will get you nowhere, McCann ... just because I'm on a desk.

SPANKY: It's a bloody operating table you want to be on, Jack. That face ... yeugh.

PHIL: You can put in for plastic surgery, you know ... on the National Health.

SPANKY: Or a 'pimplectomy'.

PHIL: It would only take about six months ...

100 SPANKY: ... and a team of surgeons ...

PHIL: ... with pliers.

JACK: (*To ALAN*) I've just got to dodge down the factory ... have a look at a couple of 'trials' ... shouldn't be too long. (*To SPANKY and PHIL*) The Boss would like you to show Alan what goes on in here ... in the way of work.

105 (*To ALAN*) Don't worry, you haven't been condemned to spend the rest of the day here ... I'll have a word with Bobby Sinclair, the colour consultant ... he could take you through the dyeing process ...

(*SPANKY collapses into PHIL's arms.*)

See you shortly ... (*Exit.*)

110 PHIL: Get a brush and some red paint, Heck.

HECTOR: What for?

SPANKY: To paint a cross on the door, stupid. To warn the villagers ...

HECTOR: What villagers?

PHIL: (*To ALAN*) OK, son, what did you say your name was again?

115 ALAN: Alan ... Alan Downie.

PHIL: Right, Eamonn ... let's show you some of the mysteries of the Slab Room. Mr Farrell ...

SPANKY: Mr Mac?

PHIL: I'm just showing young Dowdalls here some of the intricacies of our work.

120 If you and the boy would care to stand to the one side ...

SPANKY: Certainly. Hector ...

PHIL: Many thanks. Right, Alec ... this here is what we call a sink ... s-i-n-k. Now I don't expect you to pick up all these terms immediately but you'll soon get the hang of it. And this (*grabs HECTOR*) is what we cry a Slab Boy.

Questions

		Marks
1.	By referring closely to lines 1–16, show how the play's setting in time is established for the audience.	3
2.	By referring to two examples of dialogue in this extract, show how the playwright establishes the character of Willie Curry.	3
3.	Analyse the effect of some of the different registers of language in dialogue spoken by the characters that are evident in this extract.	4
4.	By referring to this extract and elsewhere in the play, discuss how the theme of bullying is developed in the text.	10

Total 20

Prose: *Sunset Song*, by Lewis Grassic Gibbon

Read the extract below and then attempt the following questions. See pages 146–148 for the answers.

This extract is from *Part I* (Ploughing).

So that was the college place at Duncairn, two Chrisses went there each morning, and one was right douce and studious and the other sat back and laughed a canny laugh at the antics of the teachers and minded Blawearie brae and the champ of horses and the smell of dung and her father's brown, grained
5 hands till she was sick to be home again. But she made friends with young Marget Strachan, Chae Strachan's daughter, she was slim and sweet and fair, fine to know, though she spoke about things that seemed awful at first and then weren't awful at all; and you wanted to hear more and Marget would laugh and say it was Chae that had told her. Always as Chae she spoke of him and that was an unco-like thing
10 to do of your father, but maybe it was because he was socialist and thought that Rich and Poor should be Equal. And what was the sense of believing that and then sending his daughter to educate herself and herself become one of the Rich?

But Marget cried that wasn't what Chae intended, she was to learn and be ready for the Revolution that was some day coming. And if come it never did
15 she wasn't to seek out riches anyway, she was off to be trained as a doctor, Chae said that life came out of women through tunnels of pain and if God had planned women for anything else but the bearing of children it was surely the saving of them. And Marget's eyes, that were blue and so deep they minded you of a well you peeped into, they'd grow deeper and darker and her sweet face grow so
20 solemn Chris felt solemn herself. But that would be only a minute, the next and Marget was laughing and fleering, trying to shock her, telling of men and women, what fools they were below their clothes; and how children came and how you should have them; and the things that Chae had seen in the huts of the blacks in Africa. And she told of a place where the bodies of men lay salted and white in
25 great stone vats till the doctors needed to cut them up, the bodies of paupers they were – *so take care you don't die as a pauper, Chris, for I'd hate some day if I rang a bell and they brought me up out of the vat your naked body, old and shrivelled and frosted with salt, and I looked in your dead, queer face, standing there with the scalpel held in my hand, and cried 'But this is Chris Guthrie!'*

30 That was awful, Chris felt sick and sick and stopped midway the shining path that led through the fields to Peesie's Knapp that evening in March. Clean and keen and wild and clear, the evening ploughed land's smell up in your nose and your mouth when you opened it, for Netherhill's teams had been out in that park all day, queer and lovely and dear the smell Chris noted. And something else she
35 saw, looking at Marget, sick at the thought of her dead body brought to Marget. And that thing was a vein that beat in Marget's throat, a little blue gathering where the blood beat past in slow, quiet strokes, it would never do that when one was dead and still under grass, down in the earth that smelt so fine and you'd never smell; or cased in the icy darkness of a vat, seeing never again the lowe of burning
40 whins or hearing the North Sea thunder beyond the hills, the thunder of it breaking through a morning of mist, the right things that might not last and so soon went by.

And they only were real and true, beyond them was nought you might ever attain but a weary dream and that last dark silence – Oh, only a fool loved being alive!

45 But Marget threw her arms around her when she said that, and kissed her with red, kind lips, so red they were that they looked like haws, and said there were lovely things in the world, lovely that didn't endure, and the lovelier for that. *Wait till you find yourself in the arms of your lad, in the harvest time it'll be with the stooks round about you, and he'll stop from joking – they do, you know, and that's just when their blood-pressure alters – and he'll take you like this – wait, there's not a body to see*
50 *us! – and hold you like this, with his hands held so, and kiss you like this!*

It was over in a moment, quick and shameful, fine for all that, tingling and strange and shameful by turns. Long after she parted with Marget that evening she turned and stared down at Peesie's Knapp and blushed again; and suddenly she was seeing them all at Blawearie as though they were strangers naked out of
55 the sea, she felt ill every time she looked at father and mother. But that passed in a day or so, for nothing endures.

Not a thing, though you're over-young to go thinking of that, you've your lessons and studies, the English Chris, and living and eating and sleeping that other Chris that stretches your toes for you in the dark of the night and whispers
60 a drowsy I'm you. But you might not stay from the thinking when all in a day, Marget, grown part of your life, came waving to you as you neared the Knapp with the news she was off to Aberdeen to live with an auntie there – *it's a better place for a scholar, Chae says, and I'll be trained all the sooner.*

And three days later Chae Strachan and Chris drove down to the station with
65 her, and saw her off at the platform, and she waved at them, bonny and young, Chae looked as numb as Chris felt. He gave her a lift from the station, did Chae, and on the road he spoke but once, to himself it seemed, not Chris: *Ay, Marget lass, you'll do fine, if you keep the lads at bay from kissing the bonny breast of you.*

Questions

		Marks
1.	By close reference to paragraphs 1 and 2, explain how the writer's language conveys a sense of Marget Strachan's character.	4
2.	By referring to at least two examples from paragraph 3, analyse how the writer conveys a sense of the contrast between life and death.	4
3.	By referring to two examples from paragraphs 4 and 5, analyse how the writer conveys Chris' perception of the incident with Marget.	2
4.	This extract refers to two aspects of Chris' character. By referring to this extract and to elsewhere in the novel, discuss how Grassic Gibbon conveys these aspects of Chris' character.	10

Total 20

Poetry: 'Nil Nil' by Don Paterson

Read the extract from Don Paterson's 'Nil Nil' printed below and then attempt the following questions. See pages 148–150 for the answers.

Unknown to him, it is all that remains
of a lone fighter-pilot, who, returning at dawn
to find Leuchars was not where he'd left it,
took time out to watch the Sidlaws unsheathed
5   from their great black tarpaulin, the haar burn off Tayport
and Venus melt into Carnoustie, igniting
the shoreline; no wind, not a cloud in the sky
and no one around to admire the discretion
of his unscheduled exit: the engine plopped out
10   and would not re-engage, sending him silently
twirling away like an ash-key,
his attempt to bail out only partially successful,
yesterday having been April the 1st –
the ripcord unleashing a flurry of socks
15   like a sackful of doves rendered up to the heavens
in private irenicon. He caught up with the plane
on the ground, just at the instant the tank blew
and made nothing of him, save for his fillings,
his tackets, his lucky half-crown and his gallstone,
20   now anchored between the steel bars of a stank
that looks to be biting the bullet on this one.

In short, this is where you get off, reader;
I'll continue alone, on foot, in the failing light,
following the trail as it steadily fades
25   *into road repairs, birdsong, the weather, nirvana,*
the plot thinning down to a point so refined
  not even the angels could dance on it. Goodbye.

Questions

		Marks
1.	By referring to specific features, explain how this extract relates to the earlier parts of the poem.	**3**
2.	By referring closely to lines 4–16, analyse the use of poetic technique to describe the fighter-pilot's experience.	**4**
3.	Evaluate how effective you find lines 16–21 of this extract. Your answer should deal with ideas and/or language.	**3**
4.	By referring to this poem and another poem by Don Paterson you have studied, discuss how he makes the reader consider the theme of time.	**10**
		Total 20

TOP TIP

Remember that the final question in this section will **always** be worth **10** marks.

The critical essay

This part of the paper is no longer quite so daunting as it used to be in previous versions of Higher English. If you have completed a National 5 English course and sat the exam that goes with that course, then you will be familiar with the demands of writing a critical essay under timed conditions. Nevertheless there are many things you can do to improve your chances of success in this part of the examination.

The critical essay section forms the second section of the Critical Reading paper. It is therefore very important that you get used to writing a successful essay in around 45 minutes. There's no point in spending so much time on your chosen Scottish text question that you run out of time and can't complete your essay. The critical essay has **20 marks** allocated to it. We will look at how the essays are marked later.

The Critical Reading paper is divided into five sub sections and these will be presented in the same order each year: drama, prose, poetry, film and TV drama, and language. You have to answer any **one** question but it must be on a genre different to the one you chose in the questions on Scottish texts section. So if you've answered on poetry in the questions on Scottish texts section you cannot choose a critical essay question from the poetry section. You are reminded of this again in the instructions printed in the exam paper itself.

The questions are designed in such a way that they test your **knowledge and understanding** of the literary texts you have studied as part of your Higher course and your ability to **analyse and evaluate** them. The essays also test your powers of expression and must be capable of being *understood at first reading* and have *only a few errors in spelling, grammar, sentence construction, punctuation and paragraphing.*

> ## TOP TIP
>
> Remember that you *can* base your critical essay on a text printed in the questions on Scottish texts section as long as you stay within the requirement to answer on **two different** genres in this paper.

Let's consider each sub section of this part of the exam paper in turn.

Drama

At the start of this section is a reminder of the dramatic techniques from the play you should address in your answer. The advice for drama is as follows:

> *Answers to questions on* **drama** *should refer to the text and to such relevant features as characterisation, key scene(s), structure, climax, theme, plot, conflict, setting ...*

There are then **three** essay questions to choose from. You should be prepared to show your knowledge of a wide range of features to be found in drama texts. The questions might make specific reference to:

- theme
- key scene
- opening scene
- concluding scene
- central character
- characterisation
- relationship between characters
- situation
- staging/set/use of acting areas
- dialogue
- plot
- structure
- conflict
- turning point
- climax
- ending
- symbolism
- recurring motifs
- lighting

Prose

This section is divided into two: fiction and non-fiction. The advice for prose fiction is as follows:

> *Answers to questions on **prose fiction** should refer to the text and to such relevant features as characterisation, setting, language, key incident(s), climax, turning point, plot, structure, narrative technique, theme, ideas, description ...*

There are then **three** questions on prose fiction. These are on the novel or short story. The questions might make specific reference to:

- plot opening
- plot ending
- characterisation/main characters/minor characters
- relationship between characters
- point of view
- setting
- narrative method
- narrative voice
- structure
- key incident or scene
- language
- theme

There are three questions on prose non-fiction. If you attempt one of them you are told that:

> *Answers to questions on **prose non-fiction** should refer to the text and to such relevant features as ideas, use of evidence, stance, style, selection of material, narrative voice ...*

The questions might make specific reference to:

- presentation of events in biography and autobiography
- portrayal of society/culture/country
- structure
- description
- emotional experience
- style
- use of humour
- insights given by travel writing
- the writer's stance
- persuasive language

TOP TIP

Studying as wide a range of texts as possible during your course will increase your options in the exam and enable you to write about texts you have genuinely enjoyed.

Poetry

Any essay on poetry should:

> ... *refer to the text and to such relevant features as word choice, tone, imagery, structure, content, rhythm, rhyme, theme, sound, ideas ...*

Sometimes a question will require you to write about **two** poems either by the same poet or by different poets. If you choose to answer such a question, make sure you can discuss both poems in sufficient depth.

The questions might make specific reference to:

- theme
- situation
- structure
- sound
- rhythm and rhyme
- form
- imagery
- word choice/diction
- tone
- closing lines
- ambiguity
- mood/atmosphere
- emotion
- poet's or speaker's stance/perspective/personality
- location/setting
- portrayal/exploration of a relationship
- an experience which prompts reflection on a theme
- description/portrayal of a scene/landscape

Film and TV drama

This section requires you to show your knowledge of media texts. **Don't** attempt a question from this section unless you have studied a media text as part of your course – however tempted you might be to 'analyse' that DVD you watched last night. Successful answers to questions from this part of the paper will:

> ... refer to the text and to such relevant features as use of camera, key sequence, characterisation, mise-en-scène, editing, setting, music/sound, special effects, plot, dialogue ...

Questions in this section require you to deal with concepts such as:

- characterisation
- central character
- music
- adaptation of novel or stage play
- setting
- atmosphere
- important sequence
- story/plot
- subject matter
- presentation of a theme

Language

Only a very few candidates attempt a question from this section each year. Successful answers require knowledge of a text you have studied:

> ... and to such relevant features as register, accent, dialect, slang, jargon, vocabulary, tone, abbreviation ...

Although the topics in this section are very interesting, they require specialist knowledge that is beyond the scope of this book.

Choosing a question

If you look at any SQA past paper or the specimen paper available on the SQA website, you will see that the questions for the critical essay tend to follow the same kind of pattern.

You are first asked to 'choose' a text. Remember that you *can* use a Scottish text but not the one that you used in section 1 of the paper.

Then there is a statement that will enable you to decide if the text you have studied is suitable to answer the question.

After this comes what you have to do in the essay. Often there will be two aspects to this.

Let's look at an example.

> The initial statement. If the play you have studied does not contain a conflict between two characters you will not be able to produce a relevant response.

Choose a play in which the conflict between two characters is an important feature. Briefly explain the nature of this conflict and discuss how the dramatist's presentation of this feature enhances your understanding of the play as a whole.

> The first part of this task requires you to describe the conflict. Note the word 'Briefly' – don't spend too long on this part of the essay.

> The second part of this task. This can often require a more 'sophisticated' response. An ability to 'analyse' and 'evaluate' is clearly required as you comment on the dramatist's techniques. You will also have to refer to the 'central concerns' of the play ('your understanding of the play as a whole').

Your essay must be a **relevant** response to the question. You must resist the temptation simply to write down everything you know about your chosen text. This is especially true when you are writing about poetry – you must avoid giving the examiner a 'guided tour' of the text, starting at the beginning and explaining all of the writer's techniques, even if that's how you were taught to analyse the poem in the first place. Although you do need to include enough **content** in order to provide evidence of your knowledge and understanding, analysis and evaluation, it is much better to write a shorter essay that is relevant than a longer one that does not get to grips with the question itself. Taking five minutes to plan your essay on this and then 40 minutes to write it is a sensible way to allocate your time in the exam and should enable you to produce a well-constructed, thoughtful answer.

Planning a critical essay

Once you have chosen a text that will allow you to produce a relevant response and have identified the key words in the question, you should then spend some time on planning the essay.

How you do this very much depends on you. Some people like to produce a mind map or spider diagram; others prefer a list of bullet points. It doesn't matter which method you choose as long as you can do it quickly and end up with the main points you are going to make. Taking five minutes to select a question and plan your essay should mean that you don't run out of steam after 20 minutes of frantic writing followed by wondering what to say next.

Let's look at an example of this in action. Look at the following critical essay question.

> *Choose a play in which the central character is heroic yet vulnerable.*
>
> *Show how the dramatist makes you aware of both qualities and discuss how they affect your response to the character's fate in the play as a whole.*

Say you were going to use Othello as an example of a character who is 'heroic yet vulnerable', you might produce the following planning diagram to remind yourself what points you intend to make:

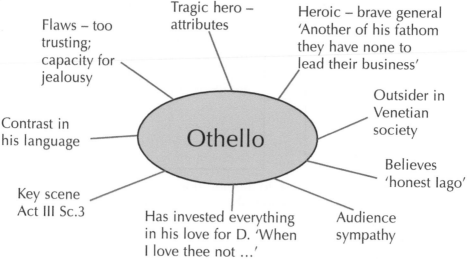

Tragic hero – attributes

Heroic – brave general 'Another of his fathom they have none to lead their business'

Flaws – too trusting; capacity for jealousy

Outsider in Venetian society

Contrast in his language

Othello

Believes 'honest Iago'

Key scene Act III Sc.3

Has invested everything in his love for D. 'When I love thee not ...'

Audience sympathy

Here are the same ideas in a list of bullet points.

Othello

- Tragic hero
- Heroic – 'Another of his fathom they have none to lead their business'
- Vulnerable: flaws – too trusting; capacity for jealousy; lacks self-knowledge
- Outsider in Venetian society
- Believes 'honest Iago'
- Has invested everything in his love for D. 'When I love thee not ...'
- Audience sympathy
- Contrast in his language (poetic style v. echoes of Iago's use of imagery)
- Key Scene: Act III Sc. 3

Once you've decided on the points you are going to make it's a good idea to **number** them so that the structure of your essay begins to take shape and you start to have an idea about how to **order** your arguments.

Writing a critical essay

Once you have a clear idea of what you are going to write, you can begin. In the potentially stress-filled environment of the examination room, it's a good idea to keep the structure of your essay as straightforward as you can.

The opening paragraph should:

* refer to the **title** of the text and its **author**
* refer to the **key words** of the question.

The main part of your essay should then develop each of the points you have decided to make. It should develop in a logical way with a clear structure. You should pay particular attention to using **topic sentences** to signpost the stages of your argument and to refer back to the **key words** of the question and incorporate a brief response to the question itself.

The final paragraph should:

* refer back to the key words of the question
* bring your argument to a logical conclusion.

As you write the essay remember to **express** the points you make as **effectively** as possible.

Try using the following expressions in your essay.

> ### TOP TIP
>
> Don't forget that it *can* sometimes be useful to think in terms of some kind of a 'formula' for your writing. You might find it helpful to think in terms of **P**oint, **E**vidence, **E**xplanation (or something similar) when constructing your paragraph. However, in the best essays such a structure shouldn't always be too obvious to the reader!

The author/poet/dramatist/director	
	• *attempts to …*
	• *develops …*
	• *demonstrates …*
	• *explores …*
	• *conveys …*
	• *exploits …*
	• *communicates …*
	• *attacks …*
	• *satirises …*
	• *utilises …*
	• *influences …*

The author/poet/dramatist/director's	
	• *aim here is to …*
	• *intention here is to …*
	• *purpose here is to …*

The author/poet/dramatist/ director's		
	• *skill*	is demonstrated by …
	• *artistry*	
	• *craft*	
	• *mastery*	

Many critics	<ul><li>*consider that …*</li><li>*believe that …*</li><li>*have stated that …*</li><li>*have expressed the view that …*</li></ul>

It is said that …

It has often been said that …

There can be little doubt that …

This could be seen as the author's attempt at …

Try using these to link paragraphs in your essay.

<ul><li>similarly</li><li>likewise</li><li>in the same way</li></ul>	<ul><li>although</li><li>for all that</li><li>however</li><li>on the contrary</li><li>otherwise</li><li>yet</li><li>but</li><li>even so</li></ul>	<ul><li>to this end</li><li>for this reason</li><li>for this purpose</li></ul>
<ul><li>accordingly</li><li>as a consequence</li><li>as a result</li><li>hence</li><li>therefore</li><li>thus</li><li>inevitably</li></ul>	<ul><li>for example</li><li>for instance</li><li>in other words</li><li>by way of illustration</li></ul>	<ul><li>as has been noted</li><li>finally</li><li>in brief</li><li>in short</li><li>on the whole</li><li>in other words</li></ul>

How to use quotations in your critical essay

Using quotations from the novel, play, poem or film that you are writing about will enable you to provide evidence to show that you have sufficient knowledge of the text and will support your analysis and evaluation of it. But the quotations you choose to include in your essay must be relevant **and** must support your line of argument. There is no point in learning 10 quotations from, say, *Othello*, and then including them in your essay if they are not relevant to the area of the text specified by the question.

It is a good idea to keep a note of useful quotations for each text you study during the course. You can do it like this:

Act, scene and line no.	Quotation	Comment
I i 65	Iago: I am not what I am.	Iago's deceitful nature is evident.
I i 88–89	Iago: … an old black ram Is tupping your white ewe.	Iago's typically coarse and bestial imagery.
I i 115–116	Iago: … your daughter and the moor are now making the beast with Two backs.	See above.
I ii 63	Brabantio: … thou hast enchanted her;	Brabantio cannot believe that his daughter would choose to marry Othello.
I iii 76–93	Othello: Most potent … … I won his daughter.	*All of this speech*. Othello's typical dignified and highly poetic style. Note that he moves into prose under the stress of emotion and degradation (IV i 35–43; 169–211).
I iii 127–169	Othello: Her father loved me … … let her witness it.	*All of this speech*. Othello's account of his courtship of Desdemona. Again, take note of the highly poetic style.
I iii 291	Brabantio: She has deceived her Father, and may thee.	Brabantio's warning to Othello. An ominous hint of what Othello will later believe.
I iii 292	Othello: My life upon her faith. Honest Iago …	Ironic, given the later events of the play. The adjective 'honest' is applied to Iago throughout the play. The audience is always aware of the irony.
I iii 395–396	Iago: … Hell and night Must bring this monstrous birth to the world's light.	Iago's plot described as a monster; something unnatural.
II i 164–173	Iago: He takes her by the palm … With As little a web as this will I Ensnare as great a fly as Cassio.	Animal imagery again. Iago as the manipulator of events and people.
II i 278–279	Iago: The Moor, howbeit that I endure him not, Is of a constant, loving, noble nature,	Even Iago recognises Othello's nobility.

II i 285–287	Iago: For that I do suspect the lusty Moor Hath leaped into my seat. The thought whereof Doth like a poisonous mineral gnaw my inwards;	A possible motive for Iago's actions? A vivid image of what it is like to be jealous. Iago's twisted mind also suspects Cassio of sleeping with his wife (297).

Or you can just annotate your text. Some or all of the texts you use might be available in digital versions so you could do all of this on your phone, tablet or laptop. Use *any* method that will make your revision easier.

When you are writing a critical essay in the external exam at Higher, it's just you, a pen, a piece of paper and what's inside your head. So you must learn the quotations to use by heart. It's a good idea to keep them short – the exam isn't really a memory test, even though it can feel a bit like that sometimes!

If the quotation is a short one (a single word or short phrase), you can simply include it in the sentence you are writing (remembering to put it inside inverted commas).

For example:

Othello's continual reference to his old comrade as 'honest Iago' is a good example of Shakespeare's use of irony in the play.

or

Brabantio believes Othello has 'enchanted' Desdemona.

or

In the expression 'the engine plopped out' Paterson uses onomatopoeia to almost comic effect.

If the quotation is a longer one (a whole line or more from the text), you can do one of the following:

Add it to the end of your sentence.

When confronted with what seems an ugly situation Othello commands everyone to 'Keep up your bright swords, for the dew will rust them'.

or

Place it, sandwiched, between the two parts of your sentence.

Othello's command

   'Keep up your bright swords, for the dew will rust them'

shows his ability to defuse a potentially ugly situation.

Introduce the quotation with a verb of saying and a colon or comma.

As MacCaig tells us,

   'She lies

   in a white cave of forgetfulness.'

or

Neil states,

'Yonder's a room with fifty rooms ... every one of them three times the size of our hut, and nearly all of them empty.'

Longer quotations like the above should be placed on a new line for the sake of clarity in your essay.

You will also see some writers simply using a colon to introduce a quotation.

For example:

Tulloch quickly takes the side of the cone-gatherers:

   'I have questioned them my lady ... and I saw what happened; and I find no fault in them.'

or

MacCaig is determined not to give in to his feelings:

   'I will not feel, I will not

   feel, until

   I have to.'

The danger with this last method is that it can make your essay seem rather staccato and disjointed as the essay becomes simply one point after another, each followed by a quotation. You will find it difficult to construct any kind of fully developed, focused argument if you rely too much on this method.

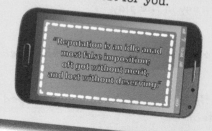

TOP TIP

To help you memorise your quotations, write them on sticky post-it notes and put them around your house in the run up to the exam. Fridge door; bathroom cabinet; bedside table – it doesn't matter where as long as they help jog your memory. You could enter and save them on your phone – as long as you remember **not** to take it with you into the exam! There are numerous free 'flash card' apps available that you could use. Search for 'flash cards' in the app store and see which ones work best for you.

"Reputation is an idle and most false imposition; oft got without merit, and lost without deserving."

Example critical essays

Finally, let's look at how all of this is put together, from reading the question to the finished essay.

> Choose a **novel** in which one character generates hostility from one or more than one other character.
>
> Explain the nature of the hostility and go on to discuss how the novelist's use of it adds to your understanding of the novel as a whole.

Example 1

We'll be using Robin Jenkins' novel *The Cone-Gatherers*, as it is an appropriate text to use, but you could use **any** novel you have studied **provided it matches the description in the first part of the question** (see the words highlighted in blue).

The key words of the question have been highlighted. Here's an example of the sort of notes you could produce to remind you of what to write.

First part of question:

- Calum generates hostility from Duror (+ Lady Runcie Campbell).
- Description of Calum.
- Why Duror hates him.
  - Personification of all that's wrong in his life.
  - Defiled his 'sanctuary'.
  - Revolted by anything misshapen or deformed.
  - Descent into madness.
  - Deer drive (LRC's hostility toward Calum).
  - Accusations against Calum.
  - End of novel – death of Calum.

Second part of question:

- Theme of good v. evil.
- Calum represents good and is sacrificed at the end.
- Closing lines – LRC's moment of catharsis.
- Jenkins' ending leaves the reader (like LRC) with hope.

TOP TIP

You should **always** take time to plan your essay – don't be put off by other people frantically scribbling as soon as the invigilator tells you to start.

With these (brief) notes in front of you, you could then write something like this in the remaining 40 minutes or so you will have left.

Opening paragraph identifies text and author and refers back to the question.

In 'The Cone-Gatherers' by Robin Jenkins we see the character Calum generate hostility from the evil gamekeeper Duror. The portrayal of the hostility adds to our understanding of the novel as a whole as Jenkins uses it as part of his exploration of the theme of good versus evil.

Jenkins makes the reader sympathise with Calum, a hunchback who is gathering cones with his brother in the woods of the Runcie Campbell estate during the

Second World War. Although he is deformed Jenkins portrays him as 'honest, generous and truly meek' and someone who is close to the world of nature. He is an expert climber and is 'as indigenous as squirrel or bird' in the trees on the estate. Jenkins effectively develops the character as someone who does not understand why there should be suffering in the world and throughout the novel he is portrayed as a 'Christ-like' figure.

> Quotations used to show knowledge of the text and to support the points made in the essay.

> Topic sentence

Calum generates hostility from Duror for many reasons. Duror 'hated and despised' the cone-gatherers and feels that they have defiled the wood which 'had always been his stronghold and sanctuary'. Through skilful characterisation, Jenkins portrays Duror's suffering. His wife has become hugely obese, their relationship has broken down and his attempts to sign up to fight in the war have been refused. Calum represents everything that is wrong in Duror's life. Jenkins tells us

'For many years his life had been stunted, misshapen, obscene and hideous; and this misbegotten creature was its personification.'

In addition to this Duror has always been revolted by anything misshapen or deformed and Jenkins even suggests that he sympathises with Hitler's treatment of 'idiots and cripples'. Duror is portrayed by Jenkins as a man descending into madness. He uses the image of a tree 'still showing green leaves' but with death 'creeping along the roots' to describe Duror and the reader is always aware of Duror's true nature and also that he is 'alone in his obsession'.

Duror uses Calum's unwilling involvement in the deer drive to try and remove him from the wood. Ironically it is at the deer drive that Duror's madness first shows in public when he kills the deer, confusing it with his wife Peggy. Calum attempts to save the deer but now also generates hostility from Lady Runcie Campbell who is annoyed that the event has become 'a shocking and demeaning spectacle'. Tulloch, a very 'moral' character, speaks up for the cone-gatherers. However, Duror's twisted mind also leads him to accuse Calum of exposing himself in the wood.

In the tense final chapter of the novel, the hostility Duror feels toward Calum leads to the killing of Calum and his own suicide.

> Now the essay begins to deal with the second part of the question.

Thus, Robin Jenkins uses this hostility to explore the theme of good versus evil and so adds to the reader's understanding of the novel as a whole. Calum's child-like goodness (a quality which he shares with Roderick) and his pity and concern for the animals of the wood make the reader sympathise with him. His 'sacrifice' at the end of the novel cleanses the wood of evil and gives hope for the future. Jenkins again suggests a similarity to Jesus' death on the Cross as 'he hung in a twisted fashion' in the tree after Duror shoots him. The cones and blood which fall from him are another suggestion of this religious symbol.

After the two deaths (and Roderick's return to safety), Lady Runcie Campbell undergoes a moment of catharsis and as she cries 'pity, and purified hope, and joy, welled up in her heart'. The reader experiences this too as we read this very powerful and thought-provoking climax to the novel.

Jenkins' ending leaves the reader (like Lady Runcie Campbell) with hope. Although he allows the hostility between Calum and Duror to culminate in their deaths, evil is defeated even if at great human cost. As a result, the reader is left with a greater understanding of the theme of good versus evil and of the novel as a whole.

> Concluding paragraph refers back to the key words of the question.

This essay is 660 words long. You should be able to write something of similar length in the time available to you in the exam.

Example 2

Here is another example of a critical essay. Read it carefully to see how the writer has constructed a relevant response to the question.

> *Choose a poem which you find emotionally unsettling or intellectually challenging.*
>
> *Show how the poem elicits the response from you and discuss how it contributes to your understanding of the central concerns of the poem.*

Donald Paterson's 'Nil Nil' is a poem the reader finds intellectually challenging. The poem presents you with what seems at first to be two separate 'stories' using a mixture of vivid and sometimes bizarre images. These stories are in fact linked and the reader is left to consider the connections between them and also the connections between them and the epigraph and the epilogue. Paterson skilfully challenges the reader to consider the central concerns of the poem: nothingness and loss.

The structure of the poem presents the reader with the first intellectual challenge as we are made to think about how the four separate sections are connected. The epigraph says it is a search for meaning but as it is attributed to the fictional literary theorist, Francois Aussemain, who appears in other Don Paterson poems, the reader is immediately suspicious. Paterson links ideas and images throughout the poem and the reader is challenged to find these patterns. In the epigraph we are told about 'abandoned histories' which 'plunge on into deeper and deeper obscurity' and we then see that these ideas are picked up in the two 'stories' of the poem: the decline of the football club and the death of the airman whose fuel tank 'blew/and made nothing of him'. Paterson's use of a vivid image in the epigraph 'the vast rustling map of Burgundy ... settling over it like a freshly starched sheet' is echoed in the second 'story' when the fighter-pilot sees 'the Sidlaws unsheathed/from their great black tarpaulin'. The epilogue addresses the reader directly 'In short, this is where you get off ...' and continues the idea of things reducing to nothingness with its references to 'failing light'; 'nirvana' and 'the plot thinning down'. This is a poem aware of itself as fiction and so we are challenged to make sense of what it really means.

Paterson also challenges the reader intellectually in his account of the long decline of the football club in the first 'story' as we are forced to consider the significance of '... the fifty year slide into Sunday League'. This section of the poem begins with a description of an old film of the club's greatest success, emphasised by Paterson's word choice: 'From the top' and 'zenith'. The long description of decline which follows includes interesting juxtapositions ('long hoick forward' and 'balletic') and vivid images:

> '... a shaky pan to the Erskine St End
>
> where a plague of grey bonnets falls out of the clouds'

Paterson's use of the word 'plague', with its connotations of disease and decay, is particularly effective here at signalling the imminent decline of the club. There is humour too, in the descriptions of

> '... grim fathers and perverts with Old English Sheepdogs
>
> lining the touch, moaning softly.'

and

> '... two little boys — Alastair Watt, —
>
> who answers to "Forty", and wee Horace Madden,
>
> so smelly the air seems to quiver above him'

This use of black humour and cartoon-like images stops the poem from becoming merely sentimental or overtly nostalgic — it forces us to reconsider Paterson's presentation of the central concerns of loss and nothingness.

References to loss and nothingness appear throughout this section of the poem: 'detaching like bubbles'; 'dwindling half-hearted kickabouts' and these are reinforced by Paterson's use of listing

> '... the stopped swings, the dead shanty-town
>
> of allotments, the black shell of Skelly dry cleaners'.

Paterson even makes Horace live in a 'cul-de-sac' — a road to nowhere.

The use of the 'stone' as the hinge between the two 'stories' is particularly effective. It is a grim reminder of all that remains of the 'lone fighter-pilot' but his is also an 'abandoned history' — his story is 'Unknown' to Horace. In this section of the poem, Paterson continues to challenge the reader to find meaning in all the negatives he uses:

> '... no wind, not a cloud in the sky
>
> and no one around'

and

> '... sending him silently
>
> twirling away like an ash-key'

But these more serious images are also undercut by Paterson's wit and humour. The bizarre image of the airman pulling his ripcord and

> '... unleashing a flurry of socks
>
> like a sackful of doves rendered up to the heavens
>
> in private irenicon'.

makes the reader try and reconcile the cartoon-like description and the formality of the word 'irenicon' — a 'proposal designed to promote peace'.

The fighter-pilot's ignominious end — 'made nothing of him, save for his fillings, / his tackets, his lucky half-crown and his gallstone' — is a stark reminder that we are all reduced to nothing at the end of our lives. The poem's title, 'Nil Nil', then seems so much more than just a reference to a football score.

In conclusion, it is clear that Don Paterson's 'Nil Nil' is a poem which challenges the reader intellectually. Through its effective use of structure and imagery, its mix of the serious and the comic, and its awareness of itself as a poem, the reader is forced to question how we interpret our 'histories' and to consider the 'dull and terrible facts' of loss and our decline into nothingness.

Preparing for the exam

It's likely you will study at least three genres during your Higher English course. Consequently you would be well advised to prepare at least one text from all three prior to the exam. Even though you will only write an essay about one of them, you need the others as an 'insurance policy' should the questions in one of your preferred sections not quite 'fit' your choice of text. It is important to revise and prepare a number of different aspects of each text (use of setting, characterisation, narrative style, theme). You will also increase your chances of success by studying as wide a range of texts as time allows during your course. That way you will be able to write

about something you have genuinely enjoyed reading or watching. The 'minimalist' approach of only studying your chosen Scottish text(s) and one other text in a different genre and then practising essay after essay on them is unlikely to give you much of an insight into the study of literature. During your course you should, depending on the resources available in your school, be able to cover say a novel, one or two short stories and/or some shorter pieces of prose fiction; a play or a film and a selection of poetry – although the number and variety of texts taught will be different from school to school.

You must revisit and revise your texts throughout your course. Just because you finish looking at a novel in class in October, don't then leave it on the shelf until just before the exam. You must take responsibility for your own learning and keep updating your notes and knowledge throughout the year.

Look carefully at the feedback you get from your teacher on any practice essays that you do

> **TOP TIP**
>
> It's a good idea to buy cheap copies of your longer texts for yourself – you'll easily find older second hand editions on sites such as Amazon and Abebooks – so you can annotate them in any ways that will make your revision easier.

(especially those in a prelim) and try to avoid making the same mistakes in your next essays; but on no account should you learn an essay off by heart in the hope of using it in the exam – even if you got a good mark for it. The critical essay question rewards your ability to think on the day of the exam and it is highly unlikely that you will find a question that corresponds exactly with one you have done earlier in your course. Your teacher will probably show you 'exemplar' essays as you prepare for the exam. They are to show you the principles of effective essay writing (structure, topic sentences, links between sections, use of evidence and quotation) but they are not designed to be memorised and reproduced on the day of the exam itself. The key thing to remember is to have enough things to say about the texts you have studied and then *select* from that body of knowledge in order to write a relevant response to the exam question.

How the critical essay is marked

All critical essays are marked on a scale of 0–20. The table below shows what markers are looking for in an essay that is just good enough to pass (10–12 marks) and what they are looking for in an essay that gets the best marks (19–20).

	Marks 20–19	Marks 12–10
Knowledge and understanding The critical essay demonstrates:	• a thorough knowledge and understanding of the text • a perceptive selection of textual evidence to support a line of argument which is fluently structured and expressed • a perceptive focus on the demands of the question	• an adequate knowledge and understanding of the text • adequate textual evidence to support a line of thought which is adequately structured and expressed • an adequate focus on the demands of the question
Analysis The critical essay demonstrates:	• a perceptive analysis of the effect of features of language/filmic techniques	• an adequate analysis of the effect of features of language/filmic techniques
Evaluation The critical essay demonstrates:	• a committed, evaluative stance with respect to the text and the task	• adequate evidence of an evaluative stance with respect to the text and the task
Technical accuracy The critical essay demonstrates:	• few errors in spelling, grammar, sentence construction, punctuation and paragraphing • the ability to be understood at first reading	

The language of the marking instructions can sometimes seem not particularly 'user-friendly' so let's think about what some aspects of these criteria actually mean.

- Demonstrating 'thorough knowledge and understanding' of the text just means you need to show that you know more than just what happens in a novel or short story or poem. You need to show understanding of the **themes or ideas** the writer explores in the text. For example, you would need to show that you understand that the play *Othello* is not just about a general who is tricked into believing his wife is unfaithful and who then kills her and then himself, but that Shakespeare is using the play to explore the corrosive effects of jealousy and the very nature of evil itself. In an essay on *Sunset Song* you would need to show that you understand not just the major events in Chris Guthrie's life but also that the novel deals with the end of a way of life for a particular section of Scottish society. An essay on Norman MacCaig's 'Visiting Hour' won't just give details about the speaker in the poem's visit to a hospital; it will also refer to MacCaig's musings on confronting our mortality.

- Demonstrating an 'analysis of the effect of features of language/filmic technique' requires you to explain the various **techniques** used by the writer or director (remember that you are given a reminder of the sort of things to mention in the boxes at the start of each section of the question paper). These explanations must be used to provide evidence for the line of argument that you adopt in response to the question.

- If you choose to write about texts you have **genuinely enjoyed and/or found interesting**, then it will be easier for you to demonstrate 'a committed, evaluative stance with respect to the text and task' and say something about its effectiveness. Don't go 'over the top' in what you say about a text or writer in an attempt to illustrate this! It always sounds artificial when candidates write things like '*Larkin's brilliant use of alliteration helps the reader to realise this*' or '*Jenkins' superb characterisation brings Calum to life.*'

- The requirement for technical accuracy recognises that you are writing in the stressful setting of the exam room with no opportunity to draft and redraft your essay. Nevertheless you must do all you can to avoid common (and, at this level, very basic) mistakes such as:

  - ➤ Comma splice – where you join ('splice') sentences together with commas rather than ending a sentence with a full stop and then starting a new one.

  - ➤ Inconsistent spelling of common words – if you know you've got problems in this area make a word list as you go through the course and make learning these spellings a part of your revision routine.

  - ➤ Using slang ('*Shakespeare uses well effective imagery ...*'), colloquial language ('*Othello thinks Desdemona is cheating on him ...*'), 'text-speak' ('*The problem 4 Othello is ...*'), abbreviations and symbols ('*Othello & Iago ...*').

  - ➤ Failure to organise your essay into paragraphs – the planning you do prior to starting the essay will give you a ready-made paragraph plan.

  - ➤ Incorrect use of apostrophes.

  - ➤ Writing expressions such as '*a lot*' as one word.

Once the marker has read the essay thoroughly he or she will then give it a mark according to the following scale (this time shown in full).

	Marks 20–19	Marks 18–16	Marks 15–13	Marks 12–10	Marks 9–6	Marks 5–0
Knowledge and understanding The critical essay demonstrates:	• a thorough knowledge and understanding of the text • use of detailed textual evidence to support your line of argument which is fluently structured and expressed • perceptive focus on the demands of the question	• a secure knowledge and understanding of the text • a perceptive selection of textual evidence to support your line of thought which is coherently structured and expressed • a secure focus on the demands of the question	• a clear knowledge and understanding of the text • use of clear textual evidence to support your line of thought which is clearly structured and expressed • clear focus on the demands of the question	• an adequate knowledge and understanding of the text • adequate textual evidence to support your line of thought which is adequately structured and expressed • an adequate focus on demands of the question	• limited evidence of knowledge and understanding of the text • limited textual evidence to support your line of thought which is structured and expressed in a limited way • limited focus on the demands of the question	• very little knowledge and understanding of the text • very little textual evidence to support your line of thought which shows very little structure or clarity of expression • very little focus on the demands of the question
Analysis The critical essay demonstrates:	• a perceptive analysis of the effect of features of language/filmic techniques	• a detailed analysis of the effect of features of language/filmic techniques	• clear analysis of the effect of features of language/ filmic techniques	• adequate analysis of the effect of features of language/filmic techniques	• limited analysis of the effect of features of language/filmic techniques	• very little analysis of features of language/filmic techniques
Evaluation The critical essay demonstrates:	• a committed, evaluative stance with respect to the text and the task	• an engaged evaluative stance with respect to the text and the task	• a clear evaluative stance with respect to the text and the task	• adequate evidence of an evaluative stance with respect to the text and the task	• limited evidence of an evaluative stance with respect to the text and the task	• little evidence of an evaluative stance with respect to the text and the task
Technical accuracy The critical essay demonstrates:	• few errors in spelling, grammar, sentence construction, punctuation and paragraphing • the ability to be understood at first reading				• significant errors in spelling, grammar, sentence construction, punctuation and paragraphing which impedes understanding	

Which mark your essay is awarded in the category is down to how confidently the marker can place the essay in that category.

Some further advice

Short stories

Don't think that just because a short story is not as long as a novel it will be an easier text to study and write about in the exam. A well-crafted short story will make effective use of techniques specific to this genre and this can make it challenging to write about. Remember that you might be required to write about **two** short stories.

Non-fiction

If you want to prepare for a question from this part of the prose section you need to study texts such as essays (very different from *your* critical essays), travel writing, biography and autobiography, works on current affairs and politics, philosophy, etc. Remember that the techniques used by the writer in these kind of texts are **different** from those used in prose fiction. You should look at the techniques mentioned in the prose non-fiction advice above as a starting point for your studies.

Poetry

The danger of the 'guided tour' has already been mentioned. You must avoid providing a line-by-line analysis of the poem. If your essay is no more than a series of quotations followed by comments it will not 'address the central concerns of the text' and will not pass. Although it is true you cannot offer an analysis of a poem without quoting from the text you must make sure these quotations are being used by you to provide evidence to support the line of argument in your essay.

Film and TV drama

Questions from this section should be dealt with just like those in the drama, prose and poetry sections. You will need to be confident that you can make effective use of the appropriate technical terms (mise-en-scène, camera angles, sound, costume, ideology, lighting, etc.) to support your argument.

Practice critical essay questions

Try these against the clock (give yourself 45 minutes).

Drama

1. Choose a play which made you reconsider your attitude to an important issue.

   Show how the dramatist introduces this issue and go on to discuss the effectiveness of the dramatic techniques employed to make you consider the issue in a new light.

2. Choose a play in which aspects of staging (lighting, music, set, stage directions …) seem particularly important.

   Discuss how effective you find the use of these in the dramatist's exploration of the central concerns of the play.

3. Choose a play in which a central character is faced with a difficult choice.

   Briefly give an outline of the circumstances which lead up to this situation and go on to discuss how the dramatist makes you aware of the consequences of the character's decision.

Prose fiction

4. Choose a **novel or short story** in which the style of writing greatly impressed you.

   Show how the writer's chosen style added to your understanding and appreciation of the central concerns of the text.

5. Choose a **novel** set in a location which is unfamiliar to you.

   Briefly describe the setting and go on to show how, despite the unfamiliarity, the novelist is able to make you consider themes which are universal.

6. Choose a **novel or short story** in which there is conflict between two characters.

   Briefly outline the nature of the conflict and go on to show how the writer uses it to develop a central concern of the text.

Prose non-fiction

7. Choose a **non-fiction text** which seems to reveal a lot about the writer's point of view on a particular topic.

   Briefly describe what this point of view seems to be and go on to discuss in detail how this is revealed through his or her writing.

8. Choose a piece of **travel writing** in which the writer's use of language gave you a new perspective on somewhere you were already familiar with.

   Describe how the writer uses language to give you this new perspective.

9. Choose a piece of **biography** or **autobiography** which includes an account of a shocking experience.

   Briefly describe the experience and then discuss how the writer conveys the shocking nature of it.

Poetry

10. Choose two poems which seem to have similar central concerns.

    Explain what the central concerns of both poems are and go on to discuss which poem you feel deals more effectively with them.

11. Choose a poem which you feel says something important to today's society.

    Discuss how effectively the poet's techniques help to convey this message.

12. Choose a poem in which you feel the content is enhanced by the poet's choice of a particular poetic form.

    Explain in detail how the choice of form adds to your understanding of the central concerns of the text.

Film and TV drama

13. Choose a **film** or **TV drama** in which a character seems isolated from the rest of society.

    Discuss how effective you find the film or programme makers' representation of this character and go on to explain how this adds to your appreciation of the text as a whole.

14. Choose a film or television drama which subverts the conventions of its own genre.

    Explain how the film or programme makers' subversion of the genre enhances your appreciation of the text as a whole.

15. Choose a film or television programme in which the opening sequence is particularly effective in introducing the central concerns of the text.

    Explain how this effective introduction to the central concerns was achieved by the film or programme makers.

How is your writing portfolio assessed?

Let's start with a reminder of the ways by which your writing is assessed as part of your Higher English course. As part of the course assessment you have to send a Portfolio of Writing to SQA. The portfolio consists of two writing pieces: one creative piece and one discursive piece.

The creative writing piece could be:

- a personal essay (an account of a personal experience and its effects on you)

  or

- a reflective essay (a bit more sophisticated than the personal essay – you could reflect on an idea; an experience; a concept or issue)

  or

- an imaginative piece (short story, drama script, poem, episode from a novel).

The discursive writing piece could be:

- an argumentative essay (exploring two or more points of view with a line of argument clearly emerging)

- a persuasive essay (in which you try to convince the reader to agree with you on a particular subject)

- a report (using information from at least two sources).

Let's consider the unit assessment in more detail. Each piece of writing you produce must be **no more than 1300** words long. **Each piece is marked out of 15**. The combined score out of **30** is added to your marks from the external exam to determine your final grade.

The following marking tables show you the differences between writing that is just good enough to pass (7–9 marks) and very good writing (13–15 marks).

Creative writing piece		
	15–13 marks	**9–7 marks**
Content	• Committed attention to purpose and audience. • Strong creative qualities. • Evident command of the genre. • Thematic concerns that are clearly introduced and developed. • Ideas/feelings/experiences which are explored with a strong degree of mature reflection/self-awareness/involvement/insight/sensitivity. • The writer's personality and individuality.	• Adequate attention to purpose and audience. • Adequate creative qualities. • Understanding of the genre. • Thematic concerns which are introduced. • Ideas/feelings/ experiences which are explored with an adequate sense of reflection and involvement. • The writer's personality.

Creative writing piece		
	15–13 marks	**9–7 marks**
Style	• Linguistic features of the chosen genre used skilfully to create a strong impact. • Confident and varied expression. • An effective structure, which enhances the purpose/meaning.	• Linguistic features of the chosen genre used successfully. • Adequate expression. • An adequate structure.

Discursive writing piece		
	15–13 marks	**9–7 marks**
Content	• Committed attention to purpose and audience. • Full understanding and engagement. • Evidence of full research and selection, as appropriate. • A clear and sustained line of thought/convincing stance.	• Adequate attention to purpose and audience. • Adequate understanding. • Evidence of relevant research and selection, as appropriate. • A line of thought/clear stance.
Style	• Linguistic features of the chosen genre used comprehensively to argue/discuss/persuade and convey depth and complexity of thought/objectivity/insight/persuasive force. • Confident and varied expression. • An effective structure, which enhances the purpose/meaning.	• Linguistic features of the chosen genre used adequately to argue/discuss/persuade and convey thought/objectivity/insight/persuasive force. • Adequate expression. • An adequate structure.

Your Portfolio of Writing must be submitted on the SQA approved template. Your teacher/lecturer will tell you more about this requirement. You can access further information and download the template from the 'Coursework' section of the SQA Higher English web page available at http://www.sqa.org.uk/sqa/47904.html

Producing pieces of writing for your portfolio

If you have done National 5 or Intermediate 2 English you will already have experience of producing pieces of writing in a number of different forms and genres so Higher English is about **refining and developing** the skills you already possess.

Since the requirement is no more detailed than for you to produce **one** broadly creative and **one** broadly discursive piece you obviously have a wide range of subjects to choose from. For example you could write:

- a short story set on a Dundee housing estate
- an opening chapter of novel about a girl's fraught relationship with her mother
- a sonnet about the passing of time
- a drama script involving three characters on a Glasgow bus
- a piece that explores the arguments for and against creating more wind farms in Scotland
- a piece that attempts to persuade the reader that schools are outdated institutions
- a piece in which you reflect on your experience of what it means to be a young adult living in Scotland today
- a report on the benefits and drawbacks of Edinburgh's new tram system

These are just examples and there are more suggestions later in this chapter.

Planning your writing

It doesn't matter **which** kind of writing you choose to do (although you are well advised to attempt something at which you are already reasonably competent), what is important is that the writing is **your** work. Your teacher should ask you for the following at each stage of the writing process in order to guarantee the authenticity of what you produce:

- a draft title and proposal
- an outline plan
- a first draft
- a final version

A draft title, proposal and outline plan for a persuasive piece of writing might look something like this:

Date:	Pupil name:	Language study unit – writing
Proposed title: *Education 2.0 – Why our schools are failing to pass the test*		Genre: persuasive

Proposal

In this essay I am going to persuade the reader to agree with my point of view that schools are no longer fit for purpose and do not provide their pupils with an education experience that is relevant to the needs of society in the twenty-first century. I will show that they are institutions that have remained largely unchanged since the early years of the last century and that our insistence on gathering large groups of young people together in huge buildings and then dividing them into groups based on arbitrary principles, rules and flawed statistics is no longer an effective way of educating young people today. I will also look at how information technology is radically altering how we learn and how we interact with others and that this means we need a complete overhaul of what we want our schools to do.

Teacher's initials:

Date:

Outline

Introduction:

- Description of typical school day from 30 years ago (classes, timetables, buildings, bells, etc.) – shows how little pupils' experience has changed – contrast with radical changes in society and technology – suggest schools need to change.

Points I intend to make:

- Maintaining school buildings is a huge drain on the public purse (use local authority statistics).

- Very few of us will ever work in such large 'communities' again – why corral young people into these buildings? Once we leave school most people now work in small teams and more than ever are working from home.

- Acknowledge the counter-argument about the 'socialising' effect of schools but dismiss this with reference to the negative aspects of school life such as bullying.

- Examples of successful learning outwith school.

- Point out how information technology is embedded within our lives – ref. to internet, social networking – how this has changed the way we interact with others.

- Point out how information technology has changed the way we learn – Wikipedia, etc. – schools' own greater use of websites, virtual learning environments, GLOW – so why the need for 'traditional' classrooms?

- Health risks – easy for viruses such as flu to spread in large schools, etc.

Conclusion

- Reiterate points made and end with strong closing statement.

Teacher's initials:

Date:

The first draft

Once your teacher has had a look at your proposals you can start work on a first draft. Remember that a word-processed draft will be easier for you to edit and amend before you produce the final version.

Let's see what the introductory paragraphs of our persuasive piece might look like. Remember to make use of the language techniques you have come across in your study of close reading passages.

Starts with a command – involves the reader

Repetition of 'dutiful'/ 'dutifully' suggests someone meekly following instructions

Paragraph ends with a thought-provoking question

Education 2.0 – Why our schools are failing to pass the test

First draft

Picture the scene. The dutiful pupil dressed in full school uniform arrives at her local secondary school. It is a large concrete and glass box; a box she shares with 1000 other dutiful souls. Her day is mapped out before her; a day delineated by the grid squares of her timetable. A bell rings and she dutifully makes her way to her registration room. Another bell rings and she dutifully carries her bag full of jotters and folders to her first class. Her teacher hands out the textbooks and the pupil dutifully begins to work through the examples …

This dutiful pupil is receiving her education in a Scottish secondary school in 2021, but the year could have been 2001, 1991, 1981 or 1971. Outwith school, however, things are very different for this pupil compared with her sisters of forty, thirty, twenty or even ten years ago. In school, she is hemmed in; at home she can roam the digital world at will. This same dutiful pupil goes home to watch her favourite TV shows online, updates her Instagram account and chats to friends and relatives in Germany and Australia. She then sharpens up her guitar playing with a quick tutorial from a useful website and ends her day by making another entry on her blog. How can imprisoning her in a concrete and glass box for six years possibly be to the benefit of this young person?

Suggests 'restriction'

Word choice suggests unflattering image of school building

Connotations of lack of freedom

List of dates suggests unchanging nature of school experience over time

Balanced sentence around a semi-colon 'hinge'

Emotive language to elicit sympathy from the reader

Chapter 9: The writing portfolio

Once a first draft has been completed, you should ensure it contains the features required for an effective piece of writing at this level. Here is a checklist for persuasive writing:

Discursive: persuasive	
Strong opening statement	
Clear structure	
Effective use of linkage between sections/arguments	
Emotive vocabulary	
Arguments supported by evidence (statistics, etc.) where appropriate	
Acknowledgement and rejection of any counter-arguments	
Direct address to the reader	
Repetition	
Climax	
Contrast	
Contrast within a list	
Use of analogy and/or illustration	
Listing for effect (especially in groups of three)	
Effective use of imagery	
Gives a clear sense that the writer is *convinced* of their case	
Effective use of 'attitude markers': *Surely, ... Clearly, ... Happily, ...*	
Strong closing statement	
Sources consulted are clearly stated	

Once you have completed a first draft of your writing your teacher will be able to give you feedback. This feedback will usually be in the form of suggesting improvements you might make to your piece. You might be asked to look again at the way you have structured your writing (perhaps you need to reorder your ideas) or you might be told that your punctuation and spelling are not yet accurate enough. Your teacher is **not**, however, allowed to indicate specific, individual errors for you to go away and correct. Proofreading and editing of your work are **your** responsibility.

Features and techniques of each genre

If you have decided what kind of writing you want to do, here's a reminder of the features and techniques to use. We've already looked at those required for persuasive writing so let's consider a short story (creative/imaginative), a reflective piece (creative/imaginative), an argumentative piece (discursive) and a drama script (creative/imaginative). There's an exemplar opening with comments and a checklist for each genre for you to refer to. You could try continuing each piece for practice. Remember to make use of the appropriate techniques.

Story starts 'in medias res' – in the middle of the action

Personification suggests hostility and amplifies the mood of tension

Showing the reader she's engaged or married, rather than telling them

The Hunted

(short story)

First draft

She turned the key. Nothing. She turned the key again. Still nothing. A small bubble of fear tried to rise in her chest. She willed herself to ignore it and turned the key again. This time the engine coughed and caught. She felt the small bubble burst and she pressed her foot down on the accelerator.

She hated driving on her own through this part of the city. She hated the empty streets; the feeling that people had given up on it. Ugly houses leered at her from either side. *Everything's fine. This is something you can do. It's not going to happen again.*

She glanced nervously in the mirror and adjusted it a fraction. The diamond on her left hand briefly caught the light as she changed gear. *Normal, normal, normal. Ordinary. It's a day like any other. It's a journey like any other. You've done this a hundred times before. Think about next week. Think about Alan. Think!*

She looked in the mirror again.

A black car.

Something quivered inside her. *It was a coincidence – that was all. There must be a hundred black cars in the city, a thousand.* She gripped the wheel more tightly.

She looked in the mirror again.

Minor sentence helps create a tense atmosphere

Italics to indicate the character's thoughts

Creative: short story	
Limited setting	
Definite shape or structure	
Few characters	
Action takes place over a relatively short space of time	
Limited number of plot 'events'	
Use of imagery, metaphor, simile, personification …	
Use of symbolism	
Provides insight into a character's life/thoughts/feelings	
Reveals or *shows* the reader things rather than telling them	
Use of believable dialogue to bring characters to life	
Credible ending	
Some sort of change evident (from the fortunes/situation/mind-set of the character(s) at the story's start)	
Spelling is consistently accurate	
Punctuation is consistently accurate	
Sentence construction is consistently accurate	

Relative Values

(reflective)

First draft

Stimulus for the reflection

It's not much to look at: just a small lapel badge made up of the letters N.U.M.

National Union of Mineworkers; and yet every time I pick it up I am reminded of the man who wore it. A man with thirty years' service 'man and boy' to his local pit. A man who loved the camaraderie of it all. A man who loved his pipe band and his football team. A man who loved his family – but never told them. Loyal to his union, to his mates, to his wife and children. Loyalty as much a part of him as the dust in his lungs that did for him in the end.

Repeated structure emphasises what was important in his life

I peer down the dim shaft of time and try to see the man that he was but I can't. I sit at my laptop looking at his picture and I feel the accumulated years lying in layer upon layer between his youth and mine. And I think about the differences between us …

Appropriate use of imagery linked to mining

The writer introduces the idea that will be at the heart of this essay

> **TOP TIP**
>
> In this kind of writing, make use of the techniques you have learned about as part of your study of prose fiction for the Critical Reading paper.

Creative: reflective	
Captures the reader's interest	
Deals with a single idea/insight/experience	
Evidence of reflection on knowledge/thoughts/feelings caused by the subject of the essay	
Uses a personal tone	
The reader gets a clear sense of the writer's personality	
Gives a sense of the writer really *thinking* about the subject of the essay	
States what has been realised/learned by the writer	
Shows difference between how experience/event was viewed *then* and how it is viewed *now* (if appropriate)	
Uses word choice to create particular effects	
Uses imagery to create particular effects	
Uses sentence structure to create particular effects	
Spelling is consistently accurate	
Sentence construction is consistently accurate	

TOP TIP

Start writing your own blog. Use it as a way of sharing your reflections on your experiences.

Tempestuous Times – are wind farms a blot on the Scottish landscape?

(argumentative)

First draft

As we move further into the twenty-first century, it is clear that we must decide how our energy needs will be met in the coming years. At the moment we think nothing of switching on a light, a cooker, a computer – but how can we ensure that our insatiable demand for power can be satisfied in the future? Fossil fuels will disappear in 50 years according to some experts. That means no more power stations fuelled by coal or gas so it is vital that we find alternative means of generating electricity if that light, cooker and computer are still going to be available to us half a century from now.

Introductory paragraph sets out the context for the essay

Renewable forms of energy sources such as wind, wave and hydro will all play a significant role in providing us with energy in future. Will this mean more and more 'wind farms' being constructed in Scotland's countryside? Proponents of such schemes trumpet their 'eco-friendly' qualities whilst others warn against the damage that might be done to precious landscape. Which side is correct?

The two arguments that will be considered in the essay

The Scottish Government want '80% of Scotland's gross annual electricity consumption' to come from renewable resources by 2020. Supporters of wind farms say that this means that we must build more turbines.

Use of official statistics

TOP TIP

In this kind of writing, remember to make use of the techniques you've learned about for the Reading for Understanding, Analysis and Evaluation exam paper.

Discursive: argumentative	
Introduces the topic clearly	
Makes use of *at least* two arguments related to the topic	
Has a clear, logical structure	
Makes effective use of linkage between sections/arguments	
Arguments supported by evidence (statistics, etc.) where appropriate	
Effective use of transition markers (*however, furthermore, in addition to this, despite this* …)	
Uses an appropriate tone (conveyed through appropriate word choice and other language features)	
Uses comparisons	
Arguments disproved by evidence (statistics, etc.) where appropriate	
Arrives at a clear conclusion having evaluated the evidence	
Spelling is consistently accurate	
Punctuation is consistently accurate	
Sentence construction is consistently accurate	
Sources consulted are clearly stated	

Flatmates

(drama script)

First draft

List of characters with brief outlines of personality and appearance

Characters:

Claire – a well-dressed, tall, dark-haired young woman in her mid-twenties. She has the air of someone always in control. Her speech should sound 'educated' and precise.

Rebecca – the same age as Claire but shorter. Her demeanour suggests a very relaxed attitude to life in general.

Amy – prospective flatmate of Claire and Rebecca.

Stage directions to establish setting

It is a weekday morning in the living room of a flat in Glasgow. The room is clean and tidy. There is a sofa facing a wall on which there is a flat screen television above a fireplace. There are two 'modern' armchairs beside a coffee table. On the coffee table there is an open laptop and a (very) neatly stacked pile of magazines. The general impression is of orderliness. The only object which seems out of place is the empty beer can lying on its side on the floor beside the sofa.

Claire enters. She glances around the room, walks over to the coffee table and straightens the pile of magazines that does not need straightening. Once she is satisfied, she looks around the room once more, biting her lower lip.

Stage directions in italics

Claire: (*noticing the beer can on the floor*) Oh not again! (*shouting*) Becca! Get through here and look at this!

Rebecca: (*off*) What?

Claire: (*picks up the can and holds it distastefully at arm's length*) This! What sort of impression do you think this is going to make?

Characters' names down the left-hand margin

Rebecca enters. She is wearing a dressing gown. Her hair is unkempt and there is clear evidence of last night's make-up all over her face. She walks wearily past Claire. She studiously ignores Claire's outstretched arm, which still holds the beer can, and slumps into an armchair.

Claire: Well?

Rebecca: (*eyes closed*) Aw jeez, Claire. Get a life. What is it this time? Your IKEA catalogues no arranged in date order on the table? The curtains two centimetres too far apart?

Claire: Don't be like that! You know exactly what I am talking about.

Rebecca: (*opening one eye and seemingly acknowledging the beer can for the first time*) Oh, is that all? Ah thought it was something serious.

Claire: This *is* serious. You know she's coming round at ten thirty sharp. That means any minute now. Do I need to remind you how much we need a third to split the rent? Have you forgotten *why* the last one left?

Rebecca: (*both eyes closed again*) Och that could have happened to anyone. She was far too sensitive that yin! (*both eyes open*) Here, is it true she's still gettin' counsellin'?

The door bell rings. Claire exits and returns, ushering in Amy, who is clearly nervous about the situation.

> Costume suggests the character's personality

> Dialogue suggests the character's personality

> Effective use of humour

Creative: drama script (single scene)	
Stage directions	
Action limited to one setting	
Definite shape or structure	
Few characters	
Action takes place over a relatively short space of time	
Limited number of plot 'events'	
Lighting effects	
Sound effects	
Dialogue reveals characters' emotions, personalities, reactions, etc.	
Climax or turning point in the action	
Satisfying ending (thought-provoking for the audience?)	
Spelling is consistently accurate	
Punctuation is consistently accurate	
Sentence construction is consistently accurate	
Script could be performed	

TOP TIP

Make a point of **watching** drama performances this year and look for techniques you could incorporate in your own script.

Ideas for writing

If you are stuck for inspiration, have a look at the following suggestions. They just might provide you with the inspiration to kick-start your writing. The more writing you do, the better you become at it. The opening lines are suggestions for practice pieces. Your teacher/assessor will give you further information about the writing and submission of pieces for the portfolio. Don't forget the importance of planning before you start!

Possible **titles** for short stories:

- Interiors
- Homecoming
- The Life and Times of Alexandra Macleod
- A Much Travelled Man
- New Year's Resolutions
- The Anti-social Network
- Waves
- Where the Dogs Howl
- An Inescapable Truth
- Daylight Robbery!
- The Examination
- Soldiers
- Wha's Like Us?
- The Road to Nowhere

Possible **opening lines** for short stories:

- John Smith caught, as he always did, the 7.58 to Paddington.
- I walk the line between our past and my present.
- Hergath watched the twin moons gradually appear above the horizon.
- She turned the key. Nothing. She turned the key again.
- The thrill of the chase is everything.
- I'm sitting at the same table in the same café at the same time of day. So far – no sign of him.
- The parcel on the doorstep was nothing special – just a slim cardboard box. What was inside, however, was anything but ordinary.
- Everyone disliked him. This was the simple truth. A simple truth in the same way that 'everyone has a father' is a simple truth – it could not be denied. He had long since stopped trying to deny it, even to himself.
- The adulation of the crowd had become essential to the girls. When they were on stage, nothing else mattered to them.
- 'Are we going to talk about this?'

  'What?'

  'You know fine what I mean.'

Possible topics for **argumentative** or **persuasive** pieces:

- The Edinburgh Tram Project.
- Scottish football referees should be awarded protected species status.
- Online 'friends' can never replace 'real' friends.
- Soap operas are a malign influence on our behaviour – we watch them at our peril.
- Wind farms are destroying our landscape.
- We should spend more money on transport systems.
- Why every Scottish city should be a green city.
- Schools should be more concerned with an individual's happiness than their academic achievement.
- What role does the church have in today's society?
- What can we do to reduce the ever-widening gulf between the rich and poor in our society?
- Do teenagers care about politics?
- Why is everyone so unpleasant to everyone else online?
- Computer gaming should be recognised for the complex entertainment art form it actually is.
- Female teachers are more effective than male teachers.
- Celebrities have forfeited their rights to privacy.
- The world of the same: why your town could be any town.

TOP TIP

Keep a writer's notebook and jot down things you overhear on the bus, in your local Starbucks, at a party … anything that you might incorporate in a story. Or keep the ideas as a memo or a recording on your phone.

Remember that it is advisable to choose a topic or issue you are interested in or feel strongly about. Try to avoid topics such as animal testing or abortion or size zero models unless you feel passionately about them and feel you will be able to write effectively about them. It will make the task, and your writing, so much better if the reader gets a sense of *your* engagement with the issue. Remember your writing needs to show **depth and complexity of thought**.

Possible scenarios for **drama scripts**:

- Two flatmates interview a third person to share with them.
- A dramatic monologue by a bus driver.
- A family gathering is disrupted by the revelation of a secret.
- Two strangers at a bus stop get talking and discover something in common.
- Three girls chat in a bar on a night out.
- A family argue in the departure lounge of an airport.
- A first date that goes wrong.
- A dramatic monologue by an O.A.P.
- A nervous employee is called into the boss' office.
- A check-out operator tries to make conversation with her customers.
- A parent tries to give their teenage child some 'good advice'.
- A passer-by comes into contact with a beggar on the street.
- Two football fans watch a game together and gradually reveal to the audience why they are addicted to their hobby.
- A taxi driver overhears one side of a mobile phone conversation with unpredictable results.
- A hill walking party gets lost and tensions within the group come to the surface.

Always bear in mind that a script is *designed to be performed*.

Ideas for **personal/reflective** writing:

It is difficult to suggest precise topics for personal reflective writing given the very personal nature of this kind of writing. You might like to think about the following possibilities.

* Reflect on your experiences as a young adult growing up in Scotland today.
* Think about an object that means a lot to you and reflect on why it is important.
* Think about how your personality has changed as you have grown older.
* Reflect on your experience of education to date.
* Reflect on your experience of love and relationships.
* What are the most important things in your life and why?
* Reflect on what you feel is the single most important experience in your life to date.
* Reflect on an experience that has changed the way you view the world.
* Reflect on your perception of religion and/or spirituality.
* Reflect on your experience of sport and/or competition.

Performance – spoken language

Although this assessment is not part of your exam, you must achieve a pass in it if you are to receive a course award. So don't give it anything less than your full attention! By the time you reach S5 or S6 you will have spent thousands of hours in school being involved in talking and listening activities. All this assessment task does is formalise that experience and allow your teacher to gather the appropriate evidence to award you a pass. If you have already done National 5 English, you should be familiar with the form of the assessment.

The Assessment

Let's look at what this assessment involves.

You can choose to take part in a group discussion or give a presentation to the class or small group.

If you take part in a group discussion it might be on:

- an issue in the news
- a local issue
- something which affects you and your classmates
- an aspect of one of the texts you are studying for the Critical Reading paper (*What does Shakespeare tell us about the nature of jealousy in Othello? What are the typical features of Don Paterson's poetry?*)

If you choose to prepare and deliver a presentation it might be on:

- something you feel strongly about
- the topic you have chosen for your discursive writing
- an aspect or aspects of the literature you are studying this year
- an important event in history
- your five suggestions to improve your school
- a person you admire

The possibilities for either the discussion or the presentation are limitless. No matter which one you choose or get involved in, you must show you can:

- employ relevant detailed and complex ideas and/or information using a structure appropriate to purpose and audience
- communicate meaning effectively through the selection and use of detailed and complex spoken language
- use aspects of non-verbal communication
- demonstrate listening skills by responding to detailed and complex spoken language

Your teacher will watch your performance and complete a detailed checklist as a record of the assessment.

Now let's look at each of the assessment criteria for this element of the course in more detail and think about what you have to do to achieve them – remember that it is probably more straightforward than you think. The only significant change from your experience of this assessment task at National 5 level is the additional requirements at Higher to use detailed *and complex* ideas and language and to be able to respond to detailed *and complex* language used by others.

Assessment criteria		What you have to do	
		Group discussion	**Presentation**
Employs relevant detailed and complex ideas and/or information using a structure appropriate to purpose and audience	**Content** can contribute a range of relevant detailed and complex ideas/views/opinions/ information – contributions could be made through a presentation or a group discussion or a series of discussion-based activities	*Get involved* in the discussion. Get your ideas out there! Don't sit back and wait to be asked and don't just stop after saying one thing!	Make sure you have prepared enough material for the presentation. You'll probably need five or six main points to cover on your chosen topic.
	Structure spoken language is structured effectively to enhance impact, and where appropriate, takes account of the contributions of others	Agree or disagree with what others say in the group. Give support where you can ('I think that's a good point, Ali …'). Ask direct questions of the others ('Why do you think that, Chris?'). Look for opportunities to summarise what others are saying if that might clarify things for the group ('So Freya, the three main objections you seem to have are …')	Make sure there is an obvious introduction, development and conclusion to your talk (people often forget about the importance of *ending* the talk effectively). Looking online at things such as TED talks is a good way of seeing effective talk structures in action.
	Relevance attention to task, purpose and audience is sustained throughout the presentation, group discussion or a series of discussion-based activities	Stay on task. Resist any temptation to tell the group about your latest followers on Instagram if you're supposed to be talking about Carol-Ann Duffy. Keep to the topic.	Stay on task. Stick to what you've set out to tell the audience about. Resist the temptation to make any comments or asides to (or about) anyone in your audience.

| Communicates meaning effectively through the selection and use of detailed and complex spoken language | Choice and use of language can select and use detailed and complex spoken language that is appropriate to purpose and audience | If you have been asked to discuss a topic based on the literature you are studying, then you *can't avoid* using 'detailed and complex language' – it would be impossible to talk about *Othello* or Don Paterson's poetry without using appropriate literary terminology such as 'protagonist'; 'dramatic foil'; 'theme'; 'symbol' and 'sonnet'. For other topics try to make sure you use the kind of vocabulary that is relevant and connected to the subject. | Use language connected to your subject and make use of topic specific vocabulary. If you have chosen to give a presentation on say, whether or not prisoners should be allowed to vote, then words such as 'justice system'; 'franchise'; 'democratic'; 'incarcerated'; 'loss of liberty' and 'penal reform' might well feature in your talk. These would be good examples of the detailed and complex vocabulary required in the assessment. Remember also that your choice of language should suit your audience, which is likely to be made up of your classmates and your teacher; in other words a group of reasonably intelligent individuals. So treat them as such! |
| | Clarity and accuracy can employ appropriate spoken language with sufficient clarity and accuracy to ensure that effective communication is achieved | This doesn't just refer to the sound of your voice and the way you pronounce your words; it's also a reminder to make sure that your ideas come across clearly to the others in the group. Don't speak too quickly! | This doesn't just refer to the sound of your voice and the way you pronounce your words; it's also a reminder to make sure that your ideas come across clearly to your audience. Pausing now and again can be very effective. |

Uses aspects of non-verbal communication	can employ appropriate non-verbal features to assist communication, meaning and/ or engagement. These might include, for example, facial expression, emphasis, gesture, eye contact	Look round at the other members of the group as much as you can when you are speaking. Maintain eye-contact with someone who is making a point – it will show you are interested in what they are saying. Smile. Nod in encouragement or shake your head when you don't agree with something. You might find yourself waving your hand about to emphasise a point or even banging on the table if things get heated – just make sure you don't overdo things.	Maintaining eye-contact with your audience is really important. If you can't look them in the eye then look just above their heads. Don't keep looking round at the screen. Don't fidget as you stand in front of the audience – just try to be as natural as possible. Use hand gestures to emphasise a point if it feels right.
Demonstrates listening skills by responding to detailed and complex spoken language	can give relevant responses to the contributions of others in group discussions or in a series of discussion-based activities OR can respond relevantly to questions which follow, for example, a presentation	You'll find yourself doing this automatically if you take a full part in the discussion but just make sure you listen carefully to what the other people in the group are saying. Respond if someone asks you a direct question. You can also display your listening skills by summarising what someone else has said ('So what you're saying is ...') or asking for clarification ('I get that point David, but what about ...?').	Ask for questions at the end of the talk. You'll need to answer two or three to provide sufficient evidence to meet this criterion. Always try to give as full a reply as possible. You might want to begin your replies with expressions such as 'I'm glad you asked me that ...' or 'That's a really good question'. Not only is this polite, it gives you a few extra moments to gather your thoughts before you answer.

While you are taking part in the discussion, your teacher will be assessing you and keeping a record of the evidence by completing a detailed checklist. Look at the example on the next two pages and you'll see the sort of things he or she is looking out for.

Higher English: performance – spoken language assessment checklist

Candidate name: *Piotr Filipek*

Activity: *Group Discussion (What do the different relationships in Othello tell us about the nature of love?)*

Higher English: performance – spoken language

Higher English: performance – spoken language	Aspect of Performance	Achieved/ not achieved	Assessor's comments
Employs relevant detailed and complex ideas and/or information using a structure appropriate to purpose and audience	**Content** can contribute a range of relevant detailed and complex ideas/views/ opinions/information – contributions could be made through a presentation or a group discussion or a series of discussion-based activities	✓	*Makes a number of relevant points:* • *romantic love between Othello and Desdemona* • *unrequited love: Bianca and Cassio* • *love gone stale – Iago and Emilia* • *paternal love – Brabantio and Desdemona*
	Structure spoken language is structured effectively to enhance impact, and where appropriate, takes account of the contributions of others	✓	*Challenges Sadi a – 'But Othello is in love with an idealised version of Desdemona . . .' and supports with refs. to text*
	Relevance attention to task, purpose and audience is sustained throughout the presentation, group discussion or a series of discussion-based activities	✓	*On task throughout.*
Communicates meaning effectively through the selection and use of detailed and complex spoken language	**Choice and use of language** can select and use detailed and complex spoken language that is appropriate to purpose and audience	✓	*Appropriate vocabulary in evidence:* *'Hamartia . . .'; 'protagonist'; 'stereotypical'; 'symbolic representation'*

Aspect of performance		Achieved/ not achieved	Assessor's comments
	Clarity and accuracy can employ appropriate spoken language with sufficient clarity and accuracy to ensure that effective communication is achieved	✓	Accurate and clear throughout.
Uses aspects of non-verbal communication	can employ appropriate non-verbal features to assist communication, meaning and/or engagement. These might include, for example, facial expression, emphasis, gesture, eye contact	✓	• Maintains eye-contact with other members of the group • Alert facial expression throughout • Nods in agreement with Sadia's statement
Demonstrates listening skills by responding to detailed and complex spoken language	can give relevant responses to the contributions of others in group discussions or in a series of discussion-based activities OR can respond relevantly to questions which follow, for example, a presentation	✓	Responds to question from Cameron. Answers in detail about Cassio's treatment of Bianca.

Additional comments:

More than merely competent. Piotr made a good number of high-quality contributions. A clear pass.

Assessor name: Ms. Anna Sessor

Assessor signature: Anna Sessor

Date: 24.3.20

'The age of the amateur has passed', by Ed Smith, pages 21–22

1. In the past it was a fashionable concept (1) but now it is looked down on as out of date nonsense (1).

2. The positioning of a cricketer's initials (1). The manner in which professionals had to address amateur players who were not as good as them (1).

3. It permitted a wide range of different types of people to be included/It promoted a person's unique talents (1) and it gave people more freedom (1).

4. They come from the elements of our characters (1) that can't be worked out logically (1).

5. They are successful because they don't have too much familiarity with their sport (1) and they don't think about their performance too much (1).

'Dangerous liaisons', by Lucy Mangan, pages 32–33

See how many of the following features you spotted.

'What you have instead in Meyer's work is a **depressingly retrograde**, **deeply anti-feminist**, **borderline misogynistic** novel that drains its heroine of life and vitality as surely **as if a vampire had sunk his teeth into her and leaves her a bloodless cipher** while the story happens around her. Edward tells her she is 'so interesting ... fascinating', but the reader **looks in vain** for his evidence.'

- List of three highly critical descriptions of the work ('depressingly retrograde ... borderline misogynistic').
- Emotive word choice: 'depressingly'.
- Appropriate use of vampire image to reinforce the writer's opinion of the poor characterisation in the novel.
- 'bloodless cipher' image suggests the character is not portrayed as someone the reader can engage with.
- 'looks in vain' suggests it's a hopeless task.

'**Alas**, the **only choice** Bella gets to make is to sacrifice herself in ever-larger increments ...'

- 'Alas ...' suggests Mangan's disappointment.
- 'only choice' suggests the constraints placed on Bella.

'It sounds **melodramatic and shrill** to say that Bella and Edward's relationship is abusive, **but as the story wears on it becomes increasingly hard to avoid the comparison** ...'

- 'melodramatic and shrill' shows Mangan acknowledges that some people might think she is going too far in her criticism. In the second half of the sentence she justifies this word choice.

'To **those less enamoured of Meyerworld** ...'

- 'those less enamoured' a good example of understatement.
- 'Meyerworld' seems dismissive – hints at a version of society that Mangan disagrees with.

'The **few signs of wit and independence** …'

- *Again, highly critical of the character suggesting there is little indication of the sort of qualities Mangan expects in a female central character.*

'**mute devotion**'

- *Suggests a passive, silent follower or disciple.*

'**slavish**'

- *Suggests Bella's lack of freedom in the relationship.*

'**Edward is no hero. Bella is no Buffy.**'

- *Parallel sentence structures again underlining how Mangan feels Twilight suffers in comparison with Buffy.*
- *Short sentences add impact.*
- *Alliteration in the second sentence draws our eye to the sentence and reinforces the point being made.*

'And *Twilight's* underlying message – **that self-sacrifice makes you a worthy girlfriend, that men mustn't be excited beyond a certain point, that men with problems must be forgiven everything, that female passivity is a state to be encouraged – are no good to anyone. It should be staked through its black, black heart.**'

- *Parenthesis (inside paired dashes) is a list of what Mangan considers to be the negative message conveyed by the book and film.*
- *It's followed by the brief and blunt statement 'are no good to anyone'.*
- *Final sentence contains another appropriate vampire image as Mangan suggests the Twilight phenomenon should be killed off in the same way a vampire is.*
- *Repetition of 'black' also serves to emphasise Mangan's (perhaps rather exaggerated) point that Twilight is almost something evil.*

Reading: 'Post-traumatic stress disorder is the invisible scar of war', pages 40–42

Re-read paragraphs 1–3.

1. a) Explain in your own words the change in Stuart Tootal's attitude to PTSD.

   This should be a fairly straightforward question to answer. The passage says that the writer 'used to be sceptical' (paragraph 1) but that later his 'cynicism had disappeared'. Having located the appropriate parts of the passage, you then translate it into your own words. Your answer might look something like this:

   The writer did not really believe PTSD was important (1) but now he is no longer scornful of it (1). The change happened because of his experiences leading soldiers in Afghanistan (1).

   b) Analyse how two examples of the writer's language in these paragraphs convey the reality of combat.

   To answer this question successfully you could comment on the writer's word choice, sentence structure and use of statistics. You could mention some of the following (remember to quote/refer to the word/technique and then comment on the connotations/effects).

   Any four of the following for (1) mark each.

Answers

Word choice

- 'intensive' (para 3) suggests the concentrated and demanding nature of the fighting.
- 'Isolated' (para 3) suggests that the soldiers were very much on their own; difficult to summon support.
- 'constant attack' (para 3) suggests the incessant nature of hostilities/no respite for the troops.
- 'close-combat' (para 3) suggests almost hand-to-hand fighting.
- 'increasing sophistication' (para 3) suggests the 'hi-tech' side to the war; that they were not fighting a primitive enemy.
- 'enduring dread' (para 3) suggests ever-present fear.

Sentence structure

- List (or triad) '... enemy assaults, mortars and rocket fire' highlights the variety of threats encountered by troops.

Use of statistics

- 'Fifteen of my battle group were killed in action ... 46 seriously wounded' suggests the high percentage of casualties sustained.

Re-read paragraph 4.

2. Analyse how the writer uses sentence structure and word choice to highlight the soldiers' experiences in Afghanistan and their experiences in the 'peacetime world'.

   (1) for each point made. Both Afghanistan and the peacetime world should be covered for full marks.

   In Afghanistan

- 'valiantly' suggests their bravery.
- 'admirably' suggests their reputations were enhanced.
- 'constant stress' highlights the inescapable nature of the difficulties.
- Colon introduces the list of negative experiences 'loss of ... serious injury'.
- Use of contrasting ideas in the first sentence 'While we ... served valiantly ...' is juxtaposed with the realities of war 'loss of ... serious injury'.
- 'left a mark' this image suggests the psychological effects suffered by the soldiers – like a stain or a scar.

   In the peacetime world

- 'readjusted ... reintegrated' contrasts with 'mental trauma'.
- 'deeply embedded' suggests how profound the problems are for sufferers of PTSD.
- Contrast in the final sentence: 'But while most of us ... for some ...' highlights the different outcomes for soldiers.

Re-read paragraphs 6–8.

3. Explain what might be a reason for the level of PTSD being 'slightly higher for infantry units and reservists'.

   *This question requires you to **infer** things from the passage. This is an important skill at Higher level. The passage won't actually give you the answer. Think carefully about what infantry are (and what they do) and how reservists are different from regular soldiers. Your answer might look like this:*

   PTSD might be higher for these groups because infantry come into contact with the enemy more directly and more frequently than other branches of the armed forces. Reservists are not full-time soldiers and so might find it more difficult to deal with the realities of combat. (2)

4. Identify and explain the writer's use of irony in paragraph 7.

   This is a straightforward question that tests your knowledge of irony. Remember to explain the effect.

   There is irony in the sentence which begins 'In 2012, 50 soldiers ...'. The irony lies in the fact that more soldiers killed themselves due to PTSD than were killed in combat. The writer makes use of irony to highlight the seriousness of the situation the veterans find themselves in (2).

5. Explain in your own words the **four** main points the writer makes in paragraph 8.

   This is another straightforward question asking you to identify some of the main ideas in the passage. Remember to 'locate' and 'translate'. Your answer might say:

   The writer thinks
   - We should look again at the numbers ('review the statistics') of soldiers suffering from PTSD (1).
   - We should improve the help offered ('address the gaps in provision') (1).
   - We should avoid making too much of the psychological effects of combat (1).
   - We should not judge those suffering from it (1).

Re-read paragraph 11.

6. The writer describes PTSD as 'an invisible scar of war.' Explain the meaning of this image and analyse its effect.

   Remember to say what is being compared to what. You can then say something about the effect of the image.

   The image compares PTSD to a mark left by a physical wound to the body that cannot be seen (1). It is effective because it describes a psychological injury in terms of a physical one — reminding us that one is just as damaging and long lasting as the other (1). Through using this image, the writer stresses the seriousness of PTSD (1).

Consider the text as a whole.

7. Identify evidence in the passage of the support offered to serving soldiers and veterans. Answer in your own words.

   There are a lot of things mentioned in the passage. You could refer to
   - Strategies have been put in place by the MoD for when soldiers return from tours of duty in a combat zone (1).
   - Soldiers are taught about the condition (1).
   - Charities attempt to deal with PTSD (1).
   - Civilian employers have special programmes for veterans (1).

   Again the important thing is to use your own words when the question demands it.

Reading for Understanding, Analysis and Evaluation exam paper, questions on passage 1, 'Only a Theory', pages 45–46

1.	Read lines 1– 6. Using your own words as far as possible, identify some of the things that make teaching Roman history and the Latin language a 'big undertaking' (lines 5).	4
	This is a straightforward 'understanding' type question so **locate** *and then* **translate** *the appropriate words in the passage.*	
	1 mark if you made the point that there is a wide range of topics/a number of complex topics to be covered and then 1 mark each for any three of the following examples/features:	
	• Poetry (the 'elegiacs' and 'odes' mentioned in the passage).	
	• Language structure ('grammar').	
	• Roman conflicts or battles (you should be able to gloss 'wars' even if you've never heard or read the word 'Punic' before — remember you will encounter unfamiliar vocabulary in this exam).	
	• Roman leaders (the 'Julius Caesar' reference).	
	• Luxurious and corrupt lives of rulers (a gloss of 'voluptuous excesses').	
	• The significant commitment/attention/focus/application/devotion required by the teacher (gloss of 'time, concentration, dedication').	
2.	Analyse the writer's use of language in lines 6–10 to convey what he feels about the threat posed by the 'ignoramuses' (line 7).	2
	Remember that any reference to the writer's 'use of language' in a question should trigger a checklist of features and techniques to start running through your mind (word choice, imagery, structure, tone, sound …). In a question like this you can score 2 marks for an 'insightful' or well-expressed point about a single feature. What makes a comment 'insightful'? It's all to do with how perceptive your understanding of the technique the writer is using seems to be and how well you express any comment about it. It's always safer to make more than one point in a 2-mark question! You need to refer to (and quote) an appropriate feature or technique and then comment on it.	
	For this question you can score up to 2 marks for a single well-expressed point. 1 mark for each more basic point. A 'reference alone' (just pointing out a feature or technique without a comment) does not score any marks (0). Each of the possible answers set out below consists of a reference and then a suggested comment.	
	Imagery *(remember to explain the 'root' of the image in your answer):*	
	• Baying pack of hounds chasing their quarry.	
	• 'Preyed upon' - predators attacking weaker animals.	
	Word choice:	
	• 'baying' — loud/menacing.	
	• 'ignoramuses' — anti-intellectual/uncivilised.	
	• 'scurry about' — animal like/unattractive/secretive/busybodies.	
	• 'tirelessly' — never giving up.	
	Sound:	
	• Alliteration — 'precious', 'preyed' catches the eye (or ear) and helps to underline the point the writer is making.	

3.	Referring to specific language features, how effective do you find lines 14–17 as an introduction to the writer's ideas?	4
	In answering a question like this you need to make sure that the features you identify and comment on relate back to what has gone before in the paragraph.	
	Up to 2 marks for a sophisticated analysis of any one feature. 1 mark for a more basic point. For full marks structure and word choice must be covered.	
	Possible answers	
	Sentence structure:	
	• Balanced structure ('Instead of devoting . . . , you are forced to . . .') highlights time wasted on answering attacks.	
	• Colon introduces expansion of the idea of the 'rearguard defence'.	
	Word choice:	
	• 'noble vocation' — higher calling/emphasises status of the Latin teacher.	
	• 'rearguard defence' — desperately fighting off attackers.	
	• 'make you weep' — suggests sense of despair engendered by ignorant attacks.	
	• 'exhibition' — shows their lack of self-awareness/sense of proportion.	
	• 'ignorant' — sums up critics' lack of knowledge.	
	• 'prejudice' — shows unthinking response/base instinct.	
	Tone:	
	• *You could also make the point that the tone of these lines (one of anger, despair or exasperation at the 'ignoramuses') is in keeping with the rest of the paragraph and support it with reference to any of the language features outlined above.*	
4.	Explain in your own words the characteristics of the 'Holocaust-deniers' (line 21).	2
	*This is another **locate** and **translate** question.*	
	1 mark each for a successful gloss of any two of:	
	• 'well-organised' — they are effectively structured.	
	• 'well-financed' — receive plenty of funding.	
	• 'politically muscular' — they are influential in the world of decision making.	
	• 'vocal' — promote their message (not just 'loud').	
	• 'superficially plausible' — believable on a very simplistic level.	
	• 'adept at seeming learned' — skilled at appearing intellectual/academic.	
5.	By referring to at least **two** features of language in lines 25–30, analyse how the writer conveys his disapproval of the situation faced by the hypothetical history teacher.	4
	*This is another question where the words **features of language** should trigger that checklist of features and techniques in your mind. Below are possible comments you could have made on word choice, punctuation and structure.*	
	*You would score up to 2 marks for a sophisticated analysis of any one feature. 1 mark for a more basic point. For full marks **two** language features must be covered.*	
	• 'continually faced with' — incessant nature of problem.	
	• 'belligerent' — aggressive.	
	• Inverted commas around 'equal time' highlight the writer's feeling that this is a waste of time.	

Answers

- Inverted commas around 'the controversy' and 'alternative theory' suggest the lack of status he awards these ideas.
- Inverted commas around 'respected' highlight his own lack of respect for the idea.
- 'Fashionably relativist' – trendy/lacking certainty/clarity.
- 'chime in' – irritating addition to the debate.
- Colon and semi-colon used to structure the relativist intellectuals' argument that 'all points of view are equally valid'.

6.	Read lines 31–41. Analyse the writer's use of language in this paragraph to highlight his feelings of sympathy for science teachers today. You should refer in your answer to such features as word choice, sentence structure, imagery …	4

This question helpfully reminds you of the sort of language features to comment on.

Up to 2 marks for a sophisticated analysis of any one feature. 1 mark for a more basic point. For full marks two language features must be covered.

Possible answers

Structure:

- Repetition 'when they … when they … when they …' shows the extent of their efforts.
- List of good they do separated by semi-colons.
- Balanced structure of second sentence in the paragraph (contrast between positive efforts followed by description of obstacles).
- Repeated structures with contrasting meanings: 'explore and explain'/'harried and stymied'/'hassled and bullied'.
- Repetition 'They are …' suggests the variety of difficulties faced.
- Contrast 'Once … now …'.

Word choice:

- 'honestly' – shows their integrity.
- 'very nature of life itself' – dealing with fundamental issues.
- 'harried' – chased.
- 'stymied' – obstructed/blocked.
- 'hassled' – bothered.
- 'bullied/threatened/menacing' – putting pressure on the teacher.
- 'wasted at every turn' – consistently interfered with.
- 'sarcastic smirks' – negative attitude of pupils/belittling teacher's efforts.
- 'close-folded arms' – body language mirrors 'closed' minds.
- 'brainwashed' – as if indoctrinated/conditioned.
- 'state-approved' – big-brother society.
- 'systematically expunged' – methodically/deliberately removed from the textbooks.
- 'bowdlerized' – altered from the original/loss of original sense or true meaning.

Punctuation:

- Inverted commas around 'change over time' suggests it is a less precise expression than 'evolution' OR inverted commas are used simply because he is quoting from a 'politically correct' textbook and wishes the reader to share his outrage at the use of the term.

7.	Re-read lines 50–59. By referring to at least one example, analyse how the writer's use of imagery reinforces his view of those who hold creationist beliefs.	2
	Remember to explain the 'root' of the image – say what is being compared to what. Make sure you justify why you think it is effective (or not).	
	Up to 2 marks for a detailed/insightful comment. 1 mark for a more basic response.	
	Creating the universe is compared to starting an engine (which runs by itself thereafter). 'Cranked' doesn't sound like a particularly 'high-tech' piece of engineering. It is effective because the image allows the writer to poke (gentle) fun at those who hold such beliefs. This lends weight to the writer's own theory.	
	Or	
	The beginning of the universe is compared to some sort of baptism ceremony ('solemnized its birth'). The writer clearly thinks this sort of personification is the wrong way to think about the universe.	
8.	Analyse the writer's use of language in the final paragraph to emphasise his position on this subject.	3
	Look carefully at the final paragraph. What aspects of language did you spot?	
	Up to 2 marks for an insightful comment on one feature. 1 mark for a more basic comment.	
	Possible answers	
	• Short, blunt first sentence states case clearly.	
	• Repetition of 'Beyond … Beyond …' shows the extent of the case for evolution/irrefutable quality of the evidence.	
	• 'Beyond sane, informed, intelligent doubt' — triad of adjectives effectively shows the quality of the evidence for his argument.	
	• Repetition of 'fact' to drive home the certainty he has.	
	• Repetition of 'cousins …' to emphasise the interrelated nature of all species.	
	• 'somewhat more distant … more distant … still … yet more distant …' suggests the breadth of the evolutionary process.	
	• Cumulative effect of 'not self-evidently, tautologically, obviously true'.	
	• Final sentence ends with simple statement reinforcing the writer's case.	

Reading for Understanding, Analysis and Evaluation exam paper, question on both passages, pages 47–48

Question on both passages Both writers express their views about the teaching of evolution and creationism. Identify key areas on which they disagree. In your answer, you should refer in detail to both passages. *The mark for this question should reflect the quality of response in two areas:* • *Identification of the key areas of agreement/disagreement in attitude/ideas.* • *Level of detail given in support.* *To answer this, look again at where the writers seem to disagree. For example, what do they say about the status of creationism and evolution as theories that are taught in schools? Do they both believe that science teachers should 'correct' students who have creationist views? What is their opinion of those with a 'creationist' world view?* **Marks are allocated as follows:** *5 marks – comprehensive identification of three or more key areas of disagreement with full use of supporting evidence.* *4 marks – clear identification of three or more key areas of disagreement with relevant use of supporting evidence.* *3 marks – identification of three or more key areas of disagreement with supporting evidence.* *2 marks – identification of two key areas of disagreement with supporting evidence.* *1 mark – identification of one key area of disagreement with supporting evidence.* *0 marks – failure to identify any key area of disagreement and/or total misunderstanding of task.*	5

How to study poetry: Asking questions about poems, 'Heliographer', page 65

1. What is the poem about?

    The poem seems to be about a child (a young boy?) looking down on his home town with his father. As he does so he learns how to drink from a bottle of lemonade. The poem seems to be about growing up — it describes a particular 'rite of passage' as the boy learns to do something in the way 'grown-ups' do. The title 'Heliographer' and the word 'decoded' suggest that the poem might also be saying something about signs and signals. What do you think?

2. Who is speaking?

    The young boy or the grown man he has become who is looking back on the incident.

3. How is the poem structured?

    The poem is divided into two stanzas, one of eight lines and one of six. The division into eight and six suggests it is a kind of sonnet although it doesn't have a sonnet's rhyme scheme. There does seem to be a change at the volta when his father intervenes. What do you think?

4. What other techniques have been used?

    Word choice/imagery

    *   'decoded' has connotations of the father reading and explaining to the boy the landscape spread out below the two of them. It also echoes the title, 'Heliographer' — a signaller who transmitted messages in Morse code by reflecting the sun's rays in a mirror. Armies used heliographers to send signals on the battlefield before the invention of radio.
    *   'bolted' describes the boy's attempts to drink from the bottle as if it is some mechanical operation.
    *   'shaky,/single-handed grip' suggests the effort needed by the boy. As well as now only needing one hand to complete the task, there are also connotations of doing something on your own in the phrase 'single-handed' — the act of drinking from the bottle becomes a symbol of the boy's increasing independence.
    *   'it detonated with light' suggests something explosive (violent?) and sudden as the sun's rays catch the bottle.

    Simile

    *   'my lips pursed like a trumpeter's' continues the idea of sending signals introduced earlier in the poem.

    Sound

    *   Onomatopoeia: 'Clunk', 'butting' suggests the boy's clumsiness.

    Sentence structure

    *   The triad of 'our tenement, the rival football grounds, / the long bridges', which suggests the setting for the incident described (it seems they are looking down from Dundee Law). The movement from home (the tenement) to the football grounds and then to the bridges suggest the boy's future progression in life and that he will grow up and ultimately leave the city.

5. How effective are the poet's methods in conveying the meaning of the text to the reader?

    The poet's methods are effective in conveying the central concerns of this text. The short, compact form he has chosen for the poem effectively brings a brief moment in time to life. The word choice and imagery suggest the significance of the incident in the speaker's growing up. The allusions to signs and symbols add a further layer of meaning to the poem.

6. What is your personal reaction to the poem?

    You will have responded to the poem in your own way. Did you like the way this incident was described? It seems a skilful evocation of a childhood experience.

How to study poetry: Asking questions about poems, 'In a snug room', pages 65–66

1. What is the poem about?

    A successful businessman enjoys a drink in a bar. He thinks about his recent successes. He awaits the arrival of his 'true love'. MacCaig suggests he is about to be punished for his complacency.

2. Who is speaking?

    A detached, neutral poetic voice. Perhaps the poet himself.

3. How is the poem structured?

    *   *The concise form of the poem adds impact to its message.*
    *   *Free verse with no regular rhythm or rhyme for most of the poem suits the 'mini-narrative' MacCaig is telling us.*
    *   *Movement in the poem from the comfortable (literal and metaphorical) position of the anonymous man to the idea that his life is about to fall apart.*

4. What other techniques have been used?

    Word choice/imagery

    *   *'snug' suggests 'sheltered'; 'cosy'; 'comfortable' (you might even have heard of the old expression 'as snug as a bug in a rug'!). 'The snug' is also the name for a separate room in an old-fashioned bar, which makes it doubly apt in this context — 'snug' refers to both the setting of the poem and how the subject of the poem feels in the first stanza.*
    *   *'He' suggests his anonymity but he is clearly a man of some importance; someone with a public profile ('flattering reference ... morning papers').*
    *   *'sips' suggests a measure of sophistication or refinement.*
    *   *'complacently' suggests he is self-satisfied or perhaps smug.*
    *   *'cronies' implies close friends (although 'cronyism' now has negative connotations and a sense of corruption).*
    *   *'profitable' suggests he's a successful businessman (a fat cat? A banker?).*
    *   *'donation' suggests his philanthropic side — his generosity. Or is he just salving a guilty conscience?*
    *   *'And he smiles ...' suggests further complacency — the day just seems to be getting better and better for this man. Notice how the poet deliberately leaves us guessing as to the identity of his 'true love'. Who's coming? His wife? His mistress? Someone (or something) else? 'true love' seems a rather old-fashioned expression.*
    *   *Reference to 'Nemesis' gives this concise narrative a sense of 'universality' — we are invited to read it as a modern morality tale; especially when we take into account the anonymity of the central character.*

    Sentence structure

    *   *Colon introduces the list of things he is pleased with.*

    Sound

    *   *Alliteration ('deal ... dotted ... donation') the repeated hard plosive 'd' sounds help to suggest the certainty of the hard-headed businessman.*

- Concluding rhyme ('gun'/'one') helps to underline the final message of the poem: a warning to the self-satisfied. You might argue that this seems a peculiarly 'Scottish' response to those who are successful!
- The word 'gun' echoes the word 'snug' in the title (Seamus Heaney does exactly the same in his poem 'Digging').

Other features include

- Placing line 10 in a line on its own:
  - ➢ allows the poet to sum up succinctly the seemingly 'perfect' day being enjoyed by the man
  - ➢ allows a dramatic pause before the climax of the poem.
- Placing the closing lines in a separate stanza provides a dramatic conclusion to the poem.
- Witty juxtaposition of ancient and modern (Greek goddess and 'two bullets ...').

5. How effective are the poet's methods in conveying the meaning of the text to the reader?

   The techniques outlined above all convey the meaning of the text effectively. The poem offers a blunt warning against being overly complacent and smug about your life and/or yourself.

6. What is your personal reaction to the poem?

   Do you like this poem or not? Do you feel sorry for the man?

Drama: *The Slab Boys*, by John Byrne, pages 76–79

	Answers	
1.	By referring closely to lines 1–16, show how the play's setting in time is established for the audience.	3
	You should refer to the following:	
	• *Spanky's hairstyle and costume ('drainpipe trousers', 'Tony Curtis hairdo', 'crepe-soled shoes') suggests the 'uniform' of a 1950s Teddy Boy.*	
	• *The use of the word 'wireless'.*	
	• *The reference to 'Luxemburg', the pirate radio station.*	
	• *The reference to 'Terry Dene' singing 'A White Sport Coat', a popular song of the day. This (originally American) song suggests the influence of American pop culture on Britain at the time.*	
	These all serve to (very economically) establish the action of the play firmly in the 1950s, with the obvious influence of American culture.	
2.	By referring to two examples of dialogue in this extract, show how the playwright establishes the character of Willie Curry.	3
	The key point to make is that he is presented almost as a caricature or stereotype of the older authority figure, forever bemoaning the behaviour of those younger than him and always harking back to a better time. This is illustrated through dialogue such as:	
	• *'If I'd had you chaps out in Burma' marks him as being of the older generation who served in the war. It suggests he feels less powerful now and is nostalgic for the army discipline he could administer in the past.*	
	• *'silly duck's arse haircuts'/'bloody contraption'/'that racket'/'gadget' suggest his dismissive contempt for current styles and technology.*	
	• *'you're for the high jump' typical of his clichéd authoritarian threats.*	
	• *'Now, get on with it …' typical of the orders he gives.*	
3.	Analyse the effect of some of the different registers of language in dialogue spoken by the characters that are evident in this extract.	4
	To answer this you could refer to:	
	• *The earthy coarseness of lines such as 'Dee-oh-raw-ho … the skitters' for humorous effect and which help to establish Phil's character.*	
	• *The use of Scots idiom/dialect to establish the setting of the play and the working class background of the characters.*	
		➢ *'Who belongs to the juke box?'*	
		➢ *'… no what you'd cry a spectator sport'*	
		➢ *'could you not've brung in'*	
		➢ *'my maw's Christmas present'*	
	• *Phil and Spanky's imitation of the language of English public school stories in lines: 'Bless my boater, did you catch that, Cherry? A yuletide cadeau for the squirt's mater …' for humorous effect but also as a marker of the theme of class and privilege that is revealed as one of the play's concerns.*	
	• *Words taken from American popular culture such as 'vamoose' (Western).*	

4.	By referring to this extract and elsewhere in the play, discuss how the theme of bullying is developed in the text.	10

You can answer this question in bullet points or in a series of linked statements.

Marks are allocated to this question (as they are for all the 10-mark Scottish text questions) as follows:

You will get up to 2 marks for identifying an area of 'commonality' – in this case you could refer to the fact the bullying (of Hector and Alan) in the extract is then developed in the treatment Hector receives at the hands of Phil and Spanky later in the play.

There are another 2 marks available for referring to the extract – you could discuss the business with the radio and Spanky's breaking of the aerial callously dismissing the fact that it was supposed to be a present for Hector's 'maw'. You might also identify that the suggestion of 'cufflinks' as a replacement present is another cruel jibe at Hector's expense (although also one designed to raise a laugh from the audience). You could point out Phil and Spanky's deliberate use of the wrong names for Alan – 'Archie', 'Andy', 'Eamonn', 'Alec' – in order to make him feel unwelcome.

Whatever references you choose to make, remember to comment on their effect.

The remaining 6 marks are allocated for your comments on other parts of the text and how they convey the theme of bullying. Effective and insightful comments will always score well. Markers will award 2 or 1 marks to each point that you make. For this question you might refer to and comment on Phil and Spanky's treatment of Hector and Alan:

- 'He was going to be a Capucci monk' — they suggest Hector is Catholic.
- Alan's Parker pen is taken off him.
- Phil and Spanky make fun of Hector's Uncle Bertie.
- Phil and Spanky make fun of Hector's intention of taking Lucille to the staff dance.
- The casual cruelty in their description of Hector 'Everything's wrong with you ...'
- The cutting of Hector's ear.
- The 'new' look created for Hector.

There are many other episodes in the play that you could refer to.

Prose: *Sunset Song*, by Lewis Grassic Gibbon, pages 80–81

	Answers	
1.	By close reference to paragraphs 1 and 2, explain how the writer's language conveys a sense of Marget Strachan's character. *In your answer you could refer to and comment on some of the following:* • List of adjectives to describe her 'slim and sweet and fair' emphasises her attractive qualities – (deliberate) echo of a description that we might find in an old folk tale or ballad. • This description is contrasted by the 'awful things' (sex and reproduction) she speaks about – she is much more 'worldly wise' than Chris. • She is ambitious ('off to be trained as a doctor') and practical – she won't wait for the arrival of her father's 'Revolution'. • The comparison used in the description of her eyes, 'blue and so deep they reminded you of a well you peered into', suggests her attractive/mysterious qualities. • These qualities are emphasised by the alliteration in the comparatives 'deeper and darker'. • Grassic Gibbon contrasts the 'solemn' and serious side of her nature with the much more light-hearted side 'laughing and fleering'. The overall impression is of a bright, lively and attractive individual. *You would be awarded up to 2 marks for a detailed or insightful comment you made and 1 mark for a more basic comment. Remember the marks are allocated for your **comment on the effect** of each feature that you identify. There are no marks just for identifying a language feature.*	4
2.	By referring to at least two examples from paragraph 3, analyse how the writer conveys a sense of the contrast between life and death. *You could refer to any of the following. The question asks about a contrast so for full marks you must offer comment on the features that refer to life and to death.* Life • Sensory experience and an acute sense of being alive suggested by the list of adjectives 'Clean and keen and wild and clear'. • Grassic Gibbon's description of 'a vein that beat in Marget's throat, a little blue gathering' suggests how small and fragile life is. • 'blood beat past in slow, quiet strokes' – the alliteration and the short simple words suggest the pulse of life. • More vivid sensory experience suggested by the descriptions 'lowe of burning whins' and 'hearing the North Sea thunder beyond the hills'. • Repetition of 'thunder' to highlight the contrast with the 'dark silence' of death. • 'morning of mist' has connotations of something transitory and insubstantial. Death • 'dead and still under grass' contrasts with the lively picture created of life above ground. • 'you'd never smell' suggests the finality of death. • 'cased' suggests being confined and enclosed. • 'icy darkness' suggests something forbidding and frightening.	4

3.	By referring to two examples from paragraphs 4 and 5, analyse how the writer conveys Chris' perception of the incident with Marget.	2
	Here you could refer to:	
	Word choice	
	• 'red' suggests both passion and life.	
	• 'kind' suggests this was not an aggressive act.	
	• 'over in a moment', 'quick' suggests transitory nature of experience.	
	• 'shameful' suggests something wrong, illicit.	
	• 'fine … tingling … shameful' effectively suggest the conflicting emotions felt by Chris.	
	Comparison	
	• 'so red they were that they looked like haws' another example of Chris seeing things in terms of the natural world.	
	Sentence structure	
	• Repetition/triad 'lovely … lovely … lovelier'.	
	• Dashes indicate the different stages of Marget's actions as she prepares to kiss Chris.	
	• Long, climactic build-up to '… and kiss you like this!'	
	Again you must remember to comment fully on your chosen examples.	
4.	This extract refers to two aspects of Chris' character. By referring to this extract and to elsewhere in the novel, discuss how Grassic Gibbon conveys these aspects of Chris' character.	10
	You can answer this question in bullet points or in a series of linked statements.	
	Marks are allocated to this question (as they are for all the 10-mark Scottish text questions) as follows:	
	You will get up to 2 marks for identifying an area of 'commonality' – in this case you could refer to the fact that this extract refers to the 'Two Chrisses' – the English Chris and the Scots Chris – and that this 'divided' Chris is also evident in other parts of the novel such as when she is torn between going off to train as a teacher when her father dies or staying and taking over the running of the croft.	
	There are another 2 marks available for referring to the extract – you could refer to the word choice in the description of Chris and her thoughts in the first paragraph:	
	English Chris	
	'douce and studious'	
	Scots Chris	
	'sat back'	
	'laughed a canny laugh'	
	'antics of the teachers'	
	You could also refer to the list 'champ of horses … smell of dung … father's brown, grained hands', which suggests her affinity with the land and those who work on it.	
	'sick to be home again' suggests the strength of her feelings for the land.	
	Whatever references you choose to make, remember to comment on their effect.	

The remaining 6 marks are allocated for your comments on other parts of the text and how they convey the two aspects of Chris' character. Effective and insightful comments will always score well. Markers will award 2 or 1 marks to each point that you make. For this question you might refer to and comment on:

- Her love/admiration for her father and her fear of him.
- When she is torn between going off to train as a teacher when her father dies or staying and taking over the running of the croft.
- The calm and collected way she deals with her relatives and the lawyer and her fight with Ewan in Seed-Time.

There are many other episodes in the novel you could refer to.

Poetry: 'Nil Nil', by Don Paterson, pages 82–83

	Answers	
1.	By referring to specific features, explain how this extract relates to the earlier parts of the poem. *In your answer you could mention:* • 'Unknown to him' echoes the 'abandoned histories' and the idea of 'deeper and deeper obscurity'. • 'him' refers to Horace Madden, mentioned in the first narrative. • 'it' refers to the stone he kicks into the gutter, which is revealed in this extract to be the pilot's gallstone. • References to place names: 'Leuchars', 'Tayport', 'Carnoustie', 'Sidlaws', echo the references to the Dundee area in the first narrative. • 'the Sidlaws unsheathed from their great black tarpaulin' repeats the image in the epigraph 'imagine the vast, rustling map of Burgundy, say, settling over it like a freshly starched sheet!'	3
2	By referring closely to lines 4–16, analyse the use of poetic technique to describe the fighter-pilot's experience. *To answer this question you might comment on some of the following:* *Word choice* • 'lone (fighter-pilot)' suggests his isolation and/or his heroic status. • 'unsheathed' suggests the hills emerge like knives or swords; suggests something threatening the pilot. • 'unscheduled' suggests the unexpected nature of his emergency. • 'flurry' suggests the socks streaming into the sky. • 'rendered' suggests something given up as an offering to someone. • 'irenicon' suggests something used to secure peace – offers a contrast to the ideas contained in 'fighter-pilot'.	4

Imagery

- 'their great black tarpaulin' suggests the hills are covered in dark mist or fog. This image echoes the reference to the giant map laid over Burgundy in the epigraph. The image also has sinister connotations of something shrouded.
- 'twirling away like an ash-key' suggests the helplessness of the pilot as the plane spirals to the ground.
- 'like a sackful of doves' conventional symbols of peace.

Sound

- Onomatopoeia 'plopped' — faintly childish or ridiculous word contrasting with the seriousness of the engine failure.

Tone

- The mix of the serious and the comic makes the reader consider anew and question the significance of Paterson's description of the pilot's experience in terms of the central concerns of the poem as a whole.

You might get up to 2 marks for a detailed, insightful comment on one feature. You will always get 1 mark for a more basic, accurate comment. Remember that there are no marks for reference/quotation alone.

3.	Evaluate how effective you find lines 16–21 of this extract. Your answer should deal with ideas and/or language.	**3**

To answer this you should refer to specific features of the text and comment on them. The question asks you to **evaluate** *so make sure you make some sort of statement about the lines being effective or very effective or fairly effective and then give your evidence to support your evaluative statement.*

You could mention:

- The cartoon-like (but still gruesome) image of the pilot and his plane hitting the ground at the same time.
- 'made nothing of him' reminds the reader of the central concerns of this poem — the idea of loss/decline/nothingness. There is also humorous allusion in the expression.
- The list — 'fillings', 'tackets', 'lucky half-crown', 'gallstone' — illustrates what the pilot is reduced to in death: a collection of fragments.
- The irony of 'lucky half-crown'.
- 'anchored' suggests something secured very strongly.
- Alliteration in 'steel bars of a stank' suggests something harsh and metallic.
- The Scots dialect word 'stank' helps establish the setting of the poem.
- The humour of 'biting the bullet' and the comparison to someone with a bullet between his teeth. This idiomatic expression also suggests the idea of having to put up with something.
- 'looks like' suggests the ambiguities and uncertainties that pervade the poem.

Answers

4. By referring to this poem and another poem by Don Paterson you have studied discuss how he makes the reader consider the theme of time.

10

You can answer this question in bullet points or in a series of linked statements.

Marks are allocated to this question (as they are for all the 10-mark Scottish text questions) as follows:

You will get up to 2 marks for commenting on an area of 'commonality', i.e. pointing out that 'Nil Nil' deals with loss and ultimate extinction over time and that '11:00: Baldovan' deals with the frightening and disconcerting changes that the passing of time can bring. A general comment on theme will be worth up to 2 marks.

There are another 2 marks available for referring to the extract – you could refer to:

- 'deeper and deeper obscurity' in the epigraph.
- The gradual extinction through the years of the football club related in the first narrative in the poem.
- The loss of identity suffered by the pilot over time.
- The 'fading', 'failing' and 'thinning down' that takes place as time passes.

*Whatever references you choose to make, remember to **comment** on their effect.*

The remaining 6 marks are allocated for your comments on the other text ('11:00: Baldovan') and its presentation of the theme of time. Effective and insightful comments will always score well. Markers will award 2 or 1 marks to each point that you make. For this question you might refer to and comment on:

- The significance of the title.
- The time shift signalled at the end of line 17 'the bus will let us down in another country' and the associated dislocation felt by the speaker.
- The changes to the world described in the poem.
- 'sisters and mothers are fifty years dead'.
- The depiction of the movement from childhood to adulthood.
- The realisation of the destructive power of the passing of time.

Higher
ENGLISH

Practice Papers

Claire Bowles, Mia Stewart,
Catherine Travis, Iain Valentine

Revision advice

Part 1: Reading for Understanding, Analysis and Evaluation

You will have one and a half hours to complete this exam. There are 30 marks available.

This is the paper which in Intermediate and the previous Higher was known as Close Reading. You will be required to read two non-fiction passages, answering questions on Passage 1 and comparing and/or contrasting Passage 1 with Passage 2 in a final 5-mark question.

The questions will cover these three areas:

- Showing your understanding of the passage by putting things in your own words, summarising and selecting key areas.

- Analysing the way the writer conveys these ideas through techniques such as word choice, imagery, sentence structure and tone.

- Evaluating how effectively the writer conveys these ideas, giving your opinion about the writer's use of language.

Part 2: Critical Reading

One and a half hours is allocated for the Scottish texts and critical essay question. It is up to you to divide your time appropriately. 45 minutes for each section is a good guide.

Section 1: Scottish texts

Here you will have approximately 45 minutes to answer questions on a text you have studied in class. In total, 20 marks are available. In this part of the exam you will be given an extract from the text or texts you have studied. You will answer questions on this extract and then, in a final 10-mark question, compare the extract to the rest of the text/the other set texts by the same writer.

This part of the paper asks you to consider:

1. Why is the extract important? What ideas does it present? How is language used?

2. How does this extract fit into the whole text or set of texts? For example, what themes or ideas in the extract relate to other stories or poems by the same writer?

Section 2: Critical essay

Here you will have approximately 45 minutes, depending on your time management, to answer a question on a text you have studied in class. 20 marks are available for this part of the paper. There will be a choice of questions in different genres: drama, prose, poetry, film and television drama or language study. You will be asked to focus on aspects of your chosen text. To be able to write a well-structured, detailed answer to the question, you will need to know the text fully, and demonstrate this with textual reference. Remembering quotations is not what you're being assessed on – it is what you do with the quotations and the comments you make about them that count. In terms of length, 1000 words is a good target; you need to show breadth and depth in your answer, which is difficult to do in shorter responses.

You should make sure that you leave sufficient time to write a strong conclusion, regardless of whether you have developed all the points in your plan or not. Remember, you need to focus on the question throughout the essay and particularly in the conclusion. Look at the SQA supplementary marking grid to understand the standards and evaluate your own work. Set yourself targets for improvement in critical essay writing and work on them in your next essay.

There is lots of advice on writing successful critical essays on pages 243–245 of this book.

You can check your answers to the practice papers online at www.leckiescotland.co.uk.

Practice Exam A

CfE Higher English

Practice Papers for SQA Exams

Exam A
Reading for Understanding, Analysis and Evaluation

Duration – 1 hour 30 minutes

Total marks – 30

Attempt ALL questions.

×Leckie
the education publisher
for Scotland

Passage 1

In the first passage Paulina Porizkova, writing for the Huffington Post, reflects on her own attitude towards beauty and ageing.

Old age is the revenge of the ugly ones is a French proverb; one that I first heard at the very advanced age of 15 upon my arrival in Paris. I had spent five years in the ugly bin at school in Sweden, and had only recently been upgraded to beautiful. My ego was still fragile and my mind still pumped full of highbrow arty self-education and nerdy jokes, which is how one gets by when one is
5   ugly. Which of course, I promptly realised, is exactly what will pay off as one ages: beauty fades, but a mind constantly energised will shine even brighter with age. I immediately took the proverb as my own personal motto and patted myself on the back with satisfaction. I will continue to be intelligent, I vowed, no matter how beautiful I become. And then at, like, the old age of 35, I'll be an incredibly smart and kinda attractive old lady.

10   In interviews I gave at the wise age of 17 and 18, I pontificated about the beauty of age and wisdom, and blabbered on about how I looked forward to my first wrinkle. What an idiot I was.

My first recognition of age setting in occurred on my 36th birthday. I have no idea why, on this day of all days, I looked in the mirror and realised my face no longer looked young. I didn't look bad; only, the freshness had somehow disappeared. I immediately became hyper-conscious of my looks
15   and went out and bought the most expensive cream on the market (for your information, it did nothing). And I began the battle of acceptance, something I have to do now almost every time I face a mirror.

Like everything else in life, there is always payback and it's a bitch. Beauty, unlike the rest of the gifts handed out at birth, does not require dedication, patience and hard work to pay off. But it's also the
20   only gift that does NOT keep on giving. It usually blossoms at an age where you're least equipped to handle its benefits and rewards and instead take it all for granted, and by the time you start understanding the value of it, it slowly trickles away. How's that for revenge of the ugly ones?

To me, to let yourself age means that you're comfortable with who you are. Yes, sorry, I do believe that all the little shots here and there, and the pulling of skin here and there, and the removal of fat
25   here and there, means you still have something to prove; you're still not comfortable in your skin. The beauty of age was supposed to be about the wisdom acquired, and with it an acceptance and celebration of who you are. Now all we want for people to see is that we have not yet attained that wisdom. Aging has become something to fight, not something to accept. Aging is a matter of control and control of matter.

30   I recently saw a comment posted on to one of the blogs I had written by a woman who stated that my problem is that I'm obviously jealous of these women I criticise, because they are not only beautiful but successful; something I'm clearly not. That gave me pause. Am I just jealous? Is my entire creative output completely reliant on this baser of emotions? It's true I'm trying to find a new place in the world that would rather I had just shut up and stayed beautiful (dying young is a terrific
35   way to achieve this, by the way), which makes me a tad resentful. It's also true I'm still very insecure and want attention and universal love and have not a friggin' clue on how to achieve it. And likewise, it is true that I am jealous, and envious, and covetous of things I don't have. Which are, or is, rather – surprise, surprise – not an unlined forehead or puffy lips, nor a hot career, but confidence. True

40 confidence: the kind that should come with age and that I keep glimpsing off in the distance, the kind I tell myself I would have developed already had I relied on wit rather than looks.

I keep a list of my "heroines," the women who have dared to age, and I'm always stupidly grateful to see these women highlighted in the media. I just found out that Jamie Lee Curtis, one of the women on my list, and Madonna are the same age. Looking at photos of them side by side is a revelation. One looks no older than 30, hard-edged, determined and hungry. The other looks like she's old

45 enough to be her mother, but radiant, confident and content.

I already know I'm too vain and too insecure to follow her footsteps. This is what and whom I'm jealous of.

But even as I struggle with the choices – age, age a little, age not at all – I realise I'm blessed to even be in the position to age. To age is a privilege, not a birthright, even though most of us in the civilised

50 world seem to forget this. This choice of "not-aging" is actually reserved for well-off women with lots of time and money. I've met a lot of these women at parties and social gatherings, and they were all lovely, gracious, generous and often way smarter than me. So when I asked them all who they would elect as their symbol of graceful aging, the overwhelmingly popular choice, Madonna, was disheartening. With all the choices we have, with all those beautiful and strong and powerful women

55 in their 40 and 50s (Oprah? Arianna Huffington? Kathryn Bigelow? Christiane Amanpour? And although I hate to include her, Sarah Palin?), the choice was the one woman who has elected to NOT age. Of course, the kicker is: artificial youth takes a lot maintenance. Maintenance takes a lot of time.

So, the more time you chase – the more time you waste.

Passage 2

In the second passage Barbara Ellen, writing in the Observer, responds to comments made by Rosie Huntington-Whiteley on beauty and ageing.

Rosie Huntington-Whiteley, the model, has been pondering that her career is limited, saying: "Looks go, and you fade." Well, good for Rosie – a canny young woman, looking for ways to maximise her earning potential, not feeling ashamed or anxious about the future, but instead thinking ahead, getting organised. Saying that, it would be a shame if the mantra "Looks go, and you fade" becomes

5   one size fits all, even for Rosie.

Who has ultimate control over the shelf life of female beauty? After all, "Looks go, and you fade" is really only applicable to model employability. It should never apply to non-models, but still in a weird way it does. This feeling, this pressure, that there is an ever-shortening shelf life for female looks, and, by association, psychosexual appeal.

10   Real lives played out against the sparkly but sinister sand of an egg timer, constantly falling: signifying, on the one hand, not just biology, but also judgment, gloating, sometimes even hate – on the other, dread and powerlessness. A pressure that taps into female vulnerability, making them feel that their very viability is determined by shadowy outside forces, and out of their control.

Of course Huntington-Whiteley was referring to her own profession – a tiny enclave mainly
15   comprised of very pretty thin young people, who do indeed usually have short shelf lives (though not all of them, as evidenced by the still-strutting Kate Moss, et al). Complaints about the fashion industry, and the toxic messages it sends out, rage on, and it's good and healthy they do. However, right now, in this flawed reality, sobbing over the short shelf lives of models seems as illogical as becoming upset that most sportspeople retire while still relatively youthful.

20   In this way, for the model, "Looks go, and you fade", is a practical career self-appraisal, akin to a footballer ruefully observing that he missed a goal because he's not as fast as he used to be. The difference being that men would respond to this, probably by yelling: "Too right, you useless overpaid prat!" You'd never get hordes of men wailing: "No, footballer, don't put yourself down, you're just displaying a different more mature, kind of footballing speed, and anyone who says
25   otherwise is ageist and sexist – and sport needs to change!"

This just wouldn't happen, and that's partly because women have vastly more to put up with on myriad levels, and thus are far more likely to support each other. But also because men would never feel that a footballer's legs directly relate to them – not in terms of getting older, or anything else.

They wouldn't say: "Oh no, that reminds me, my legs are ageing too!" Odd then that a model's, or
30   any other famous female's comment, about her looks fading, so often automatically becomes framed as an anguished lament applicable to all womankind – not just by paranoid women, but by those particular men who seek to keep them paranoid.

In truth, outside professional modelling, "You lose your looks, and you fade" is not a reasonable or logical mantra, rather, it's self-defeating and self-hating. This also applies to Huntington-Whiteley –
35   who, even once she's left modelling would doubtless be turning heads, nowhere near "fading", for years to come.

For a non-model, it should be even simpler. All a woman has to do is look around and notice that she's being suckered – that men also don't stay in the same physical shape as in their youth, and they don't seem too bothered. So, isn't it about time the specious concept of a shelf life specifically 40 for female beauty was similarly marginalised? This is what the smart females have known all along: that in all the important ways, female ageing is really not that different from the male variety. Not only that, perception is completely in women's own power, and always has been.

MARKS

DO NOT
WRITE IN
THIS
MARGIN

Practice Papers for SQA Exams: Higher English Practice Exam A

Passage 1 questions

1. Re-read lines 1–11.

    (a) Explain what the writer's attitude was towards 'beauty' at the age of 15.   **2**

    (b) Analyse how the writer's use of language in lines 2–11 reveals the wavering self-confidence she felt as a young woman. You should refer to such features as word choice, imagery, tone …   **4**

2. 'What an idiot I was.'
   Re-read lines 10–11. Analyse how the writer's use of language introduces this idea.   **2**

3. Re-read **paragraph 3**.
   Explain fully how the writer reacts to ageing.   **2**

4. Re-read lines 18–22.
   Explain fully what the writer means by the 'payback' of beauty.   **3**

5. Re-read lines 23–29.
   By referring to at least one example, analyse the writer's use of sentence structure to develop her argument.   **2**

6. By referring to at least two features of language in lines 30–40, analyse how the writer creates tone in this section.   **4**

7. Re-read lines 41–47.

    (a) In your own words, explain the contrast between Madonna and Jamie Lee Curtis.   **2**

    (b) Identify what the writer is jealous of.   **2**

8. Explain fully the irony of the choice of Madonna as a symbol of graceful ageing.   **2**

Question on both passages

9. Both writers express their views about ageing. Identify three key areas on which they agree and/or disagree. In your answer you should refer to both passages.   **5**

CfE Higher English

Practice Papers for SQA Exams

Exam A
Critical Reading

Duration – 1 hour 30 minutes

Total marks – 40

SECTION 1 – Scottish text – 20 marks

Read an extract from a Scottish text you have previously studied and attempt the questions.

Choose ONE text from either

Part A – Drama

or

Part B – Prose

or

Part C – Poetry

Attempt ALL the questions for your chosen text.

SECTION 2 – Critical essay – 20 marks

Attempt ONE question from the following genres – Drama, Prose, Poetry, Film and Television Drama, or Language.

Your answer must be on a different genre from that chosen in Section 1.

You should spend approximately 45 minutes on each section.

×Leckie
the education publisher
for Scotland

Section 1 – Scottish text – 20 marks

Choose one text from Drama, Prose or Poetry.

Read the text extract carefully and then attempt ALL the questions for your chosen text.

You should spend about 45 minutes on this section.

Text 1: Drama

If you choose this text you may not attempt a question on drama in Section 2.

Read the extract below and then attempt the following questions.

The Slab Boys by John Byrne

	Phil:	Hey, Spanks.
	Spanky:	What?
	Phil:	D'you think going off your head's catching?
	Spanky:	Eh? You mean like crabs or Jack's plooks?
5	Phil:	No, I'm serious … d'you think it is?
	Spanky:	How … who do you know that's off their head apart from everybody in … 's not your maw again, is it?
	Phil:	Yeh … they took her away last night.
	Spanky:	Christ …
10	Phil:	She wasn't all that bad either … not for her, that is. All she done was run up the street with her hair on fire and dive through the Co-operative windows.
	Spanky:	Thought that was normal down your way?
	Phil:	Yeh … but that's mostly the drink.
	Spanky:	How long'll she be in this time?
15	Phil:	Usual six weeks, I expect. First week tied to a rubber mattress, next five wired up to a generator.
	Spanky:	That's shocking.
	Phil:	That's when we get in to see her. Never knew us the last time. Kept looking at my old man and saying, 'Bless me, Father, for I have sinned.' Course, he's hopeless …
20		thinks it's like diphtheria or something. 'The doctors is doing their best, Annie … you'll be home soon. You taking that medicine they give you?' Medicine? Forty bennies crushed up in their cornflakes before they frogmarch them down to the 'Relaxation Classes', then it's back up to Cell Block Eleven for a kitbagful of capsules that gets them bleary-eyed enough for a chat with the consultant psychiatrist.
25	Spanky:	Not much of a holiday, is it?

	Phil:	Did I ever tell you about that convalescent home my maw and me went to? At the seaside … West Kilbride …
	Spanky:	Don't think so.
30	Phil:	I was about eleven at the time. Got took out of school to go with her … on the train. Some holiday. Place was chock-a-block with invalids … headcases soaking up the Clyde breeze before getting pitched back into the burly-burly of everyday life … Old-age pensioners, their skulls full of mush … single guys in their forties in too-short trousers and intellects to match … Middle-aged women in ankle socks roaming about looking for a letterbox to stick their postcards through. Abject bloody misery, it was. Dark-brown waxcloth you could see your face in … bathroom mirrors you couldn't. Lights out at half seven … no wireless, no comics, no nothing. Compulsory hymn-singing for everybody including the bedridden. Towels that tore the skin off your bum when you had a bath. Steamed fish on Sundays for a special treat …
35		
	Spanky:	Bleagh …
40	Phil:	The one highlight was a doll of about nineteen or twenty … There we all were sitting in our deckchairs in the sun lounge … curtains drawn … listening for the starch wearing out on the Matron's top lip … when this doll appears at the door, takes a coupla hops into the room, then turns this cartwheel right down the middle of the two rows of deckchairs … lands on her pins … daraaaaa! Brilliant! I started to laugh and got a skelp on the nut. The Matron was heeling …
45		
	Spanky:	About the skelp?
	Phil:	About the doll's cartwheel, stupid. Two old dears had to get carried up to their rooms with palpitations and a guy with a lavvy-brush moustache wet himself. It was the high spot of the holiday.
50	Spanky:	What was it got into her?
	Phil:	Who knows? Maybe she woke up that morning and seen her face in the waxcloth … remembered something … 'Christ, I'm alive!' Everybody hated her after that.
	Spanky:	Did you have much bother when they took your maw away last night?
	Phil:	No … they gave her a jag to knock her out.
55	Spanky:	Eh?
	Phil:	So they could sign her in as a 'Voluntary Patient'.

MARKS

Questions

1. By referring to two examples, explain how the dialogue in lines 1–17 creates black humour.

   4

2. By referring to lines 18–24, analyse how Byrne's use of language creates an effective portrayal of Phil's father.

   4

3. Explain fully how irony is created in lines 54–56.

   2

4. By referring to this extract and to elsewhere in the play, discuss the development of Phil's character.

   10

Text 2: Drama

If you choose this text you may not attempt a question on drama in Section 2.

Read the extract below and then attempt the following questions.

The Cheviot, the Stag and the Black, Black Oil by John McGrath

Enter PATRICK SELLAR and JAMES LOCH, looking very grand. SELLAR sniffs the bucket, ignores the women, who are huddled under their shawls.

SELLAR (*with a Lowland Scots accent*): Macdonald has told me, Mr Loch, there are three hundred illegal stills in Strathnaver at this very moment. They claim they have no money for
5   rent – clearly they have enough to purchase the barley. The whole thing smacks of a terrible degeneracy in the character of these aboriginals …

LOCH: The Marquis is not unaware of the responsibility his wealth places upon him, Mr Sellar. The future and lasting interest and honour of his family, as well as their immediate income, must be kept in view.

10 *They freeze. A phrase on the fiddle. Two SPEAKERS intervene between them, speak quickly to the audience.*

SPEAKER 1: Their immediate income was over £120,000 per annum. In those days that was quite a lot of money.

SPEAKER 2: George Granville, Second Marquis of Stafford, inherited a huge estate in Yorkshire; he
15   inherited another at Trentham in the Potteries; and he inherited a third at Lilleshall in Shropshire, that had coal-mines on it.

SPEAKER 1: He also inherited the Bridgewater Canal. And, on Loch's advice, he bought a large slice of the Liverpool-Manchester Railway.

SPEAKER 2: From his wife, Elizabeth Gordon, Countess of Sutherland, he acquired three-quarters of a
20   million acres of Sutherland – in which he wanted to invest some capital.

Another phrase on the fiddle: they slip away. SELLAR and LOCH re-animate.

SELLAR: The common people of Sutherland are a parcel of beggars with no stock, but cunning and lazy.

LOCH: They are living in a form of slavery to their own indolence. Nothing could be more at variance
25   with the general interests of society and the individual happiness of the people themselves, than the present state of Highland manners and customs. To be happy, the people must be productive.

SELLAR: They require to be thoroughly brought to the coast, where industry will pay, and to be convinced that they must worship industry or starve. The present enchantment which keeps them down must be broken.

30 LOCH: The coast of Sutherland abounds with many different kinds of fish. (*LOCH takes off his hat, and speaks directly to the audience.*) Believe it or not, Loch and Sellar actually used these words. (*Puts hat on again.*) Not only white fish, but herring too. With this in mind, His Lordship

is considering several sites for new villages on the East Coast – Culgower, Helmsdale, Golspie, Brora, Skelbo and Knockglass – Helmsdale in particular is a perfect natural harbour for a
35 fishing station. And there is said to be coal at Brora.

SELLAR: You will really not find this estate pleasant or profitable until by draining to your coast-line or by emigration you have got your mildewed districts cleared. They are just in that state of society for a savage country, such as the woods of Upper Canada – His Lordship should consider seriously the possibility of subsidising their departures. They might even be inclined
40 to carry a swarm of dependants with them.

LOCH: I gather you yourself Mr Sellar, have a scheme for a sheep-walk in this area.

SELLAR: The highlands of Scotland may sell £200,000 worth of lean cattle this year. The same ground, under the Cheviot, may produce as much as £900,000 worth of fine wool. The effects of such arrangements in advancing this estate in wealth, civilisation, comfort, industry, virtue and
45 happiness are palpable.

Fiddle in – Tune, 'Bonnie Dundee', quietly behind.

LOCH: Your offer for this area, Mr. Sellar, falls a little short of what I had hoped.

SELLAR: The present rents, when they can be collected, amount to no more than £142 per annum.

LOCH: Nevertheless, Mr Sellar, His Lordship will have to remove these people at considerable
50 expense.

SELLAR: To restock the land with sheep will cost considerably more.

LOCH: A reasonable rent would be £400 per annum.

SELLAR: There is the danger of disturbances to be taken into account. £300.

LOCH: You can depend on the Reverend David Mackenzie to deal with that. £375.

55 SELLAR: Mackenzie is a Highlander. £325.

LOCH: He has just been rewarded with the parish of Farr – £365.

SELLAR: I shall have to pay decent wages to my plain, honest, industrious South-country shepherds – £350.

LOCH: You're a hard man, Mr Sellar.

60 SELLAR: Cash.

LOCH: Done.

Questions

5. From the outset it is suggested that the men of the upper classes scorned the Highlanders. With reference to the stage directions and dialogue, analyse how this is revealed.

3

6. The action is paused so that the two speakers can reveal important information to the audience. With reference to at least two examples, explain how these details are relevant to a theme of the play.

3

7. Both Sellar and Loch appear very confident and certain in their view of the best course of action for those living in the North. With reference to one example of the dialogue between them, explain what is revealed about their proposals for the Highlands.

2

8. With close reference to the text, explain how McGrath highlights the ruthless approach taken by the upper classes at this time.

2

9. Throughout this play, McGrath allows the flow of events to be broken and interrupted through such features as sudden shifts in time or location, and songs or music. With reference to this extract and elsewhere in the play, discuss how this is used to develop theme.

10

Text 3: Drama

If you choose this text you may not attempt a question on drama in Section 2.

Read the extract below and then attempt the following questions.

Men Should Weep by Ena Lamont Stewart

In this extract from Act I, Scene 1, Lily and Maggie are in the kitchen, talking. Edie has just told them that a classmate has nits.

Edie drifts around.

	EDIE:	Ma, I canna find the flannel.
	MAGGIE:	Noo, whaur did I lay it doon? I did Christopher before he went oat ta-tas …
	LILY:	How you ever find onythin in this midden beats me.
5	MAGGIE:	Oh, here it is. It beats me tae sometimes. Edie, bend ower the sink till I scart some o this dirt aff ye.
	LILY:	D'ye no tak aff her dress tae wash her neck?
	MAGGIE:	Awa for Goad's sake! It's no Setterday nicht.
10	LILY:	She's old enough tae dae it hersel. The way you rin efter they weans is the bloomin limit. Nae wunner y're hauf-deid.
	MAGGIE:	I'm no hauf-deid!
	LILY:	Well, ye look it.
	MAGGIE:	I canna help ma looks any mair than you can help yours.
	LILY:	The difference is, I try. Heve ye looked in the mirror since ye rose the morn?
15	MAGGIE:	I havena time tae look in nae mirrors and neither would you if ye'd a hoose an a man an five weans.
	LILY:	Yin o they days your lovin Johnnie's gonna tak a look at whit he married and it'll be ta-ta Maggie.
20	MAGGIE:	My lovin Johnnie's still ma loving Johnnie, whitever I look like. (*Finishing off Edie*) Comb yer hair noo, Edie … I wonder whaur it's gottae?

They both look for the comb.

	EDIE:	I canna find it Ma. Auntie Lily, could you lend us yours?
	LILY:	(*starting to look in her bag, then thinking better of it*) I didna bring it the night.
	EDIE:	I've nae beasts, Auntie Lily.
25	LILY:	Jist the same, I didnae bring it. Scram aff tae yer bed.
	MAGGIE:	Aye, Edie, get aff afore yer feyther comes in frae the library.
	LILY:	Oh, is that whaur he is?

Edie takes down from wall key to the outside WC and goes off.

MAGGIE: Whaur else wad he be? He disna go tae the pubs noo.

30 LILY: Oh aye! I'd forgot he'd went TT.

MAGGIE: Ye ken fine he's TT; but ye jist canna resist a dig at him. He hasna been inside a pub since Marina was born.

LILY: That's whit he tells you, onywey.

MAGGIE: My the tongue you have on you, Lily; it's a pity ye had yon disappointment; ye might
35 hev been real happy wi the right man and a couple weans.

Lily holds out her sleeve and laughs up it.

LILY: Dae you think you're happy?

MAGGIE: Aye! I'm happy!

LILY: In this midden?

40 MAGGIE: Ye canna help havin a midden o a hoose when there's kids under yer feet a day. I dae the best I can.

LILY: I ken ye do. I'd gie it up as hopeless. Nae hot water. Nae place tae dry the weans' clothes, nae money. If John wad gie hissel a shake …

MAGGIE: You leave John alane! He does his best for us.

45 LILY: No much o a best. OK. OK. Keep yer wig on! Ye're that touchy ye'd think ye wis jist new merriet. I believe ye still love him!

MAGGIE: Aye. I still love John. And whit's more, he loves me.

LILY: Ye ought tae get yer photies took and send them tae the Sunday papers! 'Twenty-five years merriet and I still love ma husband. Is this a record?'

50 MAGGIE: I'm sorry for you, Lily. I'm right sorry for you.

LILY: We're quits then.

MAGGIE: Servin dirty hulkin brutes o men in a Coocaddens pub.

LILY: Livin in a slum and slavin efter a useless man an his greetin weans.

MAGGIE: They're my weans! I'm workin for ma ain.

55 LILY: I'm paid for ma work.

MAGGIE: So'm I! No in wages – I'm paid wi love. (*Pause*) And when did you last have a man's airms roon ye?

LILY: Men! I'm wantin nae man's airms roon me. They're a dirty beasts.

MAGGIE: Lily, yer mind's twisted. You canna see a man as a man. Ye've got them a lumped
60 thegether. You're daft!

LILY: You're saft! You think yer man's wonderful and yer weans is a angels.

MARKS

DO NOT
WRITE IN
THIS
MARGIN

Practice Papers for SQA Exams: Higher English Practice Exam A

Questions

10. Referring closely to the extract, explain why Lily is frustrated with Maggie in lines 1–27.

2

11. By referring closely to this extract, explain what Maggie's responses show about her character and/or her feelings about her life.

4

12. Referring closely to this extract, analyse Lily's attitudes to men and/or love.

4

13. Lamont Stewart uses the relationship between the sisters Maggie and Lily to develop both characters. Referring to this extract and the play as a whole, discuss how the relationship between Maggie and Lily adds to your appreciation of the play. You should refer to **both** Maggie and Lily in your answer.

10

Text 1: Prose

If you choose this text you may not attempt a question on prose in Section 2.

Read the extract below and then attempt the following questions.

Mother and Son by Iain Crichton Smith

His mind now seemed gradually to be clearing up, and he was beginning to judge his own
actions and hers. Everything was clearing up: it was one of his moments. He turned round on his
chair from a sudden impulse and looked at her intensely. He had done this very often before, had
tried to cow her into submission: but she had always laughed at him. Now however he was looking

5   at her as if he had never seen her before. Her mouth was open and there were little crumbs upon
her lower lip. Her face had sharpened itself into a birdlike quickness: she seemed to be pecking at
the bread with a sharp beak in the same way as she pecked cruelly at his defences. He found himself
considering her as if she were some kind of animal. Detachedly he thought: how can this thing make
my life a hell for me? What is she anyway? She's been ill for ten years: that doesn't excuse her. She's

10 breaking me up so that even if she dies I won't be any good for anyone. But what if she's
pretending? What if there is nothing wrong with her? At this a rage shook him so great that he
flung his half-consumed cigarette in the direction of the fire in an abrupt, savage gesture. Out of the
silence he heard a bus roaring past the window, splashing over the puddles. That would be the boys
going to the town to enjoy themselves. He shivered inside his loneliness and then rage took hold of

15 him again. How he hated her! This time his gaze concentrated itself on her scraggy neck, rising like a
hen's out of her plain white nightgown. He watched her chin wagging up and down: it was stained
with jam and flecked with one or two crumbs. His sense of loneliness closed round him, so that
he felt as if he were on a boat on the limitless ocean, just as his house was on a limitless moorland.
There was a calm, unspeaking silence, while the rain beat like a benediction on the roof. He walked

20 over to the bed, took the tray from her as she held it out to him. He had gone in answer to words
which he hadn't heard, so hedged was he in his own thoughts.

'Remember to clean the tray tomorrow,' she said. He walked back with the tray fighting back the
anger that swept over him carrying the rubbish and debris of his mind in its wake. He turned back to
the bed. His mind was in a turmoil of hate, so that he wanted to smash the cup, smash the furniture,

25 smash the house. He kept his hands clenched, he the puny and unimaginative. He would show her,
avenge her insults with his unintelligent hands. There was the bed, there was his mother. He walked
over.

She was asleep, curled up in the warmth with the bitter, bitter smile upon her face. He stood there
for a long moment while an equally bitter smile curled up the edge of his lips. Then he walked to the

30 door, opened it, and stood listening to the rain.

Questions

14. Look at lines 1–9.
At the beginning of the extract John, the main character, has a revelation.
Explain what the revelation is and analyse how it is conveyed through the writer's use of language.

4

15. By referring closely to lines 11–25, analyse how the writer's use of language is effective in making the reader aware of John's attitude towards his mother.

4

16. Evaluate the effectiveness of lines 25–30 as a conclusion to the story. Your answer should deal with ideas and/or language.

2

17. Repression of the individual is a common theme in Iain Crichton Smith's short stories. By referring to this and at least one other short story by Crichton Smith, discuss how he develops this theme.

10

Text 2: Prose

If you choose this text you may not attempt a question on prose in Section 2.

Read the extract below and then attempt the following questions.

The Eye of the Hurricane by George Mackay Brown

Chapter Five got wedged in some deep rut of my mind. I sat most of a morning with my black biro poised over the writing pad. The phrases and sentences that presented themselves were dull, flaccid, affected. I looked blankly at the crucifix on the wall, but the Word that spanned all history with meaning was only a tortured image. The words I offered to the Word were added
5 insults, a few more random thorns for the crown. I scored out everything I had written since breakfast-time.

It flatters us writers to think of ourselves as explorers, probing into seas that have never been mapped, or charted with only a few broken lines. But the spacious days of 'Here be Whales', cherubs puffing gales from the four quarters, mid-ocean mermaids, are gone for ever. There is nothing new
10 to find; every headland has been rounded, every smallest ocean current observed, the deepest seas plumbed. Chaucer, Cervantes, Tolstoy, Proust charted human nature so well that really little is left for a novelist like myself to do. For the most part we voyage along old trade routes, in rusty bottoms; and though we carry cargoes of small interest to anyone – coal or wheat – we should be glad that hungry cupboards here and there are stored with bread and there are fires burning in cold snow
15 villages of the north.

Miriam came in without knocking. 'The captain's had a terrible night, the poor man,' she said. 'There's six broken cups in the sideboard. The rug's saturated. He was trying to make himself a pot of tea, and his hands all spasms. He never so much as closed an eye.' She had her coat on to go home for, as I said, she only works in the house mornings.

20 'He wanted me to get him more rum,' I said, 'two bottles, but I wouldn't do it. '

'You were right,' said Miriam.

'He's going to put me out on the road,' I said.

'Don't worry about that,' said Miriam. 'That was the devil talking, not the poor captain at all. Once he's better he won't know a thing he's said this past day or two.'

25 'I'm glad,' I said, 'because I like it here.'

'It must be lonely for you,' said Miriam. 'You should come to our Joy Hour some Thursday evening. There's choruses and readings from the Good Book, and O, everybody's so happy!' Her eyes drifted uneasily over the crucifix and the Virgin.

I said nothing.

30 'I'm pleased with you,' said Miriam, 'for saying No to him. He'll suffer, but his bout'll be over all the sooner. Tomorrow, or the day after, he'll be his old self again.'

There came a violent double thump on the ceiling. 'Get off, you bitch!' roared Captain Stevens. 'What are you talking to that pansy for? This is my house. Away home with you!'

MARKS

DO NOT
WRITE IN
THIS
MARGIN

Practice Papers for SQA Exams: Higher English Practice Exam A

35   Miriam lowered her voice. 'Be firm for one day more,' she whispered. 'He'll try to wheedle you in the afternoon for sure. I know him. Just keep saying No.'

'I will,' I said.

'If only Robert Jansen and Stony Hackland keep away,' whispered Miriam. 'You mustn't let them in. If they come to the door, just send them packing. Be very firm.'

'Who are they?' I said.

40   'Seamen who used to sail in his ships,' she whispered. 'They carry the drink in to him whenever he has a bout.'

'They won't get in,' I said. When she smiled her plain little face shone for a moment like one of Botticelli's angels.

If she had been born in a Breton village, I thought, she would be a devout Catholic girl, and rosary
45   and image and candle – that she shied away from with such horror – would be the gateway to her dearest treasures and delights. As it was, she merely touched the hem of Christ's garment in passing.

Questions

18. By referring closely to two examples from lines 1–5, analyse how Mackay Brown conveys Barclay's feelings about his writing.   **4**

19. Mackay Brown uses the metaphor of the writer as sailor in lines 7–15. By referring closely to the extract, explain what he means by his comparison of:

(i)   The writer as explorer

(ii)   The writer as voyager of 'old trade routes'.   **4**

20. By referring closely to one example of Mackay Brown's description of Miriam, explain how he conveys her religious conviction.   **2**

21. Alcohol and its effects is a frequent theme in George Mackay Brown's writing. With reference to this story and to at least one other by George Mackay Brown, discuss how this theme is developed.   **10**

Text 3: Prose

If you choose this text you may not attempt a question on prose in Section 2.

Read the extract below and then attempt the following questions.

The Strange Case of Dr Jekyll and Mr Hyde by Robert Louis Stevenson

In this extract, Mr Utterson receives a visitor.

Mr. Utterson was sitting by his fireside one evening after dinner, when he was surprised to receive a visit from Poole.

'Bless me, Poole, what brings you here?' he cried; and then taking a second look at him, 'What ails you?' he added; 'is the doctor ill?'

5   'Mr. Utterson,' said the man, 'there is something wrong.'

'Take a seat, and here is a glass of wine for you,' said the lawyer. 'Now, take your time, and tell me plainly what you want.'

'You know the doctor's ways, sir,' replied Poole, 'and how he shuts himself up. Well, he's shut up again in the cabinet; and I don't like it, sir – I wish I may die if I like it. Mr. Utterson, sir, I'm afraid.'

10   'Now, my good man,' said the lawyer, 'be explicit. What are you afraid of?'

'I've been afraid for about a week,' returned Poole, doggedly disregarding the question, 'and I can bear it no more.'

The man's appearance amply bore out his words; his manner was altered for the worse; and except for the moment when he had first announced his terror, he had not once looked the
15   lawyer in the face. Even now, he sat with the glass of wine untasted on his knee, and his eyes directed to a corner of the floor. 'I can bear it no more,' he repeated.

'Come,' said the lawyer, 'I see you have some good reason, Poole; I see there is something seriously amiss. Try to tell me what it is.'

'I think there's been foul play,' said Poole, hoarsely.

20   'Foul play!' cried the lawyer, a good deal frightened and rather inclined to be irritated in consequence. 'What foul play! What does the man mean?'

'I daren't say, sir,' was the answer; 'but will you come along with me and see for yourself?'

Mr. Utterson's only answer was to rise and get his hat and greatcoat; but he observed with wonder the greatness of the relief that appeared upon the butler's face, and perhaps with no less,
25   that the wine was still untasted when he set it down to follow.

It was a wild, cold, seasonable night of March, with a pale moon, lying on her back as though the wind had tilted her, and flying wrack of the most diaphanous and lawny texture. The wind made talking difficult, and flecked the blood into the face. It seemed to have swept the streets unusually bare of passengers, besides; for Mr. Utterson thought he had never seen that part of
30   London so deserted. He could have wished it otherwise; never in his life had he been conscious of so sharp a wish to see and touch his fellow-creatures; for struggle as he might, there was borne in upon his mind a crushing anticipation of calamity. The square, when they got there, was full of wind and dust, and the thin trees in the garden were lashing themselves along the railing. Poole,

who had kept all the way a pace or two ahead, now pulled up in the middle of the pavement,
35 and in spite of the biting weather, took off his hat and mopped his brow with a red pocket-handkerchief. But for all the hurry of his coming, these were not the dews of exertion that he wiped away, but the moisture of some strangling anguish; for his face was white and his voice, when he spoke, harsh and broken.

'Well, sir,' he said, 'here we are, and God grant there be nothing wrong.'

40   'Amen, Poole,' said the lawyer.

Thereupon the servant knocked in a very guarded manner; the door was opened on the chain; and a voice asked from within, 'Is that you, Poole?'

'It's all right,' said Poole. 'Open the door.'

The hall, when they entered it, was brightly lighted up; the fire was built high; and about
45 the hearth the whole of the servants, men and women, stood huddled together like a flock of sheep. At the sight of Mr. Utterson, the housemaid broke into hysterical whimpering; and the cook, crying out 'Bless God! it's Mr. Utterson,' ran forward as if to take him in her arms.

'What, what? Are you all here?' said the lawyer peevishly. 'Very irregular, very unseemly; your master would be far from pleased.'

50   'They're all afraid,' said Poole.

Blank silence followed, no one protesting; only the maid lifted her voice and now wept loudly.

'Hold your tongue!' Poole said to her, with a ferocity of accent that testified to his own jangled nerves; and indeed, when the girl had so suddenly raised the note of her lamentation, they had all
55 started and turned towards the inner door with faces of dreadful expectation. 'And now,' continued the butler, addressing the knife-boy, 'reach me a candle, and we'll get this through hands at once.' And then he begged Mr. Utterson to follow him, and led the way to the back garden.

Questions

22. Look at lines 1–19.
     By referring to at least **two** examples, analyse how the writer uses language to convey Poole's emotions or feelings.   **4**

23. Look at lines 26–38.
     By referring to at least **two** examples, analyse how the writer uses language to create a mood or atmosphere of unease.   **4**

24. Look at lines 41–57.
     By referring to **two** examples, analyse how the writer uses language to suggest the feelings of the servants.   **2**

25. By referring to this extract and to elsewhere in the novel, discuss how the writer makes effective use of setting to explore the central concerns of the text.   **10**

Text 4: Prose

If you choose this text you may not attempt a question on prose in Section 2.

Read the extract below and then attempt the following questions.

Sunset Song by Lewis Grassic Gibbon

In this extract, which is from Part III (Seed-Time), Chris sets out to rescue her horses from lightning.

It was then, in a lull of the swishing, she heard the great crack of thunder that opened the worst
storm that had struck the Howe in years. It was far up, she thought, and yet so close Blawearie's
stones seemed falling about her ears, she half-scrambled erect. Outside the night flashed,
flashed and flashed, she saw Kinraddie lighted up and fearful, then it was dark again, but not

5 quiet. In the sky outside a great beast moved and purred and scrabbled, and then suddenly it
opened its mouth again and again there was the roar, and the flash of its claws, tearing at the
earth, it seemed neither house nor hall could escape. The rain had died away, it was listening –
quiet in the next lull, and then Chris heard her Auntie crying to her *Are you all right, Chrissie?*
and cried back she was fine. Funny Uncle Tam had cried never a word, maybe he was still in the

10 sulks, he'd plumped head-first in when he'd heard of the old woman that Semple was sending to
help keep house in Blawearie. They were off to Auchterless the morn, and oh! she'd be glad to see
them go, she'd enough to do and to think without fighting relations.

The thunder clamoured again, and then she suddenly sat shivering, remembering something –
Clyde and old Bob and Bess, all three of them were out in the ley field there, they weren't taken

15 in till late in the year. Round the ley field was barbed wire, almost new, that father had put up in
the Spring, folk said it was awful for drawing the lightning, maybe it had drawn it already.

She was out of bed in the next flash, it was a ground flash, it hung and it seemed to wait, sizzling,
outside the window as she pulled on stockings and vest and knickers and ran to the door and
cried up *Uncle Tam, Uncle Tam, we must take in the horses!* He didn't hear, she waited, the

20 house shook and dirled in another great flash, then Auntie was crying something, Chris stood as
if she couldn't believe her own ears. Uncle Tam was feared at the lightning, he wouldn't go out,
she herself had best go back to her bed and wait for the morning.

She didn't wait to hear more than that, but ran to the kitchen and groped about for the box of
matches and lighted the little lamp, it with the glass bowl, and then found the littlest lantern and

25 lighted that, though her fingers shook and she almost dropped the funnel. Then she found old
shoes and a raincoat, it had been father's and came near to her ankles, and she caught up the
lamp and opened the kitchen door and closed it quick behind her just as the sky banged again
and a flare of sheet lightning came flowing down the hill-side, frothing like the incoming tide at
Dunnottar. It dried up, leaving her blinded, her eyes ached and she almost dropped the lantern

30 again.

In the byre the kye were lowing fit to raise the roof, even the stirks were up and stamping about
in their stalls. But they were safe enough unless the biggings were struck, it was the horses she'd
to think of.

MARKS

DO NOT
WRITE IN
THIS
MARGIN

Practice Papers for SQA Exams: Higher English Practice Exam A

35 Right athwart her vision the haystacks shone up like great pointed pyramids a blinding moment, vanished, darkness complete and heavy flowed back on her again, the lantern-light seeking to pierce it like the bore of a drill. Still the rain held off as she stumbled and cried down the sodden fields. Then she saw that the barbed wire was alive, the lightning ran and glowed along it, a living thing, a tremulous, vibrant serpent that spat and glowed and hid its head and quivered again to sight. If the horses stood anywhere near to that they were finished, she cried to them again and

40 stopped and listened, it was deathly still in the night between the bursts of the thunder, so still that she heard the grass she had pressed underfoot crawl and quiver erect again a step behind her. Then, as the thunder moved away – it seemed to break and roar down the rightward hill, above the Manse and Kinraddie Mains, – something tripped her, she fell and the lantern-flame flared up and seemed almost to vanish; but she righted it, almost sick though she was because

45 of the wet, warm thing that her body and face lay upon.

Questions

26. Referring closely to the extract, analyse one example of the imagery used in lines 1–12 to convey the ferocity of the storm. **2**

27. By referring to at least one example from lines 17–30, explain how the writer's sentence structure conveys Chris' panic. **2**

28. Referring closely to the extract, explain Chris' opinion of Uncle Tam. Give at least two examples to support your answer. **2**

29. By referring closely to lines 31–45, analyse how Grassic Gibbon conveys the danger of the situation Chris is in. **4**

30. Chris is both independent and practical. By referring to this extract and elsewhere in the novel, discuss how Grassic Gibbon conveys these aspects of Chris' personality. **10**

Text 5: Prose

If you choose this text you may not attempt a question on prose in Section 2.

Read the extract below and then attempt the following questions.

The Cone-Gatherers by Robin Jenkins

In this extract, from the opening scene of the novel, Neil and Calum are returning to their hut after a day of cone gathering.

'This wood,' said Neil, 'it's to be cut down in the spring.'

'I ken that,' whimpered Calum.

'There's no sense in being sorry for trees,' said his brother, 'when there are more men than trees being struck down. You can make use of a tree, but what use is a dead man? Trees can be replaced
5 in time. Aren't we ourselves picking the cones for seed? Can you replace dead men?'

He knew that the answer was: yes, the dead men would be replaced. After a war the population of the world increased. But none would be replaced by him. To look after his brother, he had never got married, though once he had come very near it: that memory often revived to turn his heart melancholy.

10 'We'd better get down,' he muttered. 'You lead the way, Calum, as usual.'

'Sure, I'll lead the way, Neil.'

Delighted to be out of this bondage of talk, Calum set his bag of cones firmly round his shoulders, and with consummate confidence and grace began the descent through the inner night of the great tree. Not once, all the long way down, was he at a loss. He seemed to find holds by instinct, and
15 patiently guided his brother's feet on to them. Alone, Neil would have been in trouble; he was as dependent on his brother as if he was blind; and Calum made no attempt to make his superiority as climber compensate for his inferiority as talker. Every time he caught his brother's foot and set it on a safe branch it was an act of love. Once, when Neil slid down quicker than he meant and stamped on Calum's fingers, the latter uttered no complaint but smiled in the dark and sucked the bruise.

20 It was different as soon as they were on the ground. Neil immediately strode out, and Calum, hurrying to keep close behind, often stumbled. Gone were the balance and sureness he had shown in the tree. If there was a hollow or a stone or a stick, he would trip over it. He never grumbled at such mishaps, but scrambled up at once, anxious only not to be a hindrance to his brother.

When they reached the beginning of the ride that divided a cluster of Norway spruces, Neil threw
25 over his shoulder the usual warning: to leave the snares alone, whether there were rabbits in them half throttled or hungry or frantic; and Calum gave the usual sad guilty promise.

During their very first day in the wood they had got into trouble with the gamekeeper. Calum had released two rabbits from snares. Neil had been angry and had prophesied trouble. It had come next evening when Duror, the big keeper, had been waiting for them outside their hut. His rage had been
30 quiet but intimidating. Neil had said little in reply, but had faced up to the gun raised once or twice to emphasise threats. Calum, demoralised as always by hatred, had cowered against the hut, hiding his face.

Duror had sworn that he would seize the first chance to hound them out of the wood; they were in it, he said, sore against his wish. Neil therefore had made Calum swear by an oath which he didn't
35 understand but which to Neil was the most sacred on earth: by their dead mother, he had to swear never again to interfere with the snares. He could not remember his mother, who had died soon after he was born.

Now this evening, as he trotted down the ride, he prayed by a bright star above that there would be no rabbits squealing in pain. If there were, he could not help them; he would have to rush past, tears
40 in his eyes, fingers in his ears.

Several rabbits were caught, all dead except one; it pounded on the grass and made choking noises. Neil had passed it without noticing. Calum moaned in dismay at this dilemma of either displeasing his brother or forsaking a hurt creature. He remembered his solemn promise; he remembered too the cold hatred of the gamekeeper; he knew that the penalty for interfering might be expulsion from
45 this wood where he loved to work; but above all he shared the suffering of the rabbit.

Questions

31. Explain how Neil's speech and actions in this extract reveal the hierarchy between the two brothers.　　　**3**

32. 'Delighted to be out of this bondage of talk'.
Explain fully what the writer means by this.　　　**2**

33. By referring closely to lines 12–23, analyse how the writer's use of language highlights the contrast between Calum in the tree and on the ground.　　　**3**

34. By referring closely to at least one example from lines 41–45, explain how the writer's use of language reveals Calum's inner turmoil.　　　**2**

35. *The Cone-Gatherers* is set during the Second World War. With reference to such features as setting, characterisation and narrative in this extract and elsewhere in the novel, explain the impact of war.　　　**10**

Text 1: Poetry

If you choose this text you may not attempt a question on poetry in Section 2.

Read the extract below and then attempt the following questions.

A Poet's Welcome to his Love-Begotten Daughter by Robert Burns

Thou's welcome, wean; mishanter fa' me,

If thoughts o' thee, or yet thy mamie,

Shall ever daunton me or awe me,

My bonie lady,

5   Or if I blush when thou shalt ca' me

Tyta or daddie.

Tho' now they ca' me fornicator,

An' tease my name in kintry clatter,

The mair they talk, I'm kent the better,

10   E'en let them clash;

An auld wife's tongue's a feckless matter

To gie ane fash.

Welcome! my bonie, sweet, wee dochter,

Tho' ye come here a wee unsought for,

15   And tho' your comin' I hae fought for,

Baith kirk and queir;

Yet, by my faith, ye're no unwrought for,

That I shall swear!

Wee image o' my bonie Betty,

20   As fatherly I kiss and daut thee,

As dear, and near my heart I set thee

Wi' as gude will

As a' the priests had seen me get thee

That's out o' hell.

25 Sweet fruit o' mony a merry dint,

My funny toil is now a' tint,

Sin' thou came to the warl' asklent,

Which fools may scoff at;

In my last plack thy part's be in't

30 The better ha'f o't.

Tho' I should be the waur bestead,

Thou's be as braw and bienly clad,

And thy young years as nicely bred

Wi' education,

35 As ony brat o' wedlock's bed,

In a' thy station.

Lord grant that thou may aye inherit

Thy mither's person, grace, an' merit,

An' thy poor, worthless daddy's spirit,

40 Without his failins,

'Twill please me mair to see thee heir it,

Than stockit mailens.

For if thou be what I wad hae thee,

And tak the counsel I shall gie thee,

45 I'll never rue my trouble wi' thee,

The cost nor shame o't,

But be a loving father to thee,

And brag the name o't.

MARKS

DO NOT
WRITE IN
THIS
MARGIN

Practice Papers for SQA Exams: Higher English Practice Exam A

Questions

36. With reference to **two** examples, explain Burns' attitude to his daughter in lines 1–6. **4**

37. How does the attitude of the community contrast with Burns' own attitude? Refer to at least one example from lines 1–24 to support your answer. **2**

38. Burns is open in his writing about sexual matters. With reference to **two** examples, explain how he does this and what this reveals about his attitude to sexual liaisons. **4**

39. Burns was outspoken in his criticism of repressive religion – Calvinism in particular. With reference to this and one other poem by Burns, discuss how he presents religion and demonstrates this criticism. **10**

Text 2: Poetry

If you choose this text you may not attempt a question on poetry in Section 2.

Read the extract below and then attempt the following questions.

In Mrs Tilscher's Class by Carol Ann Duffy

You could travel up the Blue Nile

with your finger, tracing the route

while Mrs Tilscher chanted the scenery.

Tana. Ethiopia. Khartoum. Aswan.

5   That for an hour, then a skittle of milk

and the chalky Pyramids rubbed into dust.

A window opened with a long pole,

The laugh of a bell swung by a running child.

This was better than home. Enthralling books.

10   The classroom glowed like a sweet shop.

Sugar paper. Coloured shapes. Brady and Hindley

faded, like the faint, uneasy smudge of a mistake.

Mrs Tilscher loved you. Some mornings, you found

she'd left a good gold star by your name.

15   The scent of a pencil, slowly, carefully, shaved.

A xylophone's nonsense heard from another form.

Over the Easter term, the inky tadpoles changed

from commas into exclamation marks. Three frogs

hopped in the playground, freed by a dunce,

20   followed by a line of kids, jumping and croaking

away from the lunch queue. A rough boy

told you how you were born. You kicked him, but stared

at your parents, appalled, when you got back home.

MARKS

DO NOT
WRITE IN
THIS
MARGIN

Practice Papers for SQA Exams: Higher English Practice Exam A

That feverish July, the air tasted of electricity.

25   A tangible alarm made you always untidy, hot,

fractious under the heavy, sexy sky. You asked her

how you were born and Mrs Tilscher smiled,

then turned away. Reports were handed out.

You ran through the gates, impatient to be grown,

30   as the sky split open into a thunderstorm.

Questions

40. Look at lines 1–16.
By referring to the poet's language, show how a positive impression of Mrs Tilscher and her classroom is presented to the reader.   **6**

41. Look at lines 17–18.
'... the inky tadpoles changed
from commas into exclamation marks.'
Evaluate the effectiveness of the poet's use of word choice and/or imagery in these lines.   **2**

42. Look at lines 24–30.
Analyse the use of language to convey the sense of restlessness felt by the speaker.   **2**

43. By referring to this poem and to at least one other poem by Carol Ann Duffy, show how she explores a darker side of growing up in her work.   **10**

Text 3: Poetry

If you choose this text you may not attempt a question on poetry in Section 2.

Read the extract below and then attempt the following questions.

Last Supper by Liz Lochhead

She is getting good and ready to renounce

his sweet flesh.

Not just for lent. (For

Ever)

5   But meanwhile she is assembling the ingredients

for their last treat, the proper

feast (after all

didn't they always

eat together

10   rather more than rather well?)

So here she is tearing foliage, scrambling

the salad, maybe lighting candles even, anyway

stepping back to admire the effect of

the table she's made (and oh yes now

15   will have to lie on) the silverware,

the nicely al-

dente vegetables, the cooked goose.

He could be depended on to bring the bottle

plus betrayal with a kiss.

20   Already she was imagining it done with, this feast, and

exactly

what kind of leftover hash she'd make of it

among friends, when it was just

The Girls, when those three met again.

25 What very good soup

she could render from the bones,

then something substantial, something extra

tasty if not elegant.

Yes, there they'd be cackling around the cauldron,

30 spitting out the gristlier bits

of his giblets;

gnawing on the knucklebone of some

intricate irony;

getting grave and dainty at the

35 petit-gout mouthfuls of reported speech.

'That's rich!' they'd splutter,

munching the lies, fat and sizzling as sausages.

Then they'd sink back

gorged on truth

40 and their own savage integrity,

sleek on it all, preening

like corbies, their bright eyes blinking

satisfied

till somebody would get hungry

45 and go hunting again.

Questions

44. In stanza 1, we are introduced to the narrator who is preparing for the 'last supper' with her lover. With close reference to this stanza, analyse how Lochhead conveys the conflict of emotions felt.

4

45. Look closely at stanza 2. Examine the use of poetic techniques in clarifying the writer's meaning.

2

46. Evaluate the effectiveness of Lochhead's use of extended metaphor in the final stanza of the poem.

4

47. In many of Lochhead's poems she examines the position and role held by women. With reference to this poem and at least one other poem by Lochhead, discuss how this theme is explored in her work.

10

Text 4: Poetry

If you choose this text you may not attempt a question on poetry in Section 2.

Read the extract below and then attempt the following questions.

Basking Shark by **Norman MacCaig**

To stub an oar on a rock where none should be,

To have it rise with a slounge out of the sea

Is a thing that happened once (too often) to me.

But not too often – though enough. I count as gain

5 That once I met, on a sea tin-tacked with rain,

That roomsized monster with a matchbox brain.

He displaced more than water. He shoggled me

Centuries back – this decadent townee

Shook on a wrong branch of his family tree.

10 Swish up the dirt and, when it settles, a spring

Is all the clearer. I saw me, in one fling,

Emerging from the slime of everything.

So who's the monster? The thought made me grow pale

For twenty seconds while, sail after sail,

15 The tall fin slid away and then the tail.

MARKS

DO NOT
WRITE IN
THIS
MARGIN

Practice Papers for SQA Exams: Higher English Practice Exam A

Questions

48. With reference to the text, explain fully MacCaig's contradictory feelings about his encounter with the basking shark in **stanzas 1** and **2**.

2

49. By referring to lines 1–6, analyse how MacCaig's use of poetic technique conveys an effective depiction of the basking shark.

3

50. Look at **stanza 3**.
'He displaced more than water.'
Explain fully what the poet means by this.

2

51. Evaluate the effectiveness of **stanza 5** as a conclusion to the poem. Your answer should deal with ideas and/or language.

3

52. By referring to this poem and at least one other by Norman MacCaig, discuss his use of nature and the natural world to develop theme in his work.

10

Text 5: Poetry

If you choose this text you may not attempt a question on poetry in Section 2.

Read the extract below and then attempt the following questions.

An Autumn Day by Sorley MacLean

On that slope

on an autumn day,

the shells soughing about my ears

and six dead men at my shoulder,

5 dead and stiff – and frozen were it not for the heat –

as if they were waiting for a message.

When the screech came

out of the sun,

out of an invisible throbbing,

10 the flame leaped and the smoke climbed

and surged every way:

blinding of eyes, splitting of hearing.

And after it, the six men dead

the whole day:

15 among the shells snoring

in the morning,

and again at midday and in the evening.

In the sun, which was so indifferent,

so white and painful;

20 on the sand which was so comfortable,

easy and kindly;

and under the stars of Africa,

jewelled and beautiful.

MARKS

DO NOT
WRITE IN
THIS
MARGIN

Practice Papers for SQA Exams: Higher English Practice Exam A

One Election took them

25 and did not take me,

without asking us

which was better or worse:

it seemed as devilishly indifferent

as the shells.

30 Six men dead at my shoulder on an Autumn day.

Questions

53. What is MacLean describing in lines 7–12? Explain your answer with reference to the text.

2

54. Comment, with reference to the text, on how MacLean's language and structure in lines 24–29 reflect the injustice of war and life in general.

4

55. Comment on the effectiveness of the final line as a conclusion to the poem.

4

56. Time is very important in Sorley MacLean's poetry. With close reference to this poem and to another poem or poems by MacLean, discuss how he develops this theme.

10

Text 6: Poetry

If you choose this text you may not attempt a question on poetry in Section 2.

Read the extract below and then attempt the following questions.

An extract from *Nil Nil* by Don Paterson

From the top, then, the zenith, the silent footage:

McGrandle, majestic in ankle-length shorts,

his golden hair shorn to an open book, sprinting

the length of the park for the long hoick forward,

5 his balletic toe-poke nearly bursting the roof

of the net; a shaky pan to the Erskine St End

where a plague of grey bonnets falls out of the clouds.

But ours is a game of two halves, and this game

the semi they went on to lose; from here

10 it's all down, from the First to the foot of the Second,

McGrandle, Visocchi and Spankie detaching

like bubbles to speed the descent into pitch-sharing,

pay-cuts, pawned silver, the Highland Division,

the absolute sitters ballooned over open goals,

15 the dismal nutmegs, the scores so obscene

no respectable journal will print them; though one day

Farquhar's spectacular bicycle-kick

will earn him a name-check in Monday's obituaries.

Besides the one setback – the spell of giant-killing

20 in the Cup (Lochee Violet, then Aberdeen Bon Accord,

the deadlock with Lochee Harp finally broken

by Farquhar's own-goal in the replay)

nothing inhibits the fifty-year slide

into Sunday League, big tartan flasks,

25 open hatchbacks parked squint behind goal-nets,

the half-time satsuma, the dog on the pitch,

then the Boys' Club, sponsored by Skelly Assurance,

then Skelly Dry Cleaners, then nobody;

stud-harrowed pitches with one-in-five inclines,

30 grim fathers and perverts with Old English Sheepdogs

lining the touch, moaning softly.

Questions

57. How effective do you find the title in conveying the main ideas of the poem?　　**2**

58. By referring closely to lines 1–7, analyse the use of language to portray the early era of the football club.　　**4**

59. Analyse the effectiveness of the poet's description of the declining club in lines 10–23 through:

(a) sentence structure　　**2**

(b) word choice.　　**2**

60. By referring to this poem and at least one other by Don Paterson, discuss the poet's use of structure to develop theme in his work.　　**10**

[END OF SECTION 1]

Section 2 – Critical essay – 20 marks

Attempt ONE question from the following genres – Drama, Prose, Poetry, Film and Television Drama, or Language.

You may use a Scottish text but NOT the one used in Section 1.

Your answer must be on a different genre from that chosen in Section 1.

You should spend approximately 45 minutes on this section.

DRAMA

Answers to questions on **drama** should refer to the text and to such relevant features as characterisation, key scene(s), structure, climax, theme, plot, conflict, setting …

1. Choose a play in which a central character feels uncertain about their position in their family/ society/workplace.

   Briefly explain the reasons for their uncertainty and discuss how the dramatist's presentation of this feature enhances your understanding of the play as a whole.

2. Choose a play in which the opening scene(s) effectively introduce the central concerns of the play.

   By referring in detail to the opening scene(s), discuss in what ways it is important for your understanding of the play as a whole.

3. Choose a play in which the setting is an important feature.

   Briefly explain how the dramatist establishes the importance of this setting and discuss how this feature enhances your understanding of the play as a whole.

PROSE – FICTION

Answers to questions on **prose fiction** should refer to the text and to such relevant features as characterisation, setting, language, key incident(s), climax, turning point, plot, structure, narrative technique, theme, ideas, description …

4. Choose a novel or short story which carries a strong message that may have a powerful impression on the reader.

   Briefly outline what this message is and discuss why the novel or short story has such an impact on the reader.

5. Choose a novel or short story which reaches a climax that is dramatic, disturbing or moving.

   Briefly explain how the writer achieves this effect and how this enhances your appreciation of the text as a whole.

6. Choose a novel or short story in which there is a character you admire.

Explain briefly why you admire this character and then, in detail, discuss how the writer achieves this.

PROSE – NON-FICTION

Answers to questions on **prose non-fiction** should refer to the text and to such relevant features as ideas, use of evidence, stance, style, selection of material, narrative voice …

7. Choose a piece of non-fiction writing in which the writer's presentation of an experience triggers an emotional response from you.

Give a brief description of the experience and then, in more detail, discuss how the writer's presentation of this description evokes this strong emotional response.

8. Choose a non-fiction text which explores a significant aspect of political or cultural life.

Discuss how the writer's presentation enhances your understanding of the chosen aspect of political or cultural life and how this impacts on your appreciation of the text as a whole.

9. Choose an example of biography or autobiography which gives you a detailed insight into a person's life.

Explain how the writer's presentation made you think deeply about the person and his or her life, enhancing your overall appreciation of the text.

POETRY

Answers to questions on **poetry** should refer to the text and to such relevant features as word choice, tone, imagery, structure, content, rhythm, rhyme, theme, sound, ideas …

10. Choose two poems which deal with an important issue such as crime or poverty.

Discuss which you find more effective in deepening your understanding of the issue.

11. Choose a poem in which form (such as a ballad, ode, sonnet, monologue …) plays a significant role.

Show how the poet uses the distinctive features of the form to enhance your appreciation of the poem.

12. Choose a poem which deals with the theme of loss **or** death **or** the end of a relationship.

Show how the content and poetic techniques used increase your understanding of the theme.

FILM AND TELEVISION DRAMA

Answers to questions on **film and television drama*** should refer to the text and to such relevant features as use of camera, key sequence, characterisation, mise-en-scène, editing, setting, music/sound, special effects, plot, dialogue …

13. Choose a film or television drama* in which the main character could be described as an antihero.

    Explain how the character is introduced and then developed throughout the film or television drama.

14. Choose a film or television drama* in which setting is used to create mood and/or atmosphere.

    Explain how the film or programme makers' use of this setting creates mood and/or atmosphere and go on to show how the mood and/or atmosphere is important to the effectiveness of the film or television drama as a whole.

15. Choose a film or television drama* which has an unexpected ending.

    By referring to key features (such as setting, characterisation, narrative …) and techniques used by the film or programme makers, explain how the ending is unexpected.

*'television drama' includes a single play, a series or a serial.

LANGUAGE

Answers to questions on **language** should refer to the text and to such relevant features as register, accent, dialect, slang, jargon, vocabulary, tone, abbreviation …

16. Consider the use of the Scots language today.

    Identify examples of its use and discuss to what extent these examples promote the language.

17. Choose at least one example of a new form of social networking.

    Identify some of the distinctive features of the language used and discuss to what extent these features contribute to effective communication.

18. Choose a speech which makes use of persuasive language.

    By referring to specific features of language in this speech, discuss to what extent you feel the speech is successful in achieving its purpose of persuasion.

[END OF SECTION 2]

Practice Exam B

CfE Higher English

Practice Papers for SQA Exams

Exam B
Reading for Understanding, Analysis and Evaluation

Duration – 1 hour 30 minutes

Total marks – 30

Attempt ALL questions.

The following two passages discuss sleep in the modern world.

Passage 1

Read the passage below and attempt questions 1–8.

In the first passage, Matthew Walker in his book 'Why We Sleep' explains why sleep is important.

Do you think you got enough sleep this past week? Can you recall the last time you woke up without an alarm clock, feeling refreshed, not needing caffeine? If the answer to any of these questions is "no," you are not alone. Two-thirds of adults throughout all developed nations fail to obtain the recommended eight hours of nightly sleep.

5 I doubt you are surprised by this fact, but you may be surprised by the consequences. Routinely sleeping less than six or seven hours a night demolishes your immune system, more than doubling your risk of cancer. Insufficient sleep is a key lifestyle factor determining whether or not you will develop Alzheimer's disease. Inadequate sleep – even moderate reductions for just one week – disrupts the blood sugar levels so profoundly that you would be classified as pre-diabetic. Short
10 sleeping increases the likelihood of your coronary arteries becoming blocked and brittle, setting you on a path toward cardiovascular disease, stroke, and congestive heart failure. Fitting Charlotte Bronte's prophetic wisdom that 'a ruffled mind makes a restless pillow', sleep disruption further contributes to all major psychiatric conditions, including depression, anxiety and suicidality.

Perhaps you have also noticed a desire to eat more when you're tired? This is no coincidence. Too
15 little sleep swells concentrations of a hormone that makes you feel hungry while suppressing a companion hormone that otherwise signals food satisfaction. Despite being full, you will still want to eat more. It's a recipe linked to weight gain in sleep-deficient adults and children alike. Worse, should you try to diet but don't get enough sleep while doing so, it is futile, since most of the weight you will lose will come from lean body mass, not fat.

20 Add the above health consequences up, and a proven link becomes easier to accept: the shorter you sleep, the shorter your life span. The old maxim 'I'll sleep when I'm dead' is therefore unfortunate. Adopt this mindset, and you will be dead sooner and the quality of that (shorter) life will be worse. The elastic band of sleep deprivation can stretch only so far before it snaps. Sadly, human beings are the only species that will deliberately deprive themselves of sleep without
25 legitimate gain. Every component of wellness, and countless seams of societal fabric, are being eroded by our costly state of sleep neglect: human and financial alike. So much so that the World Health Organization (WHO) has now declared a sleep loss epidemic throughout industrialised nations. It is no coincidence that countries where sleep time has declined most dramatically over the past century, such as the US, the UK, Japan, and South Korea, and several in Western Europe,
30 are also those suffering the greatest increase in rates of the aforementioned physical diseases and mental disorders.

Scientists have even started lobbying doctors to start 'prescribing'. As medical advice goes, it's perhaps the most painless and enjoyable to follow.

Approximately one out of every nine people you pass on the street will meet strict clinical criteria
35 for insomnia. While the reasons remain unclear, insomnia is almost twice as common in women than in men, and it is unlikely that a simple willingness of men to admit sleep problems explains

this very sizeable difference between the two sexes. Race and ethnicity also make a significant difference, with African Americans and Hispanic Americans suffering higher rates of insomnia than Caucasian Americans – findings that have important implications for well-recognised health

40 disparities in these communities, such as diabetes, obesity, and cardiovascular disease, which have known links to a lack of sleep.

Society's apathy toward sleep has, in part, been caused by the historic failure of science to explain why we need it. Sleep remained one of the last biological mysteries. All of the mighty problem-solving methods in science – genetics, molecular biology, and high-powered digital technology –

45 have been unable to unlock the stubborn vault of sleep.

Sleep is infinitely more complex, profoundly more interesting, and alarmingly more health-relevant. We sleep for a rich litany of functions, plural – an abundant constellation of nighttime benefits that service both our brains and our bodies. There does not seem to be one major organ within the body or process within the brain that isn't optimally enhanced by sleep (and

50 detrimentally impaired when we don't get enough). That we receive such a bounty of health benefits each night should not be surprising. After all, we are *awake* for two-thirds of our lives, and we don't just achieve one useful thing during that stretch of time. We accomplish myriad undertakings that promote our own well-being and survival. Why, then, would we expect sleep – and the twenty-five to thirty years, on average, it takes from our lives – to offer one function only?

Passage 2

Read the passage below and attempt question 9. While reading, you may wish to make notes on the main ideas and/or highlight key points in the passage.

In the second passage, from the Guardian, the columnist reflects on our understanding of sleep deprivation.

Obesity used to be regarded as a disease of affluent societies. In a sense, of course, this is true: you cannot be obese if you cannot afford enough calories. But we now understand that the story is more complex, and that children from low-income groups are more likely to be obese than those from the highest-income groups.

5 Our understanding of sleep deprivation has yet to see a similar evolution. Almost half the British population say they get six hours' sleep a night or less, compared with around a twelfth in 1942. Experts blame developments such as electrification and the proliferation of entertainment; one neuroscientist went so far as to warn of a "catastrophic sleep-loss epidemic" recently. We need sleep for mental and physical recovery; for cognitive control, memory and learning. Sleep loss is associated

10 with everything from obesity and Alzheimer's disease to diabetes and poor mental health.

Sleep evangelists such as Arianna Huffington portray a world of busy professionals sending emails into the early hours, teenagers watching televisions in their bedrooms and parents shopping online when they should be winding down. The solutions are obvious, even if we struggle to find the discipline to implement them: turn off your phone and for goodness sake go to bed.

15 The truth is that poorer people sleep worse. You cannot buy sleep itself, but you must pay for the circumstances likely to induce it. Overcrowded, noisy, cold or unsafe housing makes sleep

harder. So does shift work – especially if it is casualised and unpredictable. Poor nutrition and stress also take their toll. We fret about reaching for our smartphone at night, while those making the devices sleep on hard beds in shared dormitories with coworkers clattering to and fro, as
20 Benjamin Reiss observes in his book Wild Nights.

"Social inequities are reproduced and even multiplied in sleep," he writes; children in bad housing will struggle to concentrate in class after a poor night's slumber. The gap is racial too. Lauren Hale, an expert on social patterns of sleep, notes that fewer black people get the recommended amount of sleep than any other ethnic group in the US, and less of it is the most restorative
25 kind. Racism may itself affect sleep, perhaps because of the stress it causes; African Americans who report discrimination are more likely to say they sleep poorly than those who do not. Sleep is a social justice issue, requiring social solutions. Telling people to cut down on coffee is easy; improving labour laws is harder. But when people's sleep problems reflect their lack of control over their lives, telling them they should change how they live is profoundly unhelpful.

30 Far worse is deliberately denying sleep – as international law recognises in listing extreme deprivation as a form of torture. Professor Reiss traces US racial sleep disparities back to slavery; Frederick Douglass said that slaves were more often whipped for oversleeping than any other reason. Such cruelties belong to another age. Yet only this year Bournemouth council installed bars on benches, so that people could sit but rough sleepers could not recline. Though it backtracked,
35 such "hostile architecture" is increasingly common. "I'm allowed to lie down, but not to close my eyes," a homeless man observed of security guards at one site. Few experiences are as delicious as good sleep to an exhausted body and soul. But those who most need to shut up sorrow's eye and equip themselves for another tough day are the ones who find it hardest to do so.

MARKS

Passage 1 questions

1. Read lines 1–4.
   Evaluate the effectiveness of these lines as an opening to the passage.   **2**

2. Read lines 5–13.
   Explain fully the consequences of getting insufficient sleep. Use your own words
   as far as possible in your answer.   **4**

3. Read lines 14–19.
   By referring to at least one example, analyse how the writer uses language to
   convey the impact of insufficient sleep in maintaining a healthy weight.   **3**

4. Read lines 20–31.
   Analyse how the writer uses language effectively to convey the serious
   implications of getting insufficient sleep.   **4**

5. Read lines 34–40.
   Explain fully the key findings about insomnia. Use your own words as far as
   possible in your answer.   **3**

6. Read lines 41–44.
   By referring to at least one example, analyse how the writer's language conveys
   how much we do not know about sleep.   **2**

7. Read lines 45–49.
   By referring to at least two examples, analyse how the writer's language shows
   the benefits of sleep.   **4**

8. Read lines 49–53.
   Explain why we should not be surprised that sleep offers 'such a bounty of health
   benefits'. Use your own words as far as possible in your answer.   **3**

Question on both passages

9. Look at both passages.
   The writers agree on the importance of sleep.
   Identify three key areas on which they agree. You should support the points you
   make by referring to important ideas in both passages.
   You may answer this question in continuous prose or in a series of developed
   bullet points.   **5**

CfE Higher English

Practice Papers for SQA Exams

**Exam B
Critical Reading**

Duration – 1 hour 30 minutes

Total marks – 40

SECTION 1 – Scottish text – 20 marks

Read an extract from a Scottish text you have previously studied and attempt the questions.
Choose ONE text from either

Part A – Drama

or

Part B – Prose

or

Part C – Poetry

Attempt ALL the questions for your chosen text.

SECTION 2 – Critical essay – 20 marks

Attempt ONE question from the following genres – Drama, Prose, Poetry, Film and Television Drama or Language.

Your answer must be on a different genre from that chosen in Section 1.

You should spend approximately 45 minutes on each section.

×**Leckie**
the education publisher
for Scotland

Section 1 – Scottish text – 20 marks

Choose one text from Drama, Prose or Poetry.

Read the text extract carefully and then attempt ALL the questions for your chosen text.

You should spend about 45 minutes on this section.

Text 1: Drama

If you choose this text you may not attempt a question on drama in Section 2.

Read the extract below and then attempt the following questions.

The Slab Boys by John Byrne

(*Enter Jack Hogg. He has a bundle of mags.*)

Jack:	Alan around?	
Phil:	Tall fat guy with scarlet fever and his nose in a sling?	
Jack:	Just tell him I've got those mags he asked about …	
5	Spanky:	What mags are these, Jacky boy?
Phil:	Yeh … how come we never get to see them?	
Spanky:	Yeh … how come?	
Jack:	They're about design … I shouldn't think you'd be remotely interested …	
Phil:	Oh, is that right? Tell him, Spanks … are we interested?	
10	Spanky:	Not really.
Phil:	So you think twice before lurching in here and accusing the brother and me of not giving a monkey's. The designing of carpets for the hoi polloi may mean nothing to you, Hogg, but it means a damn sight less to us. Right, Spanky?	
Spanky:	Roger.	
15	Phil:	Sorry … Roger.
Jack:	You're so smart, aren't you? So bloody smart, the pair of you. You're just pea green if anyone takes an interest in things …	
Spanky:	Pea green? That's a new one …	
Jack:	You nobbled Hector when he first started, didn't you? He used to come out to my desk, we'd go through some carpet mags together … but, oh no, you soon put a stop to that … called him for everything … made his life a misery. A pair of bully boys, that's what you are. Hector could've been a pretty good designer by now … yes, he could! Better than either of you, anyway. When was the last time you were down the Showroom … eh? Neither of you takes the least interest in any trials that come up. In fact, I bet you don't even know what any of us is working on out there …	

Phil: (*Producing tatty piece of carpet*) Fourteen and eleven the square furlong.

Jack: That's right … go on, make a fool of things. Some of us take a pride in what we do!

Phil: Ach, pish, Jack! 'Some of us take a pride in what we do' … You? You lot! You're a bunch of no-talent, no-hopers, arse-licking your way up the turkey runner to
30   Barton's office, a fistful of brushes in this hand and the other one tugging at the forelock … 'Good morning, Sir Wallace, by Christ but that's a snazzy Canaletto print up there on the wall next to that big clock that says a quarter to eight … Suffering Jesus, is that the time already? My, but how time flies when you're enjoying yourself. Pardon me, while I flick this shite off my boot … Just after stepping on one
35   of Jimmy Robertson's sketches … it'll wash off, I'm sure. What? No, no, not at all, Sir Wallace … of course I don't mind putting in a bit of unpaid overtime … it's results that count, isn't it?' Jack, you wouldn't know a good design from a plate of canteen mince. Interest? As soon as Barton starts revving up his Jag you're the first one out the door and the leg over the bike before Miss Walkinshaw's even got her teeth out
40   of her water jug!

Jack: Yeh … yeh … very noble … very smart. Listen, you ned, I went to night school for three and a half years … I've got a Diploma in Wool Technology!

Phil: So, what does that mean?

Spanky: He's haun-knitted.

45 Jack: One day you're going to go too far, Farrell. When you do … watch out. That's all I'm saying … watch out. As for you, McCann … grow up. There's a real world out there. Some of us have to live in it. (*Exit.*)

Spanky: It's hard to believe he was ever a Slab Boy, isn't it? You don't suppose there's any truth in the rumour that he's really the love-child of Miss Walkinshaw and Plastic
50   Man? No? Well, I think I'll stroll down the Showroom and have a look at the new rugs …

Phil: Eh?

Spanky: I'm going for a smoke … hold the fort. D'you want me to have a skite for Hector?

Phil: Christ, I forgot all about him …

MARKS

DO NOT
WRITE IN
THIS
MARGIN

Practice Papers for SQA Exams: Higher English Practice Exam B

Questions

1. Explain fully, with close reference to the extract, why Spanky and Phil find it hard to believe that Jack was ever a 'Slab Boy'. **2**

2. By referring closely to lines 19–25, explain the impact Jack feels Phil and Spanky have had on Hector. **4**

3. By referring to at least two examples from lines 28–40, analyse how the writer's use of language conveys Phil's attitude towards Jack. **4**

4. By referring to this extract and elsewhere in the play, analyse how Phil and Spanky use humour to distance themselves from their misfortune and uninspiring circumstances. **10**

Text 2: Drama

If you choose this text you may not attempt a question on drama in Section 2.

Read the extract below and then attempt the following questions.

The Cheviot, the Stag and the Black, Black Oil by John McGrath

Enter WHITEHALL, a worried senior Civil Servant.

WHITEHALL: You see we just didn't have the money to squander on this sort of thing.

TEXAS JIM: That's my boy.

WHITEHALL: And we don't believe in fettering private enterprise: after all this is a free country.

5   TEXAS JIM: Never known a freer one.

WHITEHALL: These chaps have the know how, and we don't.

TEXAS JIM: Yes sir, and we certainly move fast.

M.C.l.: By 1963 the North Sea was divided into blocks.

M.C.2.: By 1964 100,000 square miles of sea-bed had been handed out for exploration.

10 WHITEHALL: We didn't charge these chaps a lot of money, we didn't want to put them off.

TEXAS JIM: Good thinking, good thinking. Your wonderful labourite government was real nice: thank God they weren't socialists.

M.C. l.: The Norwegian Government took over 50% of the shares in exploration of their sector.

M.C.2.: The Algerian Government control 800k of the oil industry in Algeria.

15 M.C.l.: The Libyan Government are fighting to control 100% of the oil industry in Libya.

Guitar.

WHITEHALL: Our allies in N.A.T.O. were pressing us to get the oil flowing. There were Reds under the Med. Revolutions in the middle-east.

TEXAS JIM: Yeah, Britain is a stable country and we can make sure you stay that way. (*Fingers pistol.*)

20 WHITEHALL: There is a certain amount of disagreement about exactly how much oil there actually is out there. Some say 100 million tons a year, others as much as 600 million. I find myself awfully confused.

TEXAS JIM: Good thinking. Good thinking.

WHITEHALL: Besides if we produce our own oil, it'll be cheaper, and we won't have to import it –
25 will we?

M.C.l.: As in all 3rd World countries exploited by American business, the raw material will be processed under the control of American capital – and sold back to us at three or four times the price –

M.C.2.: To the detriment of our balance of payments, our cost of living and our way of life.

30   TEXAS JIM: And to the greater glory of the economy of the U.S. of A.

Intro to song. Tune: souped-up version of 'Bonnie Dundee'. *TEXAS JIM and WHITEHALL sing as an echo of LOCH and SELLAR.*

TEXAS JIM & WHITEHALL:

As the rain on the hillside comes in from the sea

35   All the blessings of life fall in showers from me

So if you'd abandon your old misery

Then you'll open your doors to the oil industry

GIRLS (as backing group): Conoco, Amoco, Shell-Esso, Texaco, British Petroleum, yum, yum, yum. (*Twice.*)

40   TEXAS JIM:

There's many a barrel of oil in the sea

All waiting for drilling and piping to me

I'll refine it in Texas, you'll get it, you'll see

At four times the price that you sold it to me.

45   TEXAS JIM & WHITEHALL: As the rain on the hillside, etc.

(*Chorus.*)

GIRLS: Conoco, Amoco, etc. (*Four times.*)

WHITEHALL:

There's jobs and there's prospects so please have no fears,

50   There's building of oil rigs and houses and piers,

There's a boom-time a-coming, let's celebrate – cheers

TEXAS JIM pours drinks of oil.

TEXAS JIM: For the Highlands will be my lands in three or four years.

No oil in can.

55   *Enter ABERDONIAN RIGGER.*

A.R.: When it comes to the jobs all the big boys are American. All the technicians are American. Only about half the riggers are local. The American companies'll no take Union men, and some of the fellows recruiting for the Union have been beaten up. The fellows who get taken on as roustabouts are on a contract; 84 hours a week in 12 hour shifts, two weeks on and one week
60 off. They have to do overtime when they're tellt. No accommodation, no leave, no sick-pay, and the company can sack them whenever they want to. And all that for £27.00 a week basic before tax. It's not what I'd cry a steady job for a family man. Of course, there's building jobs going but in a few years that'll be over, and by then we'll not be able to afford to live here. Some English property company has just sold 80 acres of Aberdeenshire for one million
65 pounds. Even a stairhead tenement with a shared lavatory will cost you four thousand pounds in Aberdeen. At the first sniff of oil, there was a crowd of sharp operators jumping all over the place buying the land cheap. Now they're selling it at a hell of a profit.

Questions

5. At this stage in the play, we are introduced to Texas Jim who represents the American investors entering the Highlands. Explain in your own words the justification given by Whitehall for allowing American investment.

2

6. By referring to two examples from the text, analyse how a contrast is created between Texas Jim and Whitehall.

2

7. At this point, Texas Jim and Whitehall burst into song. By referring to at least two examples, analyse how this song is relevant to the themes of the play.

3

8. From his opening speech, what is revealed about the Aberdonian Rigger's attitude towards working life on the rigs? You should support your answer with evidence from the text.

3

9. Many of McGrath's characters are presented as clear stereotypes. With reference to this extract and elsewhere in the play, discuss how such characters are used to develop theme.

10

Text 3: Drama

If you choose this text you may not attempt a question on drama in Section 2.

Read the extract below and then attempt the following questions.

Men Should Weep by Ena Lamont Stewart

This extract is from Act III and is the end of the play. Jenny has returned home on Christmas Eve to offer her parents money for a council house.

JOHN: I tellt you tae keep oot o this!

LILY: Why should I? Maggie's ma sister! An I've had tae fight hauf your battles for ye, John Morrison, or the hale lot o ye would hae been oot on the street mair than once!

*John cannot answer: his hatred of Lily and her truth turns his mouth to a grim line: his hands open
5 and close, open and close. The others wait for him to speak.*

MAGGIE: (*with a placating smile and a note of pleading*) John, it's juist a wee help till we get a Cooncil hoose wi a wee bit garden at the front and a real green tae hang oot the washin.

JENNY: (*holding out her fat roll of notes*) I've got the cash. Ca it a loan if ye like.

10 MAGGIE: There's plenty for the flittin and the key money.

JENNY: Fifty pounds. (*She comes forward and offers it to John*)

JOHN: Ye can tak that back tae yer fancy man. We're wantin nane o yer whore's winnins here.

MAGGIE: John!

15 LILY: (*shouting*) It's no for you! It's for Bertie an the ither weans, ye pigheided fool!

JOHN: (*to Jenny*) If ye'd earned it, I'd be doon on ma knees tae ye. But ye're no better than a tart. We tried wur best tae bring you up respectable so's ye could marry a decent fella –

JENNY: Marry a decent fella! I never had a chance! Every time I got whit you would ca a
20 decent fella an he saw me hame frae the dancin, he'd tak one look at the close an that's the last I'd see o him. Did you ever provide me wi a hoose I could bring a decent fella hame to? Did ye?

JOHN: I done ma best! There's naebody can ca me a lay-about! I worked when there wis work tae get!

25 LILY: Oh, ye must mind, Jenny, he's no tae blame. Nae man's evertae blame.

               It's they dirty rotten buggers in Parliament, or they stinkin rich bosses –

JOHN: Haud yer rotten tongue, ye frozen bitch!

JENNY: (*with a sudden sour laugh*) I've often thought the way it would be when
I came hame. I was gonna make up for the way I left ye. An here we are,
30 Christmas Eve, fightin ower ma – whit is it? – ma whore's winnins. I've been savin an
savin so's I could help ye, an mak friends again, an be happy.

*She cries, head bent, standing forlornly before John who looks down on her grimly. Maggie watches,
waits: then suddenly she stops combing her hair and rises. She takes the money out of Jenny's hand
and interposes herself between them.*

35 MAGGIE: (*with uncharacteristic force*) An so we wull be happy! Whore's winnins, did ye ca
this? An did I hear ye use the word "tart"? Whit wis I, when we was coortin, but
your tart?

John is startled and shocked.

(*In an urgent whisper imitating the John of her "coortin" days*) Let me, Maggie, g'on,
40 let me! I'll mairry ye if onythin happens –

JOHN: (*a hurried, shamed glance towards Lily*) Stop it, Maggie! Stop it!

*He moves away from Maggie, but she follows, still whispering. Lily, arms akimbo, eyes a-gleam, laughs
coarsely, and hugs herself.*

MAGGIE: Aye, I wis your whore. An I'd nae winnins that I can mind o. But mebbe it's a right
45 bein a whore if ye've nae winnins. Is that the way it goes, John? (*Pause. She draws
breath and her voice is now bitter*) And don't you kid yersel that I didna see the way
ye looked at yer ain son's wife trailin aboot the hoose wi her breasts fa'in oat o her
fancy claes. (*Coming right up to him and completing his humiliation before Lily and
Jenny*) I'm no sae saft I didna ken why it wis. (*Urgent whisper*) Maggie! Come on,
50 quick, ben the back room … lock the door … it'll no tak minutes –

JENNY: Mammy, Mammy! Stop!

*John has sunk into a chair. He covers his face with his hands. There is a silence: Maggie's breathing
loses its harshness: she looks down upon him: she sags.*

MAGGIE: Aw … aw … (*She wipes her face with her hands and sighs*) Aw, I shouldna have said
55 they things.

LILY: Why no? Ye wouldna hae said them if they wisna true.

MAGGIE: (*shaking her head*) Naw. There's things atween husbands an wives shouldna
be spoke aboot. I'm sorry. I lost ma heid.

JENNY: (*kneeling at her father's feet*) Daddy … Daddy … forget it. It disnae matter. Daddy?
60 (*She tries to draw his hands from his face*) When I wis wee, you loved me, an I loved
you. Why can we no get back?

MARKS

He does not answer, but he lets her take one of his hands from his face and hold it in both of hers.

MAGGIE: Dinna fret yersel, Jenny. I can manage him … I can aye manage him.

She is still holding the roll of notes. She looks away into her long-ago dream and a smile breaks
65 *over her face.*

(*Very softly*) Four rooms, did ye say, Jenny? (*Pause*) Four rooms. Four rooms … an a park forbye! There'll be flowers come the spring!

CURTAIN

Questions

10. Explain why John hates Lily and 'her truth', referring closely to the extract.   **2**

11. Referring closely to the extract, explain why John will not take Jenny's money.   **2**

12. Referring closely to the extract, analyse how the stage directions show a change in Maggie's character in lines 32–35.   **2**

13. Referring closely to the text, show how Jenny's character is developed in this extract.   **4**

14. Discuss the effectiveness of this ending to the play with detailed reference to this extract and the play as a whole.   **10**

Text 1: Prose

If you choose this text you may not attempt a question on prose in Section 2.

Read the extract below and then attempt the following questions.

Home by Iain Crichton Smith

As he turned away from the coal-house door he saw the washing hanging from the ropes on the green.

'Ye widna like to be daeing that noo,' he told his wife jocularly.

'What would the Bruces say if they saw you running about in this dirty place like a schoolboy?'
5 she said coldly.

'What dae ye mean?'

'Simply what I said. There was no need to come here at all. Or do you want to take a photograph and show it to them? "The Place Where I Was Born".'

'I wasna born here. I just lived here for five years.'

10 'What would they think of you, I wonder.'

'I don't give a damn about the Bruces,' he burst out, the veins on his forehead swelling. 'What's he but a doctor anyway? I'm not ashamed of it. And, by God, why should you be ashamed of it? You weren't brought up in a fine house either. You worked in a factory till I picked you up at that dance.'

She turned away.

15 'Do you mind that night?' he asked contritely. 'You were standing by the wall and I went up to you and I said, "Could I have the honour?" And when we were coming home we walked down lovers' lane, where they had all the seats and the statues.'

'And you made a clown of yourself,' she said unforgivingly.

'Yes, didn't I just?' remembering how he had climbed the statue in the moonlight to show off.
20 From the top of it he could see the Clyde, the ships and the cranes.

'And remember the flicks?' he said. 'We used tae get in wi jam jars. And do you mind the man who used to come down the passage at interval spraying us with disinfectant?'

The interior of the cinema came back to him in a warm flood: the children in the front rows keeping up a continual barrage of noise, the ushers hushing them, the smoke, the warmth, the
25 pies slapping against faces, the carved cherubs in the flaking roof blowing their trumpets.

'You'd like that, wouldn't you?' she said. 'Remember it was me who drove you to the top.'

'Whit dae ye mean?' – like a bull wounded in the arena.

'You were lazy, that was what was wrong with you. You'd go out ferreting when you were here. You liked being with the boys.'

30 'Nothing wrong with that. What's wrong wi that?'

'What do you want? That they should all wave flags? That all the dirty boys and girls should line the street with banners five miles high? They don't give a damn about you, you know that. They're all dead and rotting and we should be back in Africa where we belong.'

Questions

15. Look at lines 1–10.
With reference to **at least two** examples, analyse how language is used to create a contrast between husband and wife.

2

16. Look at lines 11–27.
With reference to **at least two** examples, analyse how language is used to convey aspects of Jackson's personality.

4

17. Look at lines 28–33.
Analyse how language is used to convey Jackson's wife's frustration.

2

18. In his writing, Crichton Smith explores the tensions caused by our desires and our reality. By referring to this extract and at least one other story by Crichton Smith, discuss how he does this.

10

Text 2: Prose

If you choose this text you may not attempt a question on prose in Section 2.

Read the extract below and then attempt the following questions.

The Wireless Set by George Mackay Brown

The first wireless ever to come to the valley of Tronvik in Orkney was brought by Howie Eunson, son of Hugh the fisherman and Betsy.

Howie had been at the whaling in the Antarctic all winter, and he arrived back in Britain in April with a stuffed wallet and jingling pockets. Passing through Glasgow on his way home he bought
5   presents for everyone in Tronvik – fiddlestrings for Sam down at the shore, a bottle of malt whisky for Mansie of the hill, a secondhand volume of Spurgeon's sermons for Mr Sinclair the missionary, sweeties for all the bairns, a meerschaum pipe for his father Hugh and a portable wireless set for his mother Betsy.

There was great excitement the night Howie arrived home in Tronvik. Everyone in the valley –
10   men, women, children, dogs, cats – crowded into the but-end of the croft, as Howie unwrapped and distributed his gifts.

'And have you been a good boy all the time you've been away?' said Betsy anxiously. 'Have you prayed every night, and not sworn?'

'This is thine, mother,' said Howie, and out of a big cardboard box he lifted the portable wireless
15   and set it on the table.

For a full two minutes nobody said a word. They all stood staring at it, making small round noises of wonderment, like pigeons.

'And mercy,' said Betsy at last, 'what is it at all?'

'It's a wireless set,' said Howie proudly. 'Listen.'

20   He turned a little black knob and a posh voice came out of the box saying that it would be a fine day tomorrow over England, and over Scotland south of the Forth-Clyde valley, but that in the Highlands and in Orkney and Shetland there would be rain and moderate westerly winds.

'If it's a man that's speaking,' said old Hugh doubtfully, 'where is he standing just now?'

'In London,' said Howie.

25   'Well now,' said Betsy, 'if that isn't a marvel! But I'm not sure, all the same, but what it isn't against the scriptures. Maybe, Howie, we'd better not keep it.'

'Everybody in the big cities has a wireless,' said Howie. 'Even in Kirkwall and Hamnavoe every house has one. But now Tronvik has a wireless as well, and maybe we're not such clodhoppers as they think.'

30   They all stayed late, listening to the wireless. Howie kept twirling a second little knob, and sometimes they would hear music and sometimes they would hear a kind of loud half-witted voice urging them to use a particular brand of tooth-paste.

MARKS

DO NOT
WRITE IN
THIS
MARGIN

Practice Papers for SQA Exams: Higher English Practice Exam B

At half past eleven the wireless was switched off and everybody went home. Hugh and Betsy and Howie were left alone. 'Men speak,' said Betsy, 'but it's hard to know sometimes
35 whether what they say is truth or lies.'

'This wireless speaks the truth,' said Howie.

Old Hugh shook his head. 'Indeed,' he said, 'it doesn't do that. For the man said there would be rain here and a westerly wind. But I assure you it'll be a fine day, and a southerly wind, and if the Lord spares me I'll get to the lobsters.'

40 Old Hugh was right. Next day was fine, and he and Howie took twenty lobsters from the creels he had under the Gray Head.

Questions

19. Referring closely to lines 1–2, analyse how George Mackay Brown presents the community of Tronvik. **2**

20. Show how the language of lines 16–17 conveys the amazement of the islanders. **4**

21. Referring to one example from the extract, explain why Howie believes that the 'wireless speaks the truth'. **2**

22. Explain the significance of the wireless weather forecast in this extract. **2**

23. George Mackay Brown wrote about Orkney, its past and its people, yet he used this 'small green world' to explore issues of universal significance. By referring to this story and at least one other story by George Mackay Brown, discuss how he achieves this. **10**

Text 3: Prose

If you choose this text you may not attempt a question on prose in Section 2.

Read the extract below and then attempt the following questions.

The Strange Case of Dr Jekyll and Mr Hyde by Robert Louis Stevenson

This extract is from Chapter 1 of the novella.

MR. UTTERSON, THE LAWYER, was a man of a rugged countenance, that was never lighted by a smile; cold, scanty and embarrassed in discourse; backward in sentiment; lean, long, dusty, dreary, and yet somehow lovable. At friendly meetings, and when the wine was to his taste, something eminently human beaconed from his eye; something indeed which never found its way into his
5   talk, but which spoke not only in these silent symbols of the after-dinner face, but more often and loudly in the acts of his life. He was austere with himself; drank gin when he was alone, to mortify a taste for vintages; and though he enjoyed the theater, had not crossed the doors of one for twenty years. But he had an approved tolerance for others; sometimes wondering, almost with envy, at the high pressure of spirits involved in their misdeeds; and in any extremity inclined to
10 help rather than to reprove. "I incline to Cain's heresy," he used to say, quaintly; "I let my brother go to the devil in his own way." In this character it was frequently his fortune to be the last reputable acquaintance and the last good influence in the lives of down-going men. And to such as these, so long as they came about his chambers, he never marked a shade of change in his demeanour.

No doubt the feat was easy to Mr. Utterson; for he was undemonstrative at the best, and even
15 his friendships seemed to be founded in a similar catholicity of good-nature. It is the mark of a modest man to accept his friendly circle ready-made from the hands of opportunity; and that was the lawyer's way. His friends were those of his own blood, or those whom he had known the longest; his affections, like ivy, were the growth of time, they implied no aptness in the object. Hence, no doubt, the bond that united him to Mr. Richard Enfield, his distant kinsman, the well-
20 known man about town. It was a nut to crack for many, what these two could see in each other, or what subject they could find in common. It was reported by those who encountered them in their Sunday walks, that they said nothing, looked singularly dull, and would hail with obvious relief the appearance of a friend. For all that, the two men put the greatest store by these excursions, counted them the chief jewel of each week, and not only set aside occasions of pleasure, but even resisted
25 the calls of business, that they might enjoy them uninterrupted.

It chanced on one of these rambles that their way led them down a by-street in a busy quarter of London. The street was small and what is called quiet, but it drove a thriving trade on the week-day. The inhabitants were all doing well, it seemed, and all emulously hoping to do better still, and laying out the surplus of their gains in coquetry; so that the shop fronts stood along that
30 thoroughfare with an air of invitation, like rows of smiling saleswomen. Even on Sunday, when it veiled its more florid charms and lay comparatively empty of passage, the street shone out in contrast to its dingy neighbourhood, like a fire in a forest; and with its freshly painted shutters, well-polished brasses, and general cleanliness and gaiety of note, instantly caught and pleased the eye of the passenger.

MARKS

DO NOT
WRITE IN
THIS
MARGIN

Practice Papers for SQA Exams: Higher English Practice Exam B

Questions

24. Look at lines 1–13.
    By referring to at least one example, analyse how the writer uses language to reveal the character and/or attitudes of Mr. Utterson.   **4**

25. Look at lines 20–23.
    Analyse how the writer's language reveals the awkwardness of Enfield and Utterson's Sunday walks.   **2**

26. Look at lines 26–34.
    By referring to at least two examples, analyse how the writer's language conveys the attractive appearance of the by-street.   **4**

27. By referring to this extract and to elsewhere in the novel, discuss how Stevenson uses contrast to explore key concerns of the novella.   **10**

Text 4: Prose

If you choose this text you may not attempt a question on prose in Section 2.

Read the extract below and then attempt the following questions.

Sunset Song by Lewis Grassic Gibbon

In this extract, which is from the Epilude, Chris, young Ewan and the folk of Kinraddie have gathered around the Standing Stones to witness the unveiling of the war memorial by the minister, Mr Colquohoun, to remember the four men from Kinraddie who died in the First World War.

And then, with the night waiting out by on Blawearie brae, and the sun just verging the coarse hills, the minister began to speak again, his short hair blowing in the wind that had come, his voice not decent and a kirk-like bumble, but ringing out over the loch:

FOR I WILL GIVE YOU THE MORNING STAR

5 *In the sunset of an age and an epoch we may write that for epitaph of the men who were of it. They went quiet and brave from the lands they loved, though seldom of that love might they speak, it was not in them to tell in words of the earth that moved and lived and abided, their life and enduring love. And who knows at the last what memories of it were with them, the springs and the winters of this land and all the sounds and scents of it that had once been theirs, deep, and a passion of their*

10 *blood and spirit, those four who died in France? With them we may say there died a thing older than themselves, these were the Last of the Peasants, the last of the Old Scots folk. A new generation comes up that will know them not, except as a memory in a song, they passed with the things that seemed good to them with loves and desires that grow dim and alien in the days to be. It was the old Scotland that perished then, and we may believe that never again will the old speech and the old*

15 *songs, the old curses and the old benedictions, rise but with alien effort to our lips. The last of the peasants, those four that you knew, took that with them to the darkness and the quietness of the places where they sleep. And the land changes, their parks and their steadings are a desolation where the sheep are pastured, we are told that great machines come soon to till the land, and the great herds come to feed on it, the crofter has gone, the man with the house and the steading of his*

20 *own and the land closer to his heart than the flesh of his body. Nothing, it has been said, is true but change, nothing abides, and here in Kinraddie where we watch the building of those little prides and those little fortunes on the ruins of the little farms we must give heed that these also do not abide, that a new spirit shall come to the land with the greater herd and the great machines. For greed of place and possession and great estate those four had little heed, the kindness of friends and the*

25 *warmth of toil and the peace of rest – they asked no more from God or man, and no less would they endure. So, lest we shame them, let us believe that the new oppressions and foolish greeds are no more than mists that pass. They died for a world that is past, these men, but they did not die for this that we seem to inherit. Beyond it and us there shines a greater hope and a newer world, undreamt when these four died. But need we doubt which side the battle they would range themselves did they*

30 *live to-day, need we doubt the answer they cry to us even now, the four of them, from the places of the sunset?*

And then, as folk stood dumbfounded, this was just sheer politics, plain what he meant, the Highland man McIvor tuned up his pipes and began to step slow round the stone circle by Blawearie Loch,

MARKS

35 slow and quiet, and folk watched him, the dark was near, it lifted your hair and was eerie and uncanny, the *Flowers of the Forest* as he played it:

It rose and rose and wept and cried, that crying for the men that fell in battle, and there was Kirsty Strachan weeping quietly and others with her, and the young ploughmen they stood with glum, white faces, they'd no understanding or caring, it was something that vexed and tore at them, it belonged to times they had no knowing of.

Questions

28. With reference to the extract, explain why the time and place of this memorial service are particularly apt.

2

29. With close reference to the extract, analyse how Grassic Gibbon's language reflects the greater significance of the deaths of these four men.

4

30. Referring closely to the extract, show how atmosphere is created in lines 32–39.

4

31. Lewis Grassic Gibbon uses symbolism a great deal in *Sunset Song*. Referring to this extract, and to the wider text, discuss how he does so and explain the effect.

10

Text 5: Prose

If you choose this text you may not attempt a question on prose in Section 2.

Read the extract below and then attempt the following questions.

The Cone-Gatherers by Robin Jenkins

In this extract, Neil and Calum are surprised at the beach hut by Lady Runcie Campbell and her two children.

The door was flung open to the accompaniment of the loudest peal of thunder since the start of the storm.

From a safe distance the little dog barked at the trespassers. The lady had only a silken handkerchief over her head; her green tweed costume was black in places with damp. In the midst of the thunder
5 she shouted: 'What is the meaning of this?' Though astonishment, and perhaps dampness, made her voice hoarse, it nevertheless was far more appalling to the two men than any thunder. They could not meet the anger in her face. They gazed at her feet; her stockings were splashed with mud and her shoes had sand on them.

Neil did not know what to do or say. Every second of silent abjectness was a betrayal of himself, and
10 especially of his brother who was innocent. All his vows of never again being ashamed of Calum were being broken. His rheumatism tortured him, as if coals from the stolen fire had been pressed into his shoulders and knees; but he wished that the pain was twenty times greater to punish him as he deserved. He could not lift his head; he tried, so that he could meet the lady's gaze at least once, no matter how scornful and contemptuous it was; but he could not. A lifetime of frightened
15 submissiveness held it down.

Suddenly he realised that Calum was speaking.

'It's not Neil's fault, lady,' he was saying. 'He did it because I was cold and wet.'

'For God's sake,' muttered the lady, and Neil felt rather than saw how she recoiled from Calum, as if from something obnoxious, and took her children with her. For both the boy and girl were present.

20 The dog had not stopped barking. Even that insult to Calum could not break the grip shame had of Neil. Still with lowered head, he dragged on his jacket. 'Get out,' cried the lady. 'For God's sake, get out.'

Neil had to help Calum on with his jacket. Like an infant Calum presented the wrong hand, so that they had to try again. The girl giggled, but the boy said nothing.

25 At last they were ready.

'I'll have to get my cones,' whispered Calum.

'Get them.'

Calum went over and picked up the bag lying beside the hamper of toys.

Neil led the way past the lady, who drew back. He mumbled he was sorry.

30 Calum repeated the apology.

She stood in the doorway and gazed out at them running away into the rain. The dog barked after them from the edge of the verandah.

'You'll hear more about this,' she said.

In the hut Sheila had run to the fire, with little groans of joy. From the corner to which he had
35 retreated Roderick watched her, with his own face grave and tense.

Their mother came in and shut the door.

'I shall certainly see to it,' she said, 'that they don't stay long in the wood after this. This week will be their last, whatever Mr Tulloch may say. I never heard of such impertinence.' She had to laugh to express her amazement. 'Your father's right. After this war, the lower orders are going to be
40 frightfully presumptuous.'

'Did you see the holes in the little one's pullover?' asked Sheila.

'I'm afraid I didn't see beyond their astonishing impudence,' replied her mother. She then was aware that Roderick still remained in the corner. 'Roderick, come over to the fire at once. Your jacket's wet through.' She became anxious as she saw how pale, miserable, and pervious to disease he looked.

45 'You'll be taking another of those wretched colds.'

He did not move.

'What's the matter?' she asked.

His response shocked her. He turned and pressed his brow against the window.

Questions

32. By referring closely to at least two examples, analyse how the writer's use of language conveys Neil's emotions in lines 9–15. **4**

33. Explain fully what crimes Lady Runcie Campbell feels Neil and Calum have committed. **2**

34. By referring closely to lines 23–48, analyse Roderick and Sheila's contrasting reactions to the expulsion of the brothers from the beach hut. **4**

35. Class difference is a significant issue in the novel. By referring to this extract and elsewhere in the novel, discuss how this theme is developed. **10**

Text 1: Poetry

If you choose this text you may not attempt a question on poetry in Section 2.

Read the extract below and then attempt the following questions.

To A Mouse by Robert Burns

Wee, sleekit, cow'rin, tim'rous beastie,

O, what a panic's in thy breastie!

Thou need na start awa sae hasty,

Wi' bickering brattle!

5 I wad be laith to rin an' chase thee,

Wi' murd'ring pattle!

I'm truly sorry man's dominion,

Has broken nature's social union,

An' justifies that ill opinion,

10 Which makes thee startle

At me, thy poor, earth-born companion,

An' fellow-mortal!

I doubt na, whiles, but thou may thieve;

What then? poor beastie, thou maun live!

15 A daimen icker in a thrave

'S a sma' request;

I'll get a blessin wi' the lave,

An' never miss't!

Thy wee bit housie, too, in ruin!

20 It's silly wa's the win's are strewin!

An' naething, now, to big a new ane,

O' foggage green!

An' bleak December's winds ensuin,

Baith snell an' keen!

25 Thou saw the fields laid bare an' waste,

An' weary winter comin fast,

An' cozie here, beneath the blast,

Thou thought to dwell –

Till crash! the cruel coulter past

30 Out thro' thy cell.

That wee bit heap o' leaves an' stibble,

Has cost thee mony a weary nibble!

Now thou's turn'd out, for a' thy trouble,

But house or hald,

35 To thole the winter's sleety dribble,

An' cranreuch cauld!

But, Mousie, thou art no thy lane,

In proving foresight may be vain;

The best-laid schemes o' mice an' men

40 Gang aft agley,

An' lea'e us nought but grief an' pain,

For promis'd joy!

Still thou art blest, compar'd wi' me

The present only toucheth thee:

45 But, Och! I backward cast my e'e.

On prospects drear!

An' forward, tho' I canna see,

I guess an' fear!

MARKS

Questions

36. Burns presents a vivid image of the mouse in lines 1–6. With reference to one example, explain how the mouse is presented and analyse how Burns does this. **2**

37. Burns is apologetic to the mouse in lines 1–36. Identify two reasons why he feels this way. **2**

38. Referring to one example, show how Burns' language suggests that he and the mouse are equals. **2**

39. The tone changes in lines 37–48. With reference to two examples, identify how the tone changes and explain why it does so. **4**

40. Burns was writing at a time when traditional hierarchies and class systems were being questioned. From your reading of this poem and at least one other poem by Burns, discuss how Burns deals with the issues of social justice and equality. **10**

Text 2: Poetry

If you choose this text you may not attempt a question on poetry in Section 2.

Read the extract below and then attempt the following questions.

***Valentine* by Carol Ann Duffy**

Not a red rose or a satin heart.

I give you an onion.
It is a moon wrapped in brown paper.
It promises light
5 like the careful undressing of love.

Here.
It will blind you with tears
like a lover.
It will make your reflection
10 a wobbling photo of grief.

I am trying to be truthful.

Not a cute card or a kissogram.

I give you an onion.
Its fierce kiss will stay on your lips,
15 possessive and faithful
as we are,
for as long as we are.

Take it.
Its platinum loops shrink to a wedding-ring,
20 if you like.
Lethal.
Its scent will cling to your fingers,
cling to your knife.

MARKS

DO NOT
WRITE IN
THIS
MARGIN

Practice Papers for SQA Exams: Higher English Practice Exam B

Questions

41. By referring closely to lines 1–6, analyse the use of poetic technique to establish an assertive tone.

3

42. With reference to **two** pieces of evidence from the poem, analyse how Duffy highlights the conflicting nature of love.

2

43. By referring closely to **one** example from the poem, analyse the poet's use of enjambment in these lines.

2

44. Evaluate the effectiveness of the final stanza as a conclusion to the poem. Your answer should deal with ideas and/or language.

3

45. In many of her poems, Duffy explores the depth and complexity of love. With reference to this poem and one other by Duffy, discuss the importance of this theme in her work.

10

Text 3: Poetry

If you choose this text you may not attempt a question on poetry in Section 2.

Read the extract below and then attempt the following questions.

My Rival's House by Liz Lochhead

is peopled with many surfaces.

Ormolu and gilt, slipper satin,

lush velvet couches,

cushions so stiff you can't sink in.

5 Tables polished clear enough to see distortions in.

We take our shoes off at her door,

shuffle stocking-soled, tiptoe – the parquet floor

is beautiful and its surface must

be protected. Dust-

10 cover, drawn shade,

won't let the surface colour fade.

Silver sugar-tongs and silver salver,

my rival serves us tea.

She glosses over him and me.

15 I am all edges, a surface, a shell

and yet my rival thinks she means me well.

But what squirms beneath her surface I can tell.

Soon, my rival

capped tooth, polished nail

20 will fight, fight foul for her survival.

Deferential, daughterly, I sip

and thank her nicely for each bitter cup.

And I have much to thank her for.

This son she bore –

25   first blood to her –

never, never can escape scot free

the sour potluck of family.

And oh how close

this family that furnishes my rival's place.

30   Lady of the house.

Queen bee.

She is far more unconscious,

far more dangerous than me.

Listen, I was always my own worst enemy.

35   She has taken even this from me.

She dishes up her dreams for breakfast.

Dinner, and her salt tears pepper our soup.

She won't

give up.

MARKS

DO NOT
WRITE IN
THIS
MARGIN

Practice Papers for SQA Exams: Higher English Practice Exam B

Questions

46. By referring to lines 1–11, analyse the use of poetic technique to establish a tense atmosphere.

4

47. In lines 12–22 we are given a sense of the attitude the speaker has towards the mother. Identify the attitude displayed and analyse how this is conveyed.

2

48. Analyse how the use of poetic technique in lines 23–35 conveys the power held by her 'rival'.

2

49. Evaluate how effective lines 36–39 are as a conclusion to the poem. Your answer may deal with ideas and/or language.

2

50. In many of Lochhead's poems, she establishes a strong sense of location. Referring closely to this poem and another poem or poems by Lochhead, discuss how the poet develops a theme or themes through her description of place.

10

Text 4: Poetry

If you choose this text you may not attempt a question on poetry in Section 2.

Read the extract below and then attempt the following questions.

Visiting Hour by Norman MacCaig

The hospital smell

combs my nostrils

as they go bobbing along

green and yellow corridors.

5 What seems a corpse

is trundled into a lift and vanishes

heavenward.

I will not feel, I will not

feel, until

10 I have to.

Nurses walk lightly, swiftly,

here and up and down and there,

their slender waists miraculously

carrying their burden

15 of so much pain, so

many deaths, their eyes

still clear after

so many farewells.

Ward 7. She lies

20 in a white cave of forgetfulness.

A withered hand

trembles on its stalk. Eyes move

behind eyelids too heavy

to raise. Into an arm wasted

25 of colour a glass fang is fixed,

not guzzling but giving.

And between her and me

distance shrinks till there is none left

but the distance of pain that neither she nor I

30 can cross.

She smiles a little at this

black figure in her white cave

who clumsily rises

in the round swimming waves of a bell

35 and dizzily goes off, growing fainter,

not smaller, leaving behind only

books that will not be read

and fruitless fruits.

Questions

51. By referring closely to lines 1–7, analyse MacCaig's use of poetic techniques to create a vivid sense of place.

3

52. Look at **stanza 3**. By referring closely to lines 8–10, analyse MacCaig's use of poetic techniques to convey his feelings at this point in the visit.

2

53. By referring to at least one example, analyse how MacCaig's admiration for the nurses is made clear in lines 11–18.

2

54. Evaluate how effective lines 19–30 are in conveying the frailty of the woman in the hospital.

3

55. By referring to this poem and at least one other by Norman MacCaig, discuss how he uses personal experience to explore theme in his work.

10

Text 5: Poetry

If you choose this text you may not attempt a question on poetry in Section 2.

Read the extract below and then attempt the following questions.

XIX I Gave You Immortality by Sorley MacLean

I gave you immortality

and what did you give me?

Only the sharp arrows of your beauty,

a harsh onset

5   and piercing sorrow,

bitterness of spirit

and a sore gleam of glory.

If I gave you immortality

you gave it to me;

10   you put an edge on my spirit

and radiance in my song.

And though you spoiled

my understanding of the conflict,

yet, were I to see you again,

15   I should accept more and the whole of it.

Were I, after oblivion of my trouble,

to see before me

on the plain of the Land of Youth

the gracious form of your beauty,

20   I should prefer it there,

although my weakness would return,

and to peace of spirit

again to be wounded.

O yellow-haired, lovely girl,

25   you tore my strength

and inclined my course

from its aim:

but, if I reach my place,

the high wood of the men of song,

30   you are the fire of my lyric –

you made a poet of me through sorrow.

I raised this pillar

on the shifting mountain of time,

but it is a memorial-stone

35   that will be heeded till the Deluge,

and, though you will be married to another

and ignorant of my struggle,

your glory is my poetry

after the slow rotting of your beauty.

MARKS

DO NOT
WRITE IN
THIS
MARGIN

Practice Papers for SQA Exams: Higher English Practice Exam B

Questions

56. Look at **stanza 1** (lines 1–15). Explain how MacLean gives his subject 'immortality'.   **2**

57. Maclean writes about a disappointed love. By referring closely to lines 16–31, discuss the speaker's attitude towards the 'yellow-haired girl'.   **4**

58. Referring to at least **two** examples, analyse MacLean's language in lines 32–39 to reveal how MacLean feels about his poetry.   **4**

59. MacLean writes this poem in the first person. Referring closely to this poem and to another poem or poems by MacLean, discuss the effect of the use of the first person in MacLean's poetry.   **10**

Text 6: Poetry

If you choose this text you may not attempt a question on poetry in Section 2.

Read the extract below and then attempt the following questions.

The Circle by Don Paterson

My boy is painting outer space,

and steadies his brush-tip to trace

the comets, planets, moon and sun

and all the circuitry they run

5 in one great heavenly design.

But when he tries to close the line

he draws around his upturned cup,

his hand shakes, and he screws it up.

The shake's as old as he is, all

10 (thank god) his body can recall

of that hour when, one inch from home,

we couldn't get the air to him;

and though today he's all the earth

and sky for breathing-space and breath

15 the whole troposphere can't cure

the flutter in his signature.

But Jamie, nothing's what we meant.

The dream is taxed. We all resent

the quarter bled off by the dark

20 between the bowstring and the mark

and trust to Krishna or to fate

to keep our arrows halfway straight.

MARKS

DO NOT
WRITE IN
THIS
MARGIN

Practice Papers for SQA Exams: Higher English Practice Exam B

But the target also draws our aim –

our will and nature's are the same;

25 we are its living word, and not

a book it wrote and then forgot,

its fourteen-billion-year-old song

inscribed in both our right and wrong –

so even when you rage and moan

30 and bring your fist down like a stone

on your spoiled work and useless kit,

you just can't help but broadcast it:

look at the little avatar

of your muddy water-jar

35 filling with the perfect ring

singing under everything.

Questions

60. Look at lines 1–5.
By referring to at least **two** examples, analyse how the poet's use of language
conveys the significance of this moment.

4

61. Look at lines 9–16.
By referring to at least **two** examples, analyse how language is used to reveal
the impact of his son's birth.

4

62. Look at lines 29–36.
By referring to at least **two** examples, evaluate the effectiveness of these lines as a
conclusion to the poem.

2

63. By referring to this poem and to at least one other poem, discuss how Paterson uses
seemingly insignificant events to explore deeper human concerns.

10

[END OF SECTION 1]

Section 2 – Critical essay – 20 marks

Attempt ONE question from the following genres – Drama, Prose, Poetry, Film and Television Drama, or Language.

You may use a Scottish text but NOT the one used in Section 1.

Your answer must be on a different genre from that chosen in Section 1.

You should spend approximately 45 minutes on this section.

DRAMA

Answers to questions on **drama** should refer to the text and to such relevant features as characterisation, key scene(s), structure, climax, theme, plot, conflict, setting …

1. Choose a play in which a central character displays clear signs of instability or weakness on one or more than one occasion.

   Briefly explain the reasons for their instability/weakness and discuss how the dramatist's presentation of this feature enhances your understanding of the play as a whole.

2. Choose a play in which emotions of one or more characters reach a clear climax.

   By referring in detail to the climax, discuss in what ways it is important for your understanding of the play as a whole.

3. Choose a play in which a power struggle between two characters is an important feature.

   Briefly explain how the dramatist establishes this power struggle and discuss how this feature enhances your understanding of the play as a whole.

PROSE – FICTION

Answers to questions on **prose fiction** should refer to the text and to such relevant features as characterisation, setting, language, key incident(s), climax, turning point, plot, structure, narrative technique, theme, ideas, description …

4. Choose a novel or short story whose setting in place and/or time is an important feature.

   Explain how the writer establishes the setting and go on to discuss its importance to your appreciation of the text as a whole.

5. Choose a novel or short story in which an incident reveals a flaw in a central character.

   Explain how the incident reveals this flaw and go on to discuss the importance of the flaw in your understanding of the character and your appreciation of the text as a whole.

6. Choose a novel in which there is a key incident involving a quarrel, an unexpected revelation or an emotional reunion.

   Briefly explain the circumstances of the incident and go on to discuss to what extent the incident is important to your understanding of the text as a whole.

PROSE – NON-FICTION

Answers to questions on **prose non-fiction** should refer to the text and to such relevant features as ideas, use of evidence, stance, style, selection of material, narrative voice …

7. Choose a work of biography or autobiography which you feel is written with great insight and/or sensitivity.

    Discuss, in detail, how the writer's presentation of the life leads you to this conclusion.

8. Choose a non-fiction text in which the writer puts forward a view on a social issue.

    Briefly explain what the issue is and then discuss how effective the writer is in influencing you to share his or her point of view.

9. Choose a non-fiction text in which the style of writing is an important factor in your appreciation of the writer's ideas.

    Discuss in detail how features of the style enhanced your appreciation of the text as a whole.

POETRY

Answers to questions on **poetry** should refer to the text and to such relevant features as word choice, tone, imagery, structure, content, rhythm, rhyme, theme, sound, ideas …

10. Choose a poem which deals with birth or adolescence or adulthood or any other relevant stage of life.

    Discuss how the poet's exploration of the stage of life has deepened your understanding of it.

11. Choose a poem in which tone is important in developing theme.

    Show how the poem creates this tone and discuss its importance in your appreciation of theme in the poem.

12. Choose a poem which features a character you admire or respect.

    Show how, through the content and poetic techniques used, the poet creates a character who you admire or respect.

FILM AND TELEVISION DRAMA

Answers to questions on **film and television drama*** should refer to the text and to such relevant features as use of camera, key sequence, characterisation, mise-en-scène, editing, setting, music/sound, special effects, plot, dialogue …

13. Choose a film or television drama* in which there is a breakdown in the relationship between two characters.

    Discuss how the film or programme makers' exploration of the breakdown of the relationship contributes to your understanding of character and/or the central concern(s) of the text.

14. Choose a film or television drama* which explores the tragic consequences of war.

    Show how the film or television programme makers explore the tragic consequences and discuss to what extent they are successful in deepening your understanding of war.

15. Choose from a film or television drama* an important sequence in which tension is created by filmic technique or by action and dialogue.

    Show how the film or programme makers create this tension and explain why the sequence is so important to the film as a whole.

*'television drama' includes a single play, a series or a serial.

LANGUAGE

Answers to questions on **language** should refer to the text and to such relevant features as register, accent, dialect, slang, jargon, vocabulary, tone, abbreviation …

16. Choose at least one example of live broadcasting.

    Identify the key features of the language used in this particular example and discuss that area's contribution to effective reporting.

17. Choose at least one example of tabloid writing.

    Identify some of the distinctive features of the language used and discuss to what extent these features contribute to effective communication.

18. Choose at least one example of a campaign speech which features emotive language.

    By referring to specific features of language in this speech, discuss to what extent you feel the speech is successful in achieving its purpose.

[END OF SECTION 2]

Hints and tips

Use these hints and tips to maximise your marks when answering questions.

Reading for Understanding, Analysis and Evaluation

HINT

R1. Looking closely at the wording of this question, you will see that it is designed to **test your understanding of the writer's ideas**. Remember that the context should be read carefully as it may provide clues.

R2. You are expected to **provide relevant quotations from the passage, identify technique(s) used and comment on the effect of their use**. Marks are awarded for these comments, with insightful/detailed comments scoring up to 2 marks. 0 marks are awarded to reference alone.

R3. **Final question**

- Candidates should identify key areas of agreement and/or disagreement in the two passages by referring in detail to both passages.

- There may be some overlap among the areas of agreement. Markers will have to judge the extent to which you have covered two points or one.

- You can use bullet points in this final question, or write a number of linked statements.

- Evidence from the passage may include quotations, but these should be supported by explanations.

- The mark for this question should reflect the quality of response in two areas:

  o identification of the key areas of agreement and/or disagreement in attitude/ideas;

  o level of detail given in support.

- The following guidelines should be used:

  o **5 marks** – comprehensive identification of three key areas of agreement with full use of supporting evidence

  o **4 marks** – clear identification of three key areas of agreement with relevant use of supporting evidence

  o **3 marks** – identification of three key areas of agreement with supporting evidence

  o **2 marks** – identification of two key areas of agreement with supporting evidence

  o **1 mark** – identification of one key area of agreement with supporting evidence

  o **0 marks** – failure to identify any key area of agreement and/or total misunderstanding of task.

Scottish set texts

HINT

S1. This question requires you to **explain** something in the text, proving that you have **understood** the writer's ideas. It is best to **use your own words**.

S2. At Higher, you are not allocated marks for quoting alone. You may be allocated 2 marks for an insightful comment with reference to the text. More basic comments with reference to the text will only score 1 mark. Bullet-pointing your answers is helpful.

S3. In 4-mark questions, marks can be allocated in the following ways: 2+2, 2+1+1, 1+1+1+1.

S4. Sentence structure questions require you to **identify the technique** and then to **explain the effect** this has, **linking to the question**. Make sure you cover all three aspects in your answer.

S5. Imagery questions require you to deconstruct the image.

S6. In tone questions, you need to identify the tone, quote an example from the text to support and explain how this quotation creates the tone you have identified. To make sure you get all marks, try setting out your answer in the following way: *TONE – EXAMPLE – EXPLANATION*.

S7. **10-mark question**

The marks are broken down as follows:

- Up to 2 marks can be awarded for identifying **commonality** between the printed text and other works/wider text.

- A further 2 marks can be achieved for **detailed reference to the extract** given. NOTE: you will not gain a mark simply for quoting here; it is the quality of your explanation that gets the marks.

- 6 additional marks can be awarded for **discussion of similar references to the other work(s)/wider text**.
  You need to refer to evidence from the text and explain: evidence with detailed, insightful explanations may achieve 3 marks; evidence with less detailed answers will achieve 2 marks. Quality comments are rewarded. Do not simply try to score marks by endlessly quoting or retelling the story.

SECTION 2 – Critical essay

Essays are marked according to the supplementary marking grid. Examiners are looking for evidence of:

- your knowledge and understanding of the text
- your ability to analyse comprehensively
- your ability to evaluate and engage with the text in a convincing way
- your ability to be understood at first reading.

When you choose which essay to do in the exam, make sure you understand the question and what your line of argument is. You must **answer the question** throughout the essay. Consistent reference must be made to relevant ideas, not just at the end.

You are not seeking to retell the story in your essay; rather you are explaining **how** the writer conveys their ideas. This is analysis and evaluation.

- **Analysis**

  This is when you deconstruct the writer's language and explain how the language creates effect. You are expected to quote and comment, referring to relevant techniques. Considering the effect of connotations *can* be helpful as can fully deconstructing imagery, particularly in poetry essays. Your analysis should always be focused on the question, otherwise it is irrelevant and will add nothing to your essay.

- **Evaluation**

  This is your engagement with the text. That means you demonstrate and validate your opinions of the text in line with the question. To do this, you need to analyse; the two are closely interrelated. By showing a clear personal response to the text and task, you will be evaluating.

Commonly asked questions

Turning point

To answer this type of question effectively you need to:

- Read the question first – some questions ask you to comment in detail about the build-up to the turning point, others ask you to begin with the turning point itself and then elaborate on the impact.

- You need to show why the turning point is significant, in terms of plot, character and theme. This means you have to bring together ideas neatly and concisely, explaining their importance as you do so.

- In drama questions, remember to consider staging and evaluate its contribution to the turning point.

- You will need to explain what impact the turning point has on the rest of the text (think about character development, relationships, plot, etc.).

Characterisation

To answer this type of question effectively you need to:

- Show an awareness of how the character is presented and how they change or develop throughout the text. This means looking at not only the character's actions and reactions, but examining other characters' reactions to them too, if applicable.

- The skill here is to analyse and show HOW you see the character changing or developing. This means detailed analysis and evaluation of specific key incidents.

- In order to show a change, you need to explain how they are presented initially, before then commenting in depth on how they develop and what factors contribute to that change.

- Often, theme is explored through characterisation. Be mindful of this; it is appropriate to comment on wider themes when discussing the impact of characterisation.

Theme

To answer this type of question effectively you need to:

- Show an awareness of how the theme is developed throughout the **whole** of the text.

- Theme can be shown through characterisation, narrative, language, setting, etc.

- You may wish to focus on **specific characters and/or key moments** in the text.

- In poetry, the writer's techniques in language and structure will be more prominent in driving the theme. Be aware of this and analyse appropriately.

- Successful responses will show thoughtful and sensitive engagement with the theme, evaluating how successfully the writer explores its ideas/concerns.

Comparative questions

To answer this type of question effectively you need to:

- Identify the key points of comparison. This can be similarities and/or differences.

- Ensure you explore the key points successfully in **both** texts. This means analysis of plot/character/language/theme or any other relevant device.

- Evaluation is a strong component in these essays; you are making a judgement about the texts and have to support your views with good, detailed textual evidence and thorough explanation.

- There must be balance in your essay – you should analyse each text equally.

© 2019 Leckie

001/02102019

10 9 8 7 6

ISBN 9780008365226

Published by
Leckie
An imprint of HarperCollinsPublishers
Westerhill Road, Bishopbriggs, Glasgow, G64 2QT
T: 0844 576 8126   F: 0844 576 8131

HarperCollins Publishers
Macken House,
39/40 Mayor Street Upper,
Dublin 1
D01 C9W8
Ireland

leckiescotland@harpercollins.co.uk
www.leckiescotland.co.uk

Publisher: Sarah Mitchell
Project Manager: Gillian Bowman

Special thanks to
Jess White (proofread)
Jouve (layout)

Printed in the United Kingdom.

A CIP Catalogue record for this book is available from the British Library.

Images
P17 twitter logo - © dolphfyn / Shutterstock.com; P19a © snig/ shutter-
stock. com; P19b © AGIF / Shutterstock.com; P22 © John Cohen /
Contributor / Getty Images; P30 © Gearstd / Shutterstock.com; P32 ©
WENN UK / Alamy; P35 © Fred Morley / Stringer / Getty Images; P41 (c)
Rob Leyland / Shutterstock.com; P49a ID1974 / Shutterstock.com; P49b ©
Bruce Glikas / Contributor / Getty Images; P50 © John Snelling /
Contributor / Getty Images; P61 © Gts / Shutterstock.com; P70a Yanliang
Tao / Shutterstock. com; P70b Vitalii Nesterchuk / Shutterstock.com; P70c
4 PM Production / Shutterstock.com; P70d mimagephotography /
Shutterstock.com; P76 © ZUMA Press, Inc. / Alamy; P83 © Planet News
Archive / Contributor / Getty Images; P85 © Igor Bulgarin / Shutter-
stock.com; P87 © Chris Bull / Alamy; P87 © Geraint Lewis / Alamy; P110
© Chris Jenner / Shutterstock.com; P123 © Maxisport / Shutterstock. com;
P123 © s_bukley / Shutterstock.com

All other images © Shutterstock.com

MIX
Paper | Supporting
responsible forestry
FSC™ C007454

This book contains FSC™ certified paper and other controlled
sources to ensure responsible forest management.

For more information visit: www.harpercollins.co.uk/green